Empowered by Empathy

25 Ways to Fly in Spirit

Rose Rosetree

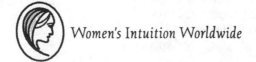

Women's Intuition Worldwide

Empowered by Empathy: 25 Ways to Fly in Spirit

Copyright© 2001 by Rose Rosetree
1st printing 2001; 2nd printing 2005, revised; 3rd printing 2006, 4th printing 2010
Illustrations© 2001 by Nicole Tadgell
Inside design by Eda Warren, Desktop Publishing Services, Inc., www.go-training.com
Editors: Martha Collins, Mitch Weber, Regina Richards, Susan Zell

Do not attempt any of the techniques in this book until you have read the section on "When to Use this Book" in Chapter 1. As explained, some readers will need to wait before it is appropriate to explore Flying in Spirit.

Library of Congress Catalog Number: 00-190155
Publisher's Cataloging-in-Publication
(Provided by Quality Books, Inc.)

Rosetree, Rose.
     Empowered by Empathy: 25 Ways to Fly in Spirit/
by Rose Rosetree. – 1st ed.
     p. cm.
          Includes bibliographical references and index.
     ISBN 0-9651145-8-9

          1.Empathy.   2. Auras.   3. Intuition
     (Psychology) I. Title.

BF575.E55R67 2001   152.41
                         QBI00000029

For **workshops, personal consultations, quantity discounts** or **foreign rights sales:**
rights@rose-rosetree.com * 703-404-4357
Women's Intuition Worldwide, LLC
116 Hillsdale Drive, Sterling, VA 20164-1201
Interact at www.rose-rosetree.com/blog

Bookstores & Libraries:
Rose Rosetree's titles are available through New Leaf, Baker & Taylor, Ingram, Quality Books and Gazelle.

$\mathcal{D}$edication

Poets, singers, artists:
you who yearn to express the truth
and yet more truth, open now
to the ways you already create and create without ceasing
through your spirit's gifts.

Dancers, actors, musicians, photographers,
creators of all kinds and intensities:
you who fervently wish that someone, that enough someones,
might give you the chance to show your talent,
open now and be refreshed.
Once upon this time, right here, in this room,
know that wherever you are, you send out your gifts
and applause for them shakes in the air
like the sound right before thunder.

Because you move as an empath,
you are an awakener,
not only through the skills that you cherish
but in all the ways that you serve, bringing light to this world
on a silver (though invisible) platter.

Even you, the hidden ones,
you who keep your gifts secret,
even you whose gifts are kept so far secret
that you do not know them yet,
stop holding back your tears.
Hear the call.
Awaken to the mystery of all you can know
and all that you share,
for our world, like you, is ready to break wide open
and show forth the full joy of God.

ℳcknowledgments

Enthusiasm from my students has motivated me to write and publish this book. They convinced me that, more than anything I've taught over the past 30 years, skilled empathy helps people live with a deeper spiritual awareness. Frankly, I've been amazed at how well my students have done.

After one workshop, it took me about a week to recover from just how well they did. Since the techniques had been a real stretch for me to discover, I expected my students to struggle at least as much. Ha! The techniques came as a relief, more than anything.

It's as if I had been a mother bird pushing little ones out of the nest, anxiously hoping my fledglings wouldn't have too much trouble working their wings. Instead they stretched and sailed like the birds they were born to be. And as we all flew together, I heard them chirp to each other, "That nest was okay but, hey, didn't it seem a little confining?"

When it comes to flying as an empath, instruction helps but the process is easy, especially when you can learn by example. This book is meant to be a process of my passing along to you the best I have learned that way; also I share intuitively discovered techniques I have tested on students.

Therefore, starting this book with acknowledgment is more than the usual convention. I'm invoking a momentum to gather force through *your* own learning, empowerment, and ability to teach by example.

Bring on the harps and trumpets, then. Let's start with my husband, Mitch Weber. He has apprenticed me as an empath ever since our first meeting in 1975. Dr. Bill Bauman and Tantra Maat have wowed me, too. I have drawn out of them all I could learn by example, including miracles done by means of highly skilled empathy.

How exactly? And is that what this book is to be about, learning to do miracles?

Yes, sometimes. And here's a hint. Tantra and Bill, like any skilled empaths, start doing miracles when they graciously step out of the way.

Other teachers have shown me about naming. Until you dare to trust the outer reaches of your perception, the naming process cannot begin. Without naming, there can be no clear conscious experience. So I honor Rev. Sandra Jean Parness and Rev. Rich Bell, instructors in Teaching of the Inner Christ, for modeling spiritual trust. This led to my ability to name empathic experience.

Susan Kingsley Rowe further awakened me with a past-life regression where I remembered being among the multitudes who heard The Sermon on the Mount—or its equivalent—the experience didn't exactly come complete with a theater marquee. The chiming presence of Jesus re-awoke in my consciousness. Ever since, it has seemed to me that what Jesus did (in part) was connect with his Source energy, then Join in Spirit with people who asked for his help: joining fearlessly, joyfully, fully. Doing this, even with a tiny fraction of his ability, sets a wonderful kind of healing into motion. I acknowledge this with amazement, even more than gratitude.

A decade before I connected with this fearless kind of empathy, Dr. David Read inspired me, week after week, with his brilliant sermons at The Madison Avenue Presbyterian Church. Not knowing he was considered one of the nation's leading preachers, I treated him simply as a friend. Once I wrote him an unintentionally outrageous thank you letter. I felt I had to share in words with *someone* the amazing thing I had noticed him doing at the end of his sermons. After giving his all, Dr. Read would step aside and let the congregation's thunderous silent applause flow right past him and straight over to God.

How, exactly, did Dr. Read make himself so transparent, to the point of being invisible? I couldn't say, but knew that I saw it somehow. He responded by writing that he treasured my letter. He called it "perceptive." Thus, he made me feel safe about presuming to explore what, in this book, I call Spiritual Oneness.

Giving thanks to the many teachers who have led me to the forms of empathy in this book (not just Spiritual Oneness but emotional, physical, and intellectual ways to Fly in Spirit), I find that one of my college professors, Dr. Allen Grossman, at Brandeis University, comes up for special recognition. Poets, he told us repeatedly, seek out the special excellence of a person or a place. They go on to find the true name for an experience.

This process of naming has taken me through poetry and religion, healing and metaphysics, relationship after relationship. Acknowledging this long journey brings joy and also healing. One instance happened just this morning, when thoughts about my journey brought back a bitter memory.

For 22 years after college I followed an Indian mystic, placing him on such a high pedestal that I believed he was my only guide to enlightenment. As a disciple, my life was devoted to teaching at his meditation centers. Sometimes, I'd study directly with him for extended retreats. And I'd wait outside his door for hours on end for a personal audience.

In all those years he granted me exactly one. The conversation lasted no more than three minutes. At the end, I asked about prayer. "Please, teach me how to pray," I implored him. My guru laughed long and hard. "Find it in a book" he said, turning away.

That memory burned for years because I heard contempt in his laughter. Hours of daily meditation, devoted service as a teacher, seven years of celibacy, work upon work and tears upon tears, despite all that, and in spite of all I had learned from my parents and teachers before him, was I such a fool that I still didn't know how to pray?

But now as I do my final draft of these pages and seal it with my thanks, I realize how my techniques to Fly in Spirit, through empathy, constitute a kind of prayer. And I hear my guru's laughter again. Only now I hear the love in it. Could it be that he foresaw and, in a twinkling, fore-read *this book*?

*C*ontents

Part One: Empathy 101

Part Two: Switch on Empathy

Part Three: Lifestyle Matters

*I*llustrations

Part I

Empathy 101

"Good fences make good neighbors."
—Robert Frost

I. *Empathy* on *Purpose*

MALLED is one word for it, that strangely mutilated psychic state some of us suffer after a trip to the mall. Emily always gets malled. Returning home after a shopping trip, she feels like an emotional basket case. No wonder she usually stays home instead.

"How can kids hang out at the malls for fun?" Emily sighs.*

Actually she isn't so much curious about how kids handle the malls as she tries to divert attention. It's hard for Emily not to blame herself. Millions of people—most people so far as she can tell—don't find shopping a major ordeal. So what's wrong with her?

Empathy is the problem, empathy that Emily hasn't yet learned to use on purpose. Many unskilled empaths interpret their talent negatively, calling themselves names like "over-sensitive," "neurotic," or "co-dependent." Ridiculous! Empaths have a gift. You can you purposely use that gift to Fly in Spirit.

Joyce first discovered empathy one lovely spring morning in 1994. She woke up feeling suicidal. "Don't get me wrong," she told me afterwards. "I have my ups and downs like everyone else. But this feeling was different.

---

* Quotations throughout the text come from my memory. Anecdotes are true, just not reported verbatim. Also, first names in this book are fictitious, unless paired with last names. And dialogues in upcoming Q&A Sections are either reconstructed or fictitious. Bottom line--I'm a teacher, not a scholar, so I've chosen anecdotes accordingly.

"For years Greg has been my hero at the newspaper where we work—you could call him my mentor. That morning, a friend of ours called me to say that Greg was in bad shape. The day before, I wasn't at work. Greg was. Apparently the pressure got to him. He walked into the newsroom and absolutely lost control. You know those things that you can say to people, the things that are true but unforgivable? Well, he said them.

"The morning after, Greg didn't know how to go on. The suicidal feelings belonged to him, not me.

"Eventually he managed to pull himself together. The feelings passed for both of us but I still remember that episode because it served as a kind of initiation for me. Ever since, I've been aware of my empathy. Every day I connect to other people's pain. I've learned to accept this. But I sure wish I could use my empathy for happy stuff, too."

That's where empathy techniques come in. First, you'll learn how to turn off unwelcome empathy. Then come the techniques to turn it on—at will—deeper and bigger and better than ever before.

Harvey has suffered from a problem related to a different form of empathy. Until recently, he thought he was a hypochondriac.

"I'd go into a business meeting and come out with weird physical ailments. For years I thought I was making this up. Eventually I realized the aches and pains were real, only they belonged to other people, not me.

"A woman where I work suffers from migraines. But when they first start to hit, this woman, Ellen, is in such denial about her body, she has no clue. By the time she notices something wrong, her headache has become a full-blown migraine and she has to go to the emergency room.

"Finally I connected all this with me. When we're together at work and her symptoms start, who else gets a headache? Me. It's her headache but I'm sharing it. Sound crazy? Then get what we do now! At *my* first sign of a headache, I call Ellen and say, "*You* have a headache. Go take your medicine. Now it never gets to the point where she goes to the hospital.

"Great, I'm glad to help Ellen. But she never pays me to be her doctor or headache wearer... whatever. How can I stop taking on people's physical symptoms when I don't want to?"

Many so-called "hypochondriacs" are really volunteers who connect empathically with other people's health problems. Having a gift for this kind of spiritual service is much more enjoyable when you learn to use the on-and-off switch.

Wishing to have control over empathy is healthy. Just because you have an empathic gift doesn't mean you must be a slave to it, on call 24/7. The solution is to use empathy in a way that empowers you.

Most empaths don't have experiences as extreme as those of Harvey, Joyce, or Emily. On the other hand, you may be misinterpreting equally pesky and solvable problems that arise in your own life due to unskilled empathy. And undoubtedly you're underestimating the joys of using empathy on purpose.

Empathy can also be your ticket to experiences of higher consciousness. Techniques in this book will show you how.

Whatever makes you curious about being empowered by empathy, there's one thing you have in common with my other students: talent that needs to be nurtured.

Welcome to Empathy 101

Whether you're a Ph.D. or a high school dropout, one class I bet you've never taken is Empathy 101. Come and learn the importance of becoming a skilled empath versus a natural empath.

SKILLED EMPATHS know enough about their gifts to use them on purpose. They taste the personal freedom, the joy. Also, these empaths can consciously appreciate the hidden spiritual ways their gifts help others.

NATURAL EMPATHS have the same gifts as skilled empaths except that they don't know how to use empathy on purpose. So they suffer unnecessarily.

The purpose of Empathy 101 is to evolve from a natural empath into a skilled empath. This book is our class together. It will help you answer questions like these:

□ What are the six major types of empathy, and which do you have?
□ How can you switch your empathy off or on at will?
□ How can different techniques enhance your empathy?
□ How can you best protect yourself?
□ Empathy can be a basis for important kinds of spiritual service. Could you have been making a contribution all along, something more individual and far reaching than you ever dreamed?
□ What will happen when you consciously use empathy to fly in spirit?

One thing's for sure. If you're reading this book, it's a little late to choose whether or not you want to *be* an empath. Assuming that you're reading of your own free will, chances are that you qualify—though probably not yet as a *skilled* empath. That's where Empathy 101 comes in. You'll explore a sequence of information and techniques that has proven effective with my students, bringing results that have ranged from merely satisfying to downright transformational.

Why Study Empathy?

Personally, I wish Empathy 101 had been part of my formal education along with reading, writing, and arithmetic. Today's elementary school children may be taught more about empathy than I was. As you can read in Daniel Goleman's *Emotional Intelligence*, being taught that Dick and Jane have feelings, just like "mine," can help kids form intellectual concepts about empathy. This is a good kind of training. It improves manners, which is nothing to sneeze at (especially without covering your mouth). However, the deeper kinds of empathy we'll explore in this book go much further than improving social skills.

EMPATHY, as discussed here, involves experience, not just concepts. Empathy, real empathy, is an experience of true otherness. Yes, that means *transpersonal* knowing, going beyond your usual boundaries to explore a completely different way to be. When you activate empathy by using techniques like those in this book, your gifts pull you out of the box of your personality, pour you into another person's reality, and eventually plonk you safely back home to your everyday energy presence. This journey is a far cry from mouthing schoolroom ideas about showing consideration for others.

Mind you, trying to be a "nice" person is fine as far as it goes; it just doesn't go very deep. The six different forms of empathy we'll explore together lead you to experiences that are either spiritual, intellectual, physical, or emotional in nature. Emotional forms of empathy are the easiest to confuse with relatively superficial ideas like good manners. By contrast, true empathy is the call of a soul's deep striving, a motivation that no schoolteacher can magically bring into being. Either your soul invites you to empathy or it doesn't.*

And, sooner or later, the souls of those who are natural empaths cry out for training. An inner discomfort prompts the realization that having a gift doesn't mean the same thing as knowing how to use it. That's what teachers are for. (You needed help learning to read, didn't you? And that was no reflection on your ability.) Teachers save us time and vexation. For those who need the knowledge, Empathy 101 is as essential as reading, writing, and arithmetic.

In a way it's more essential. As millions of illiterate Americans can attest, it's frustrating not to know how to read—also inconvenient, limiting, even humiliating at times. Situations come up where you wish you

---

* As described later in more detail, your **soul** expresses your spirit in its complete human form—it's an earthy, here-and-now part of you. By contrast, your **spirit** is the unique spark of God that makes you an individual. Thus, your spirit offers wings; your soul demands roots.

could read but the ability just won't switch on. Empathy, by contrast, is always switched on.

That's right, empathy comes to us plugged in and switched on. Apparently the only way God can give it to us is for us to have it installed from Day One. As we'll explain in more detail later, empathy could be compared to Christmas presents. That wondrous machine your kid finds under the tree requires that Santa (or someone you, personally, know) will read the operating instructions, assemble the toy, and put in the batteries. Unless you set up the toy to run, it won't work. Mysteriously, our Christmas gifts of empathy come in a different manner—fully assembled, batteries included. The trick is to learn how to switch the gift off. Maybe you've already noticed: If you don't know how to use empathy on purpose, your empathy is going to use you.

When you can switch a gift off or on at will, that could be called having CONTROL. However, I'm not crazy about using the word control in conjunction with empathy. Control has two connotations, doesn't it? One is skill, which applies very nicely to an empath's training. But the other connotation is exerting your will over other people or yourself, which definitely doesn't apply.

A more useful understanding, I think, involves FREEDOM. When you can fly into another person's mind or heart—whether to give a gift of service or to learn something outrageously new—control is too heavy a burden to bring along. It's better to travel light, with innocence. Just as skilled empathy helps you to use your free will, one requirement for using your gifts is that you respect the free will of others. Freedom all around!

Freedom also describes the relief you will feel when you learn to switch off your inner Tickle Me, Elmo©— or whatever else you name the empathic toy within that keeps on mechanically doing its thing (even when you feel like it's driving you nuts). Considering how little most empaths today know about their gifts, no wonder it takes some doing to recognize how empathy works in the first place.

Self-Recognition

Unskilled empaths suffer. It's that simple. Ironically, these days you can go through school and learn more about computers than about your own psychic and spiritual software. Knowledge of empathy sure wasn't taught to me. Even on the college level, there was no elective on Empathic Development. At Brandeis, my favorite classes initiated me into the wonders of literature, motivation and social psychology, even secrets of nonverbal communication. I'll be forever grateful. But for the purpose of empathy education, it was like preschool.

After my B.A., I did graduate study in education and social work. These academic pursuits were interspersed with years of training as a meditation teacher plus impassioned study of many religions and techniques for personal development. Unfortunately all of them taught me the same amount about becoming a skilled empath: zilch.

In fact, my first class in Empathy 101 started quite by accident and didn't even take place until I was 45 years old.

Picture the scene. It's a Christmas party at the home of Steve and Birdie Piecezenick, where I've been hired as a party entertainer to do professional Face Reading.

At first I think this gig is going to be pretty routine. Stationed at a table, I'm giving guests private readings about the talents and tribulations that show in their face data.* Although my work at this party is typical, the host is not. For the entire time I do my readings he observes me and my subjects with rapt attention. Guests may come and guests may go but this guy goes on forever. After the first two hours, the gig is extended for another couple of hours and my host, Steve, keeps on observing, quiet except for occasional exclamations of "That's exactly right!"

When the party is over Steve Pieczenik tells me why he finds my work so interesting. (By the way, don't let this tongue twister of a last name

---

* Face Reading Secrets® is my version of the age-old art of physiognomy. It's a system to interpret significant physical face data, like ear position and lip proportions. You can learn to do it from the how-to, *The Power of Face Reading*.

make your eyes glaze over. Just pronounce it *pih-CHE-nik*.) Dr. Pieczenik is a best-selling novelist, sometimes co-authoring with Tom Clancy, sometimes on his own. Pieczenik's thrillers make use of his rare background as a Harvard-trained psychiatrist, a Ph.D. in International Relations, even four assignments as Deputy Assistant Secretary of State.

What does Dr. Pieczenik do professionally, when he isn't writing? He psychs out international leaders, helping our security advisors and politicians to figure out the best way to handle them, especially the weirdly dangerous ones like Saddam Hussein or Muammar Qadhafi.

Here's how I remember our conversation:

"Your sensitivity amazes me" he said.

"Thanks. But it's no big deal. I just do my work."

"Listen," he said. "*My* work is to deal with people at the highest levels of national security. It's my responsibility to know about people. I'm telling you that your gifts are really extraordinary. How do you manage to hold it together?"

"Huh?"

"Being that ultra sensitive, how do you keep yourself in balance? It must be very difficult."

What an awakening! In the first place, I had never considered myself particularly sensitive, let alone gifted. After all, there's no version of an IQ test for that. As we've already discussed, there aren't even classes. So I had no clue. Thank you forever, Steve Pieczenik, for calling this undefined thing about me a gift! I hope to do unto others as you have done to me.

Dr. Pieczenik also brought up a concept that was totally new to me: *The more sensitive you are, the harder it is to handle.*

Gee, the very idea made me want to cry. For years I had denied this sensitive part of myself. Whenever it showed up, I called myself neurotic, unstable, weird, embarrassing, fussy, moody, or weak. I blamed myself for every social situation where I reacted in a way that made me seem different. Not once had I framed these sad parts of my life story in terms of exceptional sensitivity.

Could this chronic condition turn out to be a talent? Wow! I started paying attention to this sensitivity stuff. What was it? What did it help me to do that, maybe, wasn't as automatic for everyone else as I had assumed? Empathy was its rightful name, I discovered. For there are many ways of being sensitive that don't involve the kind of gift that Steve Pieczenik noticed.

It has now been seven years since this perceptive man gave me the gentle equivalent of a Zen master's whack on the head. I signed up for empathy class (self-taught), and began to explore my gifts.

Recognizing these gifts can be tricky. Inadvertently, we empaths play a form of Pin the Tail on the Donkey. Remember it? The picture of a donkey hangs on a wall in front of you. You're holding an essential part of it, ready to pin it where it belongs. But before your turn to do this ridiculously simple thing, someone blindfolds you and spins you around until you're dizzy. Then you lurch forward—or sideways—and usually miss the mark.

That's life here on The Learning Planet. All of us born as natural empaths must learn to recognize what would be spiritually obvious if only we weren't too blind and dizzy to tell. Empathy, for us, is like the tail that belongs to that donkey. How satisfying to put it in place! That includes becoming clear about the difference between empathy and sensitivity.

Sensitivity

Empaths are driven to constantly seek more spiritual truth. We're fascinated by those aspects of reality that are the least obvious, the most secret, sacred, and tender. One tool for our search is sensitivity.

SENSITIVITY means a way of being neurophysiologically wired to be extra-responsive, as described in Dr. Elaine Aron's groundbreaking book *Highly Sensitive Persons*. Her research has shown that 1 or 2 people in

10 can qualify as a HIGHLY SENSITIVE PERSON (HSP).* If you're an HSP, things bother you that don't bother others. You notice more, consciously and physiologically. Overstimulation happens. Hurt feelings happen. So do exceptional abilities—if you let them. Nevertheless, as noted by Dr. Aron, American society, on the whole, is prejudiced against those who are sensitive.

Empaths are a special group within the HSP category. When it comes to social problems, we get a double whammy: problems related to being sensitive, then problems related to empathy. Ironically, you may be the last one to know you're either empathic or sensitive. Why? Even the world's most talented empaths aren't sensitive to absolutely everything. Remember what Thoreau said about some people marching to the beat of a different drummer? Whatever kind of information you specialize in receiving, your empathy causes you to tune out other kinds of information. This doesn't make you insensitive, though sometimes it may seem that way.

An extreme example of specialized sensitivity is Alex Mont, a high-functioning autistic nine-year-old who also happens to be a math genius. In minutes he masters the same concepts that his father's students at Cornell University would take days to comprehend.

But Alex forgets the non-mathematical rules. A profile in *The Washington Post* illustrated how inconvenient this might be. Shopping for clothes at J.C. Penney, for instance, Mr. Mont pulled some pants off the rack and asked Alex to try them on. Oops, Alex started to take off his clothes right where they were standing.

"Alex!" his Dad exclaimed. "You need to go to the dressing room."

"Oh, I forgot," Alex apologized. "You're not supposed to take your pants off in public. I forgot that rule."

---

* When I first read Dr. Aron's book, what shocked me most was her finding that 42% of the people she questioned said "they were not sensitive at all." Apparently they weren't ashamed to say so, either. At first I couldn't compute this. How could someone not feel shattered, embarrassed, at least *reluctant* to admit to not being sensitive? America's cultural bias against sensitivity (even among psychologists, Aron points out) makes this easier to understand.

Alex's talents are probably more lopsided than yours. And they move in the opposite direction. While his numerical sensitivity can be measured on tests; your empathic sensitivity cannot. Alex tops out on the national math Olympiad. *What intellectual or psychological test can you take to tell how you rate empathically?*

Myers-Briggs may be the best test currently available, since empaths often share *one* score on *one* of the variables (N for intuition rather than S for sensing). However, Myers-Briggs was designed to type personalities, not to discern the scope and specialties of empathic gifts.

So here you are, empathic and anonymous, in a society loaded with hype for just about every other kind of ability that exists. Anything from math Olympics to mud wrestling, be it a skill or a hobby, can rate tests, competitions, awards, maybe also songs or demonstrations or parades or conventions or websites or celebrities and, undoubtedly, some kind of support group.

Empathy, however, is not a club (yet). No big deal! Don't let the lack of outer recognition cause you to belittle your gifts. They are part of the distinctive beauty of your spirit.

Recognizing Empaths

When you're searching for your fellow empaths, how can you recognize them if there is no official standardized test, no way of dressing the part? For clues, you'll have to look inside. And what I'm about to say may come as a surprise but it's important. Forget about facial expressions of concern or other ways that people act sympathetic. Acting means nothing.

Once I was interviewed by a TV talk show host with a flair for this sort of acting. On screen she comes across as highly sympathetic, even verging on saccharine. Person to person, I found that her lack of human feeling made her about as huggable as a packet of fake sugar. Immediately after asking me questions, she would withdraw so completely that my empathic self had no way to merge with her. Golly, was that ever scary!

Watching the broadcast later, I saw how my face froze into a mask of fear. This was no mere stage fright. I'd already given hundreds of media interviews. This was The Twilight Zone. When my interviewer refused to accept me empathically, I was utterly unprepared.

Most of the techniques in this book would have made it possible to predict this kind of behavior. But no technique will work if you don't remember to use it. Because I forgot to pay attention to the empathic level, my strength became my weakness. *Empathy doesn't necessarily show in a person's expression, although often we're fooled into thinking it does.* Whenever we assume that the presence or absence of empathy will show in external behavior, it's a mistake.

If you were to take one of my seminars in person (rather than joining a virtual classroom via this book) you might be shocked to meet your classmates. Who are they to think they are empaths? That woman? That guy? Are they kidding?

Turns out, the usual ways we've learned to read people are misleading when you're looking for empaths. It has nothing to do with having an expressive face like my aforementioned talk show host.

EXPRESSIVENESS in itself shows neither the presence nor absence of empathy. All it shows is a person's comfort level with the kind of communication where you let feelings show through your face.

Other factors are DISPLAY RULES* about how much emotion we're taught to show (e.g., girls who are taught that it's okay to act hurt, just not angry) and the everyday slips of face called MICRO-EXPRESSIONS (short bursts of emotion that flicker by fast and are read mostly unconsciously).

Psychologist Paul Eckman trains people to read them by showing videotapes, then using the pause button to catch moods that otherwise flash by unnoticed. You can do something similar at home, using your VCR. Reading micro-expressions is fascinating. Still, it won't necessarily show you who is an empath. Nor will reading the micros help you *become* an empath.

---

*Daniel Goleman, *Emotional Intelligence* (New York: Bantam, 1995), p. 113

Although anyone can become an expert at reading facial expression, not everyone can develop the gifts of an empath. In general, it's a mistake to imagine that you can tell empaths of any kind by their personalities. Sure, some remind you of fluffy, soft critters, like kittens. But turtles have bodies that are even softer and more vulnerable—empathy alone can show you what lies beneath the protective shell. Techniques in later chapters, like The Heart Journey, will bring that deeper truth within reach.

Psychic Ability

What does being an empath have to do with PSYCHIC ABILITY? Information from the psychic level is what people call a sixth sense. It involves specifics, like flashing on the location of your lost suitcase or predicting that tomorrow it will rain.

By contrast, empathy comes under the category of SPIRITUAL EXPERIENCE, something that contributes to the evolution of consciousness. As discussed more fully in the next chapter, whenever you work or play as an empath, your consciousness shifts. Consequently your way of experiencing life is forever altered (even if the changes are so subtle they are routinely overlooked). Thus, every step in the direction of empathy moves you forward spiritually.

Therefore, a simple way of distinguishing psychic experience from empathy is that the former adds to your collection of information whereas the latter irrevocably changes the knower.

Another difference is TIMING. Psychic experience pops like a photo flash. By contrast, empathy dawns. Gradually. Even when you're skilled, sometimes you'll slowly wake up to a feeling of "There it goes again." Only then will you recognize that you have been traveling. Either you wake up to someone else's experience in terms of *your* body-mind-spirit package or else you awaken inside *another person's package* entirely. Well, that's interesting....

The relatively slow-motion timing for empathy comes with one delightful advantage over a quick psychic flash. Skilled empaths have the choice to linger.

Another difference between psychic and empathic abilities involves practical usefulness. I may as well break it to you now— if there's a competition about usefulness, psychics win hands down. Laura Day, for instance, makes a point of how useful psychic information can be for making business decisions. Well, empathy doesn't necessarily help you pick winning stocks. Accuracy (truth that you can test) is a non-issue. Genuineness (truth that resonates within you) matters far more. Empathy reveals the deepest truth that you can hold and, like virtue, is its own reward.

SERVICE is yet another point of difference. For a psychic, service is optional—desirable, prudent, definitely wise, yet optional. I think of Betty, a friend who used her considerable psychic gifts in a way that may surprise you. She was a madam. Betty would use psychic abilities to tip her off when calls for her "girls" came from detectives. For years Betty's accuracy prevailed, helping her to foil the police. Eventually she sold her business to a non-psychic and, within two weeks, police raided the joint.

Ethically mixed situations like these are perfectly compatible with psychic development, even if not ideal. Empathy, however, demands that you be scrupulously ethical. The style of knowing is so personal that consequences of questionable choices will come back to you fast and hard.

Perhaps the most fascinating difference between psychics and empaths is DETACHMENT. When it comes to giving service, psychics help others best by staying neutral. The crystal-clear quality of their information is what counts. In *Anatomy of the Spirit*, Caroline Myss explains, "For me, a clear impression has *no* emotional energy connected to it whatsoever. If I feel an emotional connection to an impression, then I consider that impression to be contaminated."[*] Her impeccable record as a medical intuitive and teacher demonstrates how a psychic can work with the utmost effective-

---

[*] Caroline Myss, Ph.D, *Anatomy of the Spirit* (New York: Harmony Books), 1996, p. 39

ness without descending into the mushy, gushy, and vulnerable realms of empathy. For some of us, however, that mode of work is inescapable, even preferable.

Fortunately there's enough work for us all, those who are talented as psychics and those who happen to be empaths. Were you to train yourself to fit Myss's mold, after great struggle, you could probably rid yourself of the "contaminated" perception that comes from sharing energy with the people you help. In doing this, you'd also lose about 80% of your effectiveness... and even more of your joy.

This prediction isn't just theoretical. I've seen this kind of numbing happen to several empaths who've wound up as my students. Before finding me, they made heroic efforts to force their soul-level gifts to match up with those of their famous psychic teachers; to their detriment, they were trying to turn apples into oranges.

Surely the orchard of God's helpers has room for us all. Some of us are psychics, others empaths. How about being both? Yes, some are gifted at both, even if they don't make a clear distinction between them. For instance, psychotherapist Belleruth Naparstek has written a brilliant how-to about intuition, *Your Sixth Sense*. In discussing terminology, she implies that those who call themselves "empaths" are using a euphemism for the more controversial term, "psychic."

Later in her book, however, Naparstek gives personal examples of both the "pop" of psychic experience and the slower dawning of empathy—as though they were one and the same process—misnaming what I call Physical Oneness so that it can conveniently fit into the category of psychic perception. In one anecdote, for example, Naparstek describes that she felt a lump in her throat while talking with a client. "How did *her* lump get into *my* throat?" she wondered. Later the client's lump left, mid-session, and so did her therapist's.

How did this happen? How, indeed! That was empathy. When you give service as a psychic, transmitting information to others, you may bring important knowledge. Joining empathically doesn't seem as flashy; you may have relatively little knowledge to report; yet by the very act of connecting, you bring healing. And that's just part of the beauty of serving others as an empath.

Serving Others

Awakening your empathic gifts means being initiated into techniques where, *effortlessly*, you can touch another person at a deeper reality. In fact, effortlessly is the best way to do it. Don't expect struggle to be the proof that you're accomplishing something. Techniques in this book are meant to be done as effortlessly as possible. When incomparable knowledge flows to you, that is a better proof of your skill than the sweat of your brow.

Empathy can be an exquisite way of serving others. Until you can use empathy on purpose, however, your service will be about as exquisite as a monkey, dressed in a tutu, trying to dance. *Your highest and best service will become available only when you can move as a skilled empath.*

Yes, for the sake of service you'll want to be skilled. With skill you'll find that, although others may use words like "strength" or "clarity" for what you do, empathy is surprisingly easy. Compare it to lifting a two-ounce barbell. (Don't compare it to trying to *find* a two-ounce barbell.) Consciously using your gifts links you up to your spiritual Source and so, paradoxically, surrendering to your gifts will increase your power for being of service.

One of my students, Olivia, also needed to learn to surrender for the sake of her mental health. Here's the story she told towards the end of one of my seminars. "By training, I'm a nurse. But whenever I'd work, something would go on that they never covered in Nursing School. I knew when people were ill. It was as if I could feel what was going on in their bodies.

"I'd walk by a patient and smell something at the head or the legs or the feet that would tell me which part of the patient was sick. As part of this, I could tell who was getting better and who wasn't. It was uncanny.

"Altogether I knew so much that it began to overwhelm me. I made the mistake of telling other nurses and doctors. They convinced me I was nuts. I even spent time in a psych. ward. Needless to say, I got out of nursing. Until today, I felt ashamed of the part of myself that used to feel things. Thank you so much for giving me permission to know what I know."

Fear of going crazy is a secret shared by many an unskilled empath. Fighting or denying your God-given gifts, however, will not add to anyone's sanity. And rich though your vocabulary may be in words that belittle empathic sensitivity, now's the time to add new concepts, new language, new techniques. They will make it safer for you to be who you already are, someone with a destiny for service as an empath.

How to Use This Book

This is the first book to present empathy as an assortment of gifts, complete with techniques to alter your reality for the bigger and better. Here are suggestions for best results:

Once you're past the browsing stage, be sure to read Part One completely. It's designed to boost self-awareness, even if you already consider yourself pretty sophisticated about empathy. The concluding chapter, "How to Switch Empathy OFF," is vital. In Driver's Ed., which part of a car do you learn to use first? The brake. It's the same with Empathy 101.

Part Two takes you on a spiritual adventure. I'll challenge you to search for your personal language. Then come the mind-bogglers—each travel technique will help you to taste a new flavor of empathy.

With experience, you'll discover that being a skilled empath amounts to more than techniques and adventures. It's a lifestyle. Part Three presents vital information for keeping yourself in balance. Pay special attention to the chapter on grounding—and not just because of the controversial Aha!s about weight.

Each of the three Parts concludes with a set of AFFIRMATIONS. These are power words that can help you to transform yourself, both subjectively and objectively. Choose your favorite affirmations from each set, alter the words until they fit you like a glove, and repeat them aloud several times a day.*

When to Use This Book

So much for HOW to use this book—how about WHEN to use it?

- When you feel more-or-less stable, that's the best time to develop empathy.
- When you feel rotten, confused, worried, angry, and so forth, surprise! This is *not* a good time to explore the techniques in this book. Avoid doing any technique except for the one to switch empathy OFF (that's in Chapter 5). You know the impact of a cool shower when you've been out too long on a hot summer day? Empathy switch-off can be very soothing.
- When your life is in crisis, don't aim for more active forms of empathy until your life settles down. Otherwise you're apt to distort the techniques, come up with inaccurate information about others, even waste time trying to escape from reality. Social workers have found that people resolve crises within six weeks, one way or another. It's worth waiting that long until you can begin properly. Your career as a skilled empath is designed to last for a lifetime.
- When you're in urgent need of healing, if you're a not-yet-recovering alcoholic, or if you take non-prescription drugs, do yourself a big favor. Wait a while. Techniques in this book are for what psychologists call *the worried well*, people who can function okay but want to become more self-actualized.

---

* For more effective techniques that have the side benefit of developing your Celestial Perception, see my companion work, *Aura Reading Through All Your Senses*, pp. 184-192.

▫ When you are suffering from co-dependence, watch out! (Mistakenly interpreting your empathy as co-dependence doesn't count. Real CO-DEPENDENCE means being obsessed about controlling another person's life and depending on others to make you happy.) Heaven forbid that someone who is actively co-dependent should fool around with more empathy! Taking care of ourselves is plenty. Otherwise we're likely to coerce others rather than help them, which is harmful for everyone concerned. When you are ready to learn about others without trying to control them or use them, or to anxiously escape from yourself, that's when you're ready to fly with your empathic gifts.

Otherness

When, above all, is the best time to fly with your gifts for empathy? For some readers, it might be when you're curious, or ready to explore higher states of consciousness, or determined to get this empathy part of your life *right* for a change.

Any answer that speaks to your deep sense of truth signals your best time. But let me tell you when, for me, has been the best time. I became empowered by empathy when I was ready for the experience of true otherness.

OTHERNESS means jumping out of the box of being yourself. You gain direct experience of another person's body or mind or heart or spirit. People talk about knowing others "in the Biblical sense" as a euphemism for sex. But maybe KNOWING IN THE BIBLICAL SENSE really should be understood to mean the spiritual experience of otherness, regardless of whether physical intimacy is involved.

Sex can be a gateway to otherness. Conveniently, though, empathy offers many alternatives that can be just as profound. Maybe not as much fun—you'll have to decide for yourself. But don't make up your mind about sex as the best form of otherness until you've had the privilege of experiencing many kinds of otherness, several times, and uninhibitedly.

Otherness is a special kind of spiritual experience. Before discovering it, personally, I'd done decades of psychological work and daily meditation, using a variety of techniques. I'd even had a modest share of transcendent experience, the kind where you breathe the breath of God and your life is changed forever.

Without meaning any disrespect, however, the breath, the hand, even the heart of God are not "other." God is at your core. Supposing that you follow your religion perfectly, you can go for years, even an entire lifetime, without once consciously getting outside the box of your human personality. It's constantly *my* thinking, *my* feeling... even *my own opening up to God*. But how about empathic travel within someone else's box? How about an entirely different way to think or feel?

- What would it be like to live in a body that is taller or heavier or with a different sexual energy or older or quicker, etc.?
- What taste would you have in your mouth?
- Would you trust life as much?
- Imagine how it would be to visit someone else's soul, consciously, assuming that you have full permission to learn all you can and serve all you can.

Otherness sets you free from the silly habit of being boringly, only, and unconsciously yourself.

Otherness is humbling and mysterious. Yet, as you'll discover, it's also very, very simple. With all the practical benefits you gain as a skilled empath, simple otherness may be your greatest reward.

2. Skeptical Interlude

"Could I be an empath?"

It's a fair question, especially since 95 people out of 100 aren't. That's right, 5% is my ballpark estimate for the number of American adults, living now, who are naturally gifted as empaths. But you don't need to know about round numbers, you need to know about you. So here are a few tests to satisfy the most skeptical part of your healthy curiosity. After each one, you'll find questions from your fellow students in our *virtual classroom*.

Empath's Test #1 - The Quick Questionnaire

Empaths can fly... in consciousness. Many times during the day they shift into another person's way of experiencing life, whether physically, mentally, emotionally, or spiritually. Do you have a talent for it? Here's a quick aptitude test.

Answer True or False:

1. When I'm with people who fascinate me, I wish I knew what it was like to *be* them.
2. It annoys (or amuses) me when people put on a show of being very tuned in to others and I can tell that they're really not.
3. I'm thin-skinned about other people, not just myself.
4. One of the best parts of falling in love, for me, is seeing the world through my lover's eyes. Everything becomes different and new.
5. Of all the compliments I've received, some of my favorites are, "You really answer my questions." or "You understand me better than others do."
6. When with different friends, I don't just talk to them. My whole wavelength shifts. For example, when I'm with an artist, colors look brighter than usual; when I'm with a musician, I'm more aware of sounds; when I'm with an athlete, I feel more physically alive.
7. If I have to give the same speech to three different strangers, it comes out differently each time. Somehow I sense information that causes me to adjust the words. With a highly educated listener, for instance, I find myself automatically using longer words—even if nobody has told me that this person is highly educated.
8. When in the presence of someone who is ill, it takes no effort for me to experience some of what that person is going through. In fact, if I were to let myself go, my experience of another person's illness could be overwhelming.
9. In certain situations (e.g., talking or dancing or teaching), I get right on another person's wavelength—how he or she thinks. This kind of sharing is very special to me.
10. I don't just talk to my plants. I feel like they talk back to me.
11. It's freeing for me to be outdoors. And more than a change of scene. The way I think and feel changes, as though I pick up on different kinds of *consciousness* expressed in animals and plants.

12. During times of closeness with my pet, I enter the pet's world. For me, that's the truly fascinating part of having a pet.
13. Looking in the mirror shocks me. "That's supposed to be me?" The truth is, I identify with being a (non-physical) energy presence more than one particular face and body.
14. Friendship, for me, goes far beyond sharing common interests. I enjoy that my friends show me different ways to be.
15. I have a longing to connect with other people who are seeking a deeper dimension to life. Whenever I encounter these kindred spirits, I feel a kind of relief. Even if our paths cross just long enough to make eye contact once, the meeting can lighten my spirit for hours.

Answers

If you answered yes to even one of these questions, you are probably a *natural* empath. And you will love how your life changes when you become a *skilled* empath.

Empath's Test #1—Q&A

Q: WHY EXPECT A SKEPTIC LIKE ME TO BE PERSUADED BY SUCH A GENERAL QUESTIONNAIRE?

A: I'm aiming for self-recognition more than persuasion. If that hasn't happened yet, let's go on to the second test, which explores this more deeply. Although it takes more effort, it will give you more precise results.

Empath's Test #2— Who-Am-I?

Find a quiet place where you can do some inner detective work for about 10 minutes. Because your eyes will be closed most of this time, you'll need to read through the following instructions in advance before you do them.

1. Sit as comfortably as you can... considering that your very existence is under scrutiny. Find a place that is quiet and private. *Close your eyes and take a few breaths.* (Sometimes people become so focused when they do any kind of inner research, they forget they're allowed to breathe. Please, take a breath, a nice deep one.)
2. Prepare to ask a question. *Ask this question mentally: "Who am I?"*
3. Take some more deep breaths and *sit there, confident that your question will be answered.* You needn't feel as though you must twist yourself into an *angst-y* posture like Rodin's sculpture, "The Thinker." Since you've asked to connect inwardly with who you are, you will.
4. After asking your question and breathing, *you will notice something.* Count this experience as your answer.
5. *Open your eyes.* Then (and not before then) read through the following comments on what you received at Step #4. Each of these responses comes with a further action item that will answer your earlier question, "Could I be an empath?" Do not read through this list until you have done Steps #1-5. Otherwise you'll diminish your experience of this test when you really do take it.

Answers

When you did the test, which of the following answers best describes your experience—choose from a, b, c, d, or e.

a) "I noticed my body."

This sense of yourself could have involved becoming aware of pain, feeling hungry or cold or handsome or fat or anything physical whatsoever.

Turn to pages 33-37 for descriptions of two gifts for physical forms of empathy, Physical Intuition and Physical Oneness. Can you relate? If so, you're an empath. If not, you're probably not. (Exception: If you're living with chronic or acute pain, that may dominate your attention. Feel free to redo this test again, and stay at Step #4 until you notice something other than the pain. Then continue.)

b) "I noticed my emotions."

This sense of yourself could have involved feeling happy or sad, remembering something from your past, saying a wistful prayer, thinking about somebody you either like or dislike, or any other experience with a strong feeling attached to it.

Turn to pages 38-43 for descriptions of two gifts for emotional forms of empathy, Emotional Intuition and Emotional Oneness. Can you relate? If so, you're an empath. If not, you're probably not.

c) "I noticed my thoughts."

This sense of yourself could have involved self-consciousness, doubts about the author's sanity for asking you to do this technique, or doubts about your own sanity for even trying. You could have had thoughts about your work, crossword puzzles, what to have for lunch—a whole series of little thoughts one after another.

Bottom line: Did you think about thinking? Was the mental part stronger than either emotions or physical sensations related to being caught up in those thoughts? Then turn to pages 43-46 for a description of Intellectual Shape Shifting. Can you relate to it? If so, you're an empath. If not, you're probably not.

d) "I noticed other things around me, but nothing to do with myself at all."

This sense of yourself could have involved wishing you were doing something other than this exercise, feeling distracted, fighting the desire to get up and tidy up the room. Or maybe you were thinking about other people, what they are doing now, or should be doing later—or remembering something rotten they've done in the past.

If none of this "self-exploration" had much to do with yourself at all, there are three strong possibilities:

▫ Someone is making you do this exercise, and you'd really rather not.

▫ You have had little or no prior experience with focused self reflection, like psychology or meditation—in which case, you're free to attempt this technique a few more times to get the hang of paying attention to your inner self; eventually you'll come up with an answer different from (d).

▫ You're not an empath.

e) "I noticed a sense of myself, but not in the ways described previously."

This sense of yourself could have involved noticing colors or some kind of inner light, hearing non-physical sounds or qualities of silence, being aware of your presence as not confined to your physical limits, even seeing yourself as a kind of cartoon. Or maybe you noticed an awareness of yourself as a pattern of energy, such as movement of scintillating little particles.

Turn to pages 46-49, where I describe Spiritual Oneness. Can you relate to it? If so, yes, you're an empath. If no, you're not.

Empath's Test #2—Q&A

Q: You make it sound so simple, "You're not an empath." What if this upsets you?

A: If the idea of *not* being an empath breaks a part of your heart, guess what? You probably are, because a non-empath will more likely say, "So I'm not an empath? Big deal." Being an empath or not involves your entire mind-body-spirit setup, which was created long before you picked up this book. Not being an empath makes you no better or worse than people who are empaths, just different. You have no further need to read this book unless you have an empath for a significant other, e.g., your mate or your child.

Q: How did your Empath's Test 2 quiz work, anyway?

A: As you'll be reading later in more detail, each person has many layers, including some that correspond to layers of the human energy field. Besides your flesh-and-blood self, you have an AURA, made up of subtle bodies that specialize in pure spiritual energy, learning, and emotions. With your human consciousness being as flexible as it is, at any moment you can identify your "self" as being any one of these bodies. But by doing the "Who am I?" technique you have directed your consciousness to the body with which you currently identify most. That's also the body you probably use most skillfully for empathic travel.

Q: Why do you go on to ask if we can relate to descriptions of different types of empathy?

A: People are very good at recognizing their inner truth, when given the chance. If my descriptions make you go Aha!, you pass the test. You are what I call an empath. If my descriptions of being an empath leave you cold, forget it.

Q: I don't mean to split hairs, but couldn't anyone do empathic travel, having those multi-layered subtle bodies and all? Doesn't that make all of us empaths, regardless of whether we consciously believe in it?

A: Theoretically, yes. For practical purposes, no. Spiritual Oneness is a particularly good example. Ultimately everyone can be a spiritual empath, and a very good one, at that. But not everyone wants to, deep down. Such a person could force himself to practice my travel techniques for Spiritual Oneness. Eventually something would come of it. More likely, though, he'd wind up forgetting about it—until he was really ready to grow in that way.

Q: HOLD ON. YOU SEEMED TO BREEZE THROUGH SOMETHING IMPORTANT ABOUT YOUR TEST. ISN'T IT A BIT STRANGE TO ASK A QUESTION AND THEN JUST BREATHE TO FIND AN ANSWER? WHAT'S GOING ON?

A: Test #2 introduced you to a technique I call QUESTIONING. It's a way to go beyond your usual boundaries of understanding life experience. Breath becomes a powerful vehicle to ride past your expectations or doubts and to arrive at a deeper truth.

Questioning is based on the fact that, to access information from a bigger part of yourself than your everyday mind, you need to let go. But how? It doesn't work to command your mind: "Relax." Commanding means doing something, whereas relaxing means *not* doing. To let go, give yourself a task entirely different from thinking—a distraction so easy it won't take any effort at all. Assuming that your lungs are in working order, that distraction is breathing.

Q: YOU'RE SAYING THAT AFTER YOU ASK A QUESTION, YOU SHOULD CONCENTRATE ON YOUR BREATH?

A: Don't concentrate. Simply shift your attention. Breath links up with your consciousness (a term we'll investigate more later). Consequently, paying effortless attention to your breath can expand your consciousness.

The formula for Questioning, then, is to ask and immediately let go by shifting awareness to your breath. Automatically your answer will come. It's as simple as blowing out the candles on a birthday cake. Just make your wish and blow.

With Questioning, you needn't wait long for the answer, either. After a breath or two, a deeper part of you than your everyday mind will speak up. This effortless response is more complete than anything you could have figured out with everyday conscious thinking. Questioning helps you to apply the spiritual law, "Let go and let God."

Empath's Test #3—The TV Quiz

Here's the simplest test of all. It's for those who wonder if they have the emotional forms of empathy, Emotional Intuition or Emotional Oneness. Answer the following questions:

1. Which long-running TV show had a main character who was a professional empath? (Hint: If you saw that show, were you fascinated by that character's job, or were you more interested in, say, the starship's captain or the adorable android?)
2. When TV talk shows come on, the kind with the highly dramatic emotional confrontations, which of the following comes closest to your typical reaction:
    a) Thank goodness! Now I can watch something to spice up my day.
    b) Hmm, that might be fun, but what's on the other talk shows or the soaps or news shows? Maybe there's something even more emotionally intense.
    c) Help! Let me outta here!

Answers

Answer I

Counselor Deanna Troi, featured in "Star Trek: The Next Generation," is a superb role model for any developing empath. You need not be "part Betazoid," or even a science fiction fan, to emulate her gifts. Her job, as the ship's resident empath, was to join her consciousness with people, experience clearly, report her findings, and facilitate healing.

When you have a chance to watch this show, and I hope you will soon, pay particular attention to the character's skill at using her gifts. Intense though her experiences are, she knows very clearly that they belong to people other than herself. Techniques in a later part of this book will help you to develop a similar objectivity as a skilled empath.

If your reaction to such a character is positive, that's a good sign that you, too, have a gift for some form of emotional empathy. On the other hand, if the parts of the show where Troi does her job make you squirm or laugh or flip the channel, emotional forms of empathy are probably *not* your calling.

Answer 2a)

One person's "spice up my day" is someone else's emotional exhibition-ism.

With all respect, if you're among the millions of viewers who love shows like "Jerry Springer," you are probably *not* an emotional empath. Just the opposite. You're so unattuned to deeper emotions that you need high drama to feel any emotions at all. (Note: Even if you chose this an-swer you still may be a different kind of empath, just not an emotional empath.)

Answer 2 b)

As a viewer who loves emotional drama—the more of it the better—you could belong to any of the following categories.

▫ You're young, and trying to learn what life is about.

▫ You're seeking emotional CATHARSIS (that's the term from classical Greek theater about the healing process that occurs when entertainment frees up your tears or laughter).

▫ You have become disconnected from life, due to watching way too much TV—okay, there could be other causes, too. In any case, you watch TV as a form of entertainment unrelated to human reality.

▫ You are volunteering to lift emotional burdens from the poor souls on the shows. In which case, you could conceivably be an emotional empath... but way overworked and not yet skilled.

Unless you belong to the last category, you're probably *not* called to emotional travel in spirit.

Answer 2c)

If you feel revulsion towards TV shows with emotional sensationalism, ta da! You're probably an emotional empath.

For you, the relationship of these shows to your emotional life is like having a professional surgeon entertain herself by taking a romp to the butcher's shop. There's already enough emotional drama in your life as it is. "Spill Your Guts TV" is a poor choice of entertainment for empaths.

Empath's Test #3—Q & A

Q: I'LL TELL YOU ABOUT ONE FEELING RIGHT NOW. I DIDN'T LIKE YOUR TEST, OKAY? I'M NOT PROUD THAT I'M TOO UNSTABLE TO BE ABLE TO ENJOY SHOWS THAT NORMAL PEOPLE WATCH.

A: Empaths often feel bad about not fitting in. We wish we could be like "everyone else," i.e., not so super sensitive. But if you're strongly empathic, it's time you accepted that your peer group is other empaths and not the American public at large.

Stop kidding yourself about this fitting-in business. Millions of people love these talk shows so much, they find them addictive. Millions can tolerate them. Millions find them mildly helpful. They are not empaths. You are.

3. Your Gifts for Empathy

Empathy 101 starts with learning to recognize different forms of empathy. Along with this, for self-defense (and also for laughs), you need to become very clear about what empathy is *not*. Some of the gifts described here will apply to you. Other descriptions will remind you of people you know. We'll start with the six most common gifts: Physical Intuition, Physical Oneness, Emotional Intuition, Emotional Oneness, Intellectual Shape Shifting, and Spiritual Oneness. Then I'll round out the picture by describing some of the rarer forms of empathy.

Physical Intuition

When was the last time you tuned into how another person physically feels? PHYSICAL INTUITION informs you about what's going on with anybody's body.

Mothers and fathers are given this type of empathy for a few years every time a new baby enters their lives, whether through physical birth or adoption. Count this gift as one of the spiritual rewards for committing to parenthood. Usually it comes as a temporary dispensation for people who are not, otherwise, Physical Intuitives.

All parents need this gift. How else are you going to care for a baby without going out of your mind?

Sleepy? "Waahhh!"

Wet? "Waahhh!"

Thirsty? "Waahhh!"

Learning the language of Cry is just the beginning.

- ▫ Parents tuned into their gift of Physical Intuition can look at a baby's face and tell that her bottom needs changing.
- ▫ Physical Intuitives can sniff the baby's feet and know he is in for a rough day of teething.
- ▫ They can also look at a baby *from the back* and know the kid needs a nap. (Looking from the front, most people can read expression. But a kid from behind? That goes far beyond mere body language.)

Mysterious though such forms of knowing may seem to the uninitiated, physical empaths just do it. When you question how your child—or anyone else in a physical body—feels right now, boing! You *know*. (How does this work? See the next chapter.)

Do parents always maintain their special dispensation for Physical Intuition? No, in fact by the time your kid is a teen, the gift is often replaced by kvetching. Think back to when you were a teenager. Did Mom ever holler dressing instructions at you?

"Take your jacket. Listen to me. You are going to freeze without that jacket."

Rules about clothing, predictions, worrying—none of this has the least connection with empathy. (Incidentally, healthy children actually stay warmer than most older people. As explained by Covert Bailey in *The New Fit or Fat*, scientists have discovered that kids have more efficient thermoregulatory units. So the jacket-less kid may know what she's doing.)

The larger point is this. When a mother, or anyone, incorrectly tells you what you're supposedly feeling, it's enough to make you highly suspicious that anyone could have such a thing as Physical Intuition. So let's be clear. Bossing you around, based on your alleged physical life, is *not* empathy. Your mother's claim that she knows how you feel when she doesn't is something else entirely—maybe misdirected affection, psychological projection, a craving to control, or an overwhelming desire to instill fashion sense into her offspring. None of this counts as Physical Intuition.

But people who have the genuine gift can make inspired mothers, fathers, healers, lovers, trainers, massage givers. They touch you as though they know exactly what you're feeling. Because they do. Grace, a massage therapist, has told me that the best part of doing her work is "taking a ride on the client's energy." Nothing she learned from her professional training compares with this intuitive learning about another person's body. "It makes me so high," she says. But her clients probably get even higher because of the extra dimension of empathic skill that Grace brings to her work.

Physical Intuition is a highly valuable form of intelligence. If you have it, learn to use it on purpose. If your Physical Intuition isn't terribly strong yet, awaken it. Techniques in a later part of this book will show you how.

Physical Oneness

Unlike Physical Intuition, which shows you another person's physical life at a distance, Physical Oneness means you can experience someone else's physical functioning in terms of *your own body*. Before becoming a skilled empath, that can be inconvenient, to say the least.

Have you ever taken on aches and pains that belonged to somebody else? The most extreme examples I've heard came from one of my students, Moira. As a massage therapist, she did body work on a client with asthma; later she woke up in the middle of the night, hardly able to breathe. She blamed her "bad" empathy for the problem.

She also told me, "Breathing problems aren't all. What really gets to me are the stools. Some of the patients I work with are in chemotherapy, and they'll describe strange bowel movements. More often than not, they'll describe one and, I swear, very the next day that same kind of stool is coming out of my body."

Not that unskilled Physical Oneness is usually so extreme—the signals are often so subtle that an unskilled empath wouldn't even notice. For example, imagine you're at a party. A highly attractive specimen strolls by and engages you in some light banter. Your sexual signals go "Yes, yes, yes." By golly, you're starting to feel mighty attractive yourself. But something inside tells you to back off. Sigh! You excuse yourself and start talking to other guests at the party. Gradually you realize that your lower back has been hurting like crazy. And that's something your particular back doesn't generally do. How will you explain all this?

Unskilled empath? You start to beat yourself up for HYPOCHONDRIA, which really means fabricating an illness by blowing ordinary physical sensations out of proportion. Physical Oneness is *not* hypochondria. The symptoms are real. Although they seem to come out of nowhere, they belong to someone—just not to you.

Skilled empath? You know enough to question, "Whose backache is this, anyway?" Using the technique for Questioning, you receive an answer. In the example here, you discover that this particular backache belongs to your potential new lover, who suffers from a host of symptoms, psychological and financial as well as physical. Thanks to your gift for Physical Oneness, you've been warned away from a potentially draining relationship.

Here's another example. You're leading an important business meeting with a dozen people. The minutes are ticking along with the comforting pace of a big schoolroom clock when, suddenly, you feel anxious.

Unskilled empath? You blame yourself for being paranoid. Nothing's wrong. What's your problem? Squash down your bad feelings. Secretly, you worry that you'll come across to others as if though you're just going through the motions, which you are.

Sure enough, eyes glaze over. Collectively, your group enters a sort of sleep state—like one of those anxiety dreams that seems to last forever—

not the sort of meeting people remember in a positive way. Collective amnesia is the best you can hope for.

Skilled empath? Interesting—anxiety seems to comes out of nowhere during your business meeting. The explorer in you asks why. While someone else talks, you question what's going on with your body. Sure enough, you find a bunch of anxiety messages: sweaty palms, shallow breathing, a dry mouth with a metallic taste, plus a wobbly feeling in your gut.

Aha! You know what that means. One meeting participant, maybe more than one, feels anxious. It's affecting you right now. If you let this situation continue, anxiety in your audience will build. So you break out of your set speech *right now* and move some energy.

You say, "Before we go any further, let's hear some reactions. Has what we've been talking about made anyone uncomfortable? Do you think this new plan will work?"

After the meeting, which winds up being uncommonly successful, participants thank you. Someone says, "I think you are reading our minds." Really, you were reading their bodies.

Skilled physical empaths know that our bodies carry priceless information. When you use your courage and curiosity, when you risk living fully in the moment, then your body can become a powerful instrument for leadership. Business leaders, parents, speakers, salespeople all benefit from using Physical Oneness on purpose.

Healers have an equally valuable use for Physical Oneness. Sometimes you'll discover this gift when doing a technique as deceptively simple as Reiki or massage. Sensations within your own body will lead you to rub a shoulder, push against a kneecap. (This is different from having your sensitivity appear in the form of Physical Intuition, where your client's body moves your hands in the right direction. With Physical Oneness you, yourself, become an extension of your client.)

Whatever your lifestyle, as a skilled physical empath, you'll find your body is God's perfect instrument—an amazing source of knowledge that you can use in service.

Emotional Intuition

One sunny spring weekend you telephone your mother. "Hello," she groans. Your next words?

"Mom, what's wrong?"

Welcome to the world of EMOTIONAL INTUITION, where you're privy to information you might prefer not knowing. Does your mother feel sad right now? That's an understatement. Something about her voice has clued you into her whole emotional story, vivid with nuances of suffering. All you needed to hear was one word.

At least, that's what happens if you're unskilled in the use of this gift. Emotional Intuition, unskilled, can switch on and off as if it has a will of its own. Bam! You're watching another person's emotions. In the case of your mother, the sound of her hello told you the whole story. Was it anger? A guilt trip she was ready to put on you? Fear? As an Emotional Intuitive, you'll know a dozen different varieties of your mother's misery.

Maybe she wants to repeat a sad story you've heard countless times before. She's hoping you will sympathize. Ha! That's like asking a graduate student in math to practice counting to 10. What makes listening to your Mom's story so exquisitely painful (or exasperating) is the sheer redundancy. Because of your gift as an Emotional Intuitive, you know what Mom is feeling full force... before she finishes her first sentence. When she goes over her story, blow by blow, it's like hitting you with a sledgehammer.

"Then he said to me, 'You're wrong.' The nerve! Can you imagine how frustrated I felt?" Imagine? You don't have to. You heard frustration loud and clear when she cleared her throat at the start of her tale. You heard it in every sentence, every period, every pause. Had she been talking of Easter bunnies and perky little sunbonnets, you still would have heard the subtext of woe.

Emotional Intuition doesn't stop with people you know as well as your mother. When you pay attention to *anyone*, you can learn what is going on with that person's emotions. Assuming that you have this gift, anything can start you journeying:

- Tone of voice
- Speed of the voice, fast or slow
- Pronunciation of speech sounds
- Odors around the body
- Subtle variations in the person's facial skin tone, etc.

Useful though facial expressions may be socially, they can seem almost superfluous to an empath. Expressions are more like a stage show, projecting emotions that may or may not be deeply felt. In fact, one of the ways you can tell if you have a strong gift for Emotional Intuition is your strong reaction when other people display *fake* Emotional Intuition.

What, is it common for people to pretend to be Emotional Intuitives when they're not? Let's put it this way. By comparison, faked orgasms are rare. Noticing another person's insincere performance, some of us Emotional Intuitives feel disgusted, others inwardly laugh. Hey, Marcel Proust wrote novels. Whatever your reaction, you're entitled to it.

Here's an example of fake Emotional Intuition. Say you're at a memorial service. Nathan has just died and mourners are saying goodbye to his widow, Sheryl. Jessica, Sheryl's neighbor, goes into a sympathy act that makes you want to throw up. "I know just how you feel," Jill keeps repeating.

Meanwhile, Emotional Intuition is telling you loud and clear that Jill's so-called "sympathy" is really self-pity, oodles of it. Altogether, the entire scene is a ludicrous talking at cross purposes (not unlike many everyday conversations, but more intense and sadder).

For sure, when you're strongly gifted at Emotional Intuition, you know it is *not* sympathy. SYMPATHY means a forced attempt at genuine Emotional Intuition. Sympathizers feel virtuous, whereas empaths actually *feel*.

Beyond confusing empathy with sympathy, people often confuse empathy with compassion. For instance, Rosie O'Donnell, the comic and TV star, said in an interview with *Parade Magazine*: "But if you never had pain, you never have empathy. I recognize [pain like mine] when I see it in the faces of children in the clinics I go to or the kids who come to the show or in the letters I get."

Yes, Rosie is recognizing pain like her own at being raised in "an aura of neglect." Yet the true name for her experience is COMPASSION, which means sharing the suffering of another. With compassion, another person's experience pushes your buttons. Emotional Intuition is bigger. You can become aware of emotions in others that you seldom, or never, visit within yourself—sometimes with great intensity.

Incidentally, Rosie's aura shows her to be a very strong Emotional Intuitive. Even without her past history of suffering, this TV phenom would be able to enter into another person's feelings. Not yet being skilled as an empath, she's finding the best words she can to describe her experience. But compassion alone isn't what has earned Rosie her reputation as "The Queen of Nice." Emotional Intuition, I suspect, has a lot more to do with it.

This gift, like all forms of empathy, need *not* only involve pain. In fact, Emotional Intuition gives you the means to discover ways of being that are freer from pain than anything in your entire emotional repertoire. Become a skilled empath and you can safely fly out of "the box," the limits of your personality. Make way for experience that is genuinely new.

For example, I have used Emotional Intuition to experience people who have well developed, highly dignified Inner Adults. Ask any of my friends. This is not Rose Rosetree's specialty. Dignified Inner Adultness lies far outside my personal boundaries. When you choose to make contact with a genuinely new way of being, you don't necessarily copy the other person's outer behavior. You stay who you are.

Compassion, like sympathy, draws on your past experience. Empathy opens you up to your future.

Here's one final *not* about empathy in general and Emotional Intuition in particular. It does *not* involve psychologizing. Intellectually figuring out what a person "must be going through" can signal good intentions. It also can come across with all the grace of a robot trying to waltz.

Once I had a job transcribing case notes for a group of psychotherapists. Hour after hour, I worked from tapes supplied by Henry, a singularly untalented therapist. One day I muttered to one of Henry's colleagues, "He doesn't have a clue, does he?" She gave a conspiratorial groan.

Of course, therapists can do a great job, provided they first use Emotional Intuition or other forms of empathy. The problem with analyzing emotions is that it can't substitute for genuine experience. Either you touch the person's emotions or you don't. All the concepts in the world won't bridge the distance.

One way to understand the gap between empathy and psychologizing is to appreciate that figuring out anything, including feelings, means that a person works on the level of the mind, whereas Emotional Intuition is spiritual in nature. Ultimately all empathic abilities are. When it comes to spiritual learning, effort is counterproductive. For best results, you get your ego out of the way, then soak up the grace as if you were dipping dry bread into gravy.

How would someone skilled at Emotional Intuition deal with Sheryl at the funeral? He would Hold a Space for her (a technique explained later). If the space is right, his presence will bring comfort—regardless of any words he does or doesn't say. Emotional Intuition, from a skilled empath, is a powerful force for healing.

Emotional Oneness

EMOTIONAL ONENESS is an inside job. You take on other people's emotions as though they belonged to you. Maybe you're often "malled," like the woman mentioned at the start of this book who blamed herself for hating shopping. Maybe you just feel like you have the wrong set of friends in your life. People can go through a period of time (sometimes, alas, a whole lifetime) where they act as energy suckers. No matter how pleasant their manners or wishes, they leave empaths feeling exhausted.

However, the number of emotional drainers in your life does *not* necessarily correspond to your amount of talent for Emotional Oneness. Maybe you're drained due to missing a few conversational skills (like saying, "No, I don't want to ever see you again"). Maybe it's time to pay for a little therapy from a sympatico professional. Or maybe you just have the sort of job that's intolerable for highly sensitive people unless they are into vengeance, such as working for the Department of Motor Vehicles.

It's also possible, however, that people drain you because you have talent as an emotional empath and you're not skilled yet.

Cheer up. The draining, the confusion, the self-doubt, the emotional roller coaster... problems you've suffered from all your life are about to come under control. Emotional Oneness *not* on purpose is misery. But life as a skilled empath is another matter entirely. Some day you will thank your lucky stars that you were born with this gift.

At least once in a lifetime everyone receives a positive experience of Emotional Oneness. This special dispensation is called "falling in love." But how about the rest of the time, when you aren't expanded by means of romantic rapture? Emotional Oneness means cascading heaps of data, like the mega-amounts of e-mail that some of us contend with on a regular basis.

Before developing skill at handling all the feelings that come to you from others, your emotional life may be exhausting. For instance, say you're riding a bus. Other people sit and gaze out the windows; you, however, don't need to look that far to see "the sights." On every side your busmates press upon you, their assorted moods spilling over into your gut. One short ride may pull you into oneness with:

- ▫ A deeply exhausted parent, asleep while clutching her toddler
- ▫ A depressed divorcee who glares competitively at every woman in sight who might qualify as a trophy wife
- ▫ The weird and wacky playfulness of teenage boys after school

▫ Uncontrollable, though silent, giggling from a teenage girl who watches them, stealing furtive glances

▫ And (scariest of all)a pleasant-faced businessman's numbed out, tranquilized emotions

Can experiences like this be nerve wracking? You bet. You may wonder if you, like the guy with the three piece suit, should put yourself in the path of some kind of tranquilizer dart. But remember, skilled empaths can switch those emotional experiences on or off at will.

Skilled Emotional Oneness means choosing when to journey into another person's consciousness, when to hold back. It can be an act of inspiration, where you spot potential teachers and, instead of admiring from afar, you can connect at will, instantly.

Perfecting yourself or protecting yourself are simple choices when you have skill at Emotional Oneness.

Intellectual Shape Shifting

INTELLECTUAL SHAPE SHIFTING is the hardest empathic gift to recognize. It means a talent for sharing another person's thought process, as though your way of thinking changes so drastically that you become a different kind of intellectual animal. This gift can make your personality seem temporarily transparent to others, and even cause people to overlook you socially. Consequently you may lack self-confidence in general, awareness of your empathic gift in particular.

Because Intellectual Shape Shifting is so abstract, maybe it's simplest to give examples in terms of the nots. For instance, Intellectual Shape Shifting is *not* the same as academic intelligence. Your IQ could be high or low. What matters is that your smarts wear traveling shoes.

Teachers are *not* necessarily Intellectual Shape Shifters. But when you encounter one who is, you'll know it. Think back to those rare teachers who changed your life; one of them may have been an Intellectual Shape

Shifter—someone who could follow the maze of your thought process and find you just when you were stuck in some dusty, unexplored corner. This intellectual empath could guide you to some fascinating new place, then effortlessly travel to someone else's completely different mind and do the same thing.

Most teachers, even good ones, aren't Intellectual Shape Shifters. Pedagogical skills keep them going. Besides, some teachers also know their subjects so thoroughly, they can serve as VCR's for each student, performing "Play," "Rewind," or "Fast Forward" on demand. Perhaps one student needs to hear the complete recitation over and over, while another prefers to hear one sentence and invent the paragraph to go with it. Mental agility and good pacing are commendable talents, but let's not confuse them with empathy. They're more management skills about how to facilitate learning, whereas an intellectual empath Joins in Spirit with the one who learns.

Intellectual Shape Shifting is also *not* related to being a "good conversationalist." Often intellectual empaths come across as indistinguishable from other people driven by intelligence: nerdy, aloof, dry, or relentlessly precise. Their personalities don't necessarily glitter. For instance, I knew Paul for years before I pegged him as an empath. Maybe it's the movies that train us to expect extraordinary people to look the part. Paul's personality doesn't reflect his inner repertoire. Musically he has perfect pitch; conversationally he speaks in a near monotone. Judging by appearances, it was easy for me to underestimate this off-the-chart gifted Intellectual Shape Shifter.

So how did I blow his cover? Different kinds of empaths learn to recognize each other instantly, in the manner of undercover agents. My own intellectual empathy could have led me to recognize him faster than you could say "synapse," except that Intellectual Shape Shifting isn't one of my major gifts. To recognize it in him, I used "I Want to Hold Your Hand," an empathy technique you'll learn later in this book. Being Paul, even for a minute, it felt like his gift for intellectual empathy hit me *inside* the head.

These questions can help you tell if you're an Intellectual Shape Shifter, too:

- Are you interested in music, math, chess, and/or computers... especially because they're different wavelengths?
- Do you intensely feel the challenge (or delight, or absence) of intellectual companionship?
- Do you have a knack for learning complex abstract operations just by being with people who can do them? Jim, a computer consultant, told me, "Basically I'm not very good at computers, but I can travel to the consciousness of people who are... and move around where they do what they do." Sounds like an easy way to fake your way to a high-paying job, doesn't it? Just one catch—a Shape Shifting gift as strong as Jim's occurs in perhaps 1 out of 10,000 people.
- Are you a knowledge seeker more than an information gatherer? Do you find that some people's minds bore you silly, even while you appreciate the interesting facts they're communicating?
- Do you make analogies? Love abstractions? Do you constantly search for underlying principles? Intellectual Shape Shifters are fascinated by the pure mechanics of thinking. And they're especially intrigued by alternate intellectual pathways.

Another aspect of Intellectual Shape Shifting is the ability to see two or more sides to a story—then make each side a very big, vivid, and accurate story. Of course there's a downside to this form of giftedness, until you become a skilled at it. Here's a clue: Does the word "indecisive" mean anything to you?

Because you slip so easily from one kind of intellectual functioning to another, you may find yourself unable to commit to one action. Different possibilities, felt oh so clearly, appeal to you differently. It may seem as though your mind is taking over your life. Or maybe it's more accurate to say that your mind is traveling, stretching, unwilling to come in for a landing. As your spirit vibrates, the gift within you cries out to be used. Imagine if you had the three-dimensional sight of an air traffic controller. How content would you be to focus on one small runway?

My friend Gwen hates making even the smallest decision, then blames herself for it. She doesn't connect this problem with her intellectual empathy, or even with her perfect SAT score or her straight A's at Stanford. The angrier she gets at her mind, the more she pushes it to stay put on one little thing at a time, and the harder her mind creaks under the strain. She calls this a memory problem. Can you relate? Then you need to know that techniques for Intellectual Shape Shifting, just 10 minutes a day, can help you to restore balance.

For starters, it would help for you to acknowledge yourself as an Intellectual Shape Shifter. Otherwise, your heavy lifting job will go unnoticed. Unfair! Those muscular guys who work for the moving van companies gain a certain measure of respect as soon as others see their bulging forearms. Well, you Intellectual Shape Shifters have equivalent muscles. They simply don't show to the naked eye... or ear or heart. Flex your empathy, use it on purpose, and you'll increase your self-respect.

Moreover, purposeful use of your Intellectual Shape Shifting can remind you to switch it off sometimes, which will give you a chance to activate your other empathic gifts. Otherwise you may forget to switch on the more common forms of empathy, which you probably have as well. Gifts like Emotional Intuition mix in a fascinating way with Intellectual Shape Shifting... provided that you remember to use them. Techniques in later chapters will help.

Spiritual Oneness

Have you ever wondered how the weird variety of human specimens could all have been created in God's image? The answer, I believe, shows in the gift of SPIRITUAL ONENESS, a God-like ability within each of us.

Switch it on and you can experience how it is to be a completely different person. What is the new texture of your silence? How does beauty impress you? Spiritual Oneness enables you to explore how different someone else is deep down, how truly *other* compared to you.

Ultimately the workings of our senses and mind depend on the spirit, that glorious distinctiveness of each person's nature. Techniques like those you'll find later in this book will allow you to test the strength of your Spiritual Oneness, which probably works far better than you now realize. And unlike other empathic gifts, Spiritual Oneness is unique in being available to everyone who cares to use it. Most commonly, it's activated by looking someone in the eyes.

By contrast, physical, emotional, and intellectual forms of empathy are part of each person's set of God-given gifts. Although you're welcome to develop what you have, you can't give yourself a gift that isn't there. Spiritual Oneness is another story, however. It's a sleeping giant within everyone, and you can definitely wake yours up.[*]

Ask for your Spiritual Oneness to become conscious. Pray to experience, from the deepest levels, how others connect with God. For fancier variations on this theme, use the techniques later in this book.

To me, connecting with others at the level of Spiritual Oneness is like rising at dawn, waking up to witness the newly created colors of the morning. No other time of day is like it. You, too, can explore the nuances of dawn, the tender aspect of spiritual-level uniqueness.

It's fascinating to explore how other people seek their spiritual truth. For instance, ever wonder how different religions work? Taste them from the inside. With empathy, you can journey into another vibration, explore what it is like to commune with masters like Buddha and Krishna, Kwan Yin and Muhammad.

---

[*] Spiritual Oneness generally arises as *unskilled* empathy, with the experience not available on a conscious level. In this book, the author has simplified terminology by not calling people empaths unless they have empathic gifts in addition to Spiritual Oneness. Although Spiritual Oneness is a universal gift, the vast majority of people today are not strongly interested in developing it.

And, please, don't worry. If you belong to Jesus or Jehovah, they won't be offended; you can explore another's spiritual truth with perfect freedom to return to your own. Your ʀᴇʟɪɢɪᴏɴ is part of your lifestyle, like the home where you live. The creeds and customs, rituals and rites become dearer over the years, as much a part of your life as the furniture in your living room. Mystical travel to other regions is just a vacation, perhaps the most refreshing one you have ever had. And Spiritual Oneness is your ticket.

Spiritual Oneness is *not* comparative religion, fascinating though that may be as a cultural adventure. The customs of a religion have little to do with its spiritual presence. *Experience* is the key here, as with all forms of empathy.

One time, I remember, my client for a spiritual healing session was a Buddhist named Karen. Connecting with her through Spiritual Oneness, I was fascinated by the power of my discernment. I started to describe in wonderment the distinctions Karen could make, how she sifted through reality as though she was using one of those old-fashioned, squeeze-em, metal mesh flour sifters. I burbled on and on, describing the mindset from different angles until Karen started to laugh.

"What did you think Buddhism was about, anyway?" she asked.

Eventually, the session stopped being helpful mostly for me and started being helpful for her. She treated all the members of her family, including her husband, Jeff, to sessions of their own. He literally found himself sitting in the Buddha's hand. Ever since that session, he has been able to contact his own inner Buddha at will. His own Spiritual Oneness has been awakened.

It's a privilege for me to facilitate sessions like this. As a skilled empath, I've been able to guide different clients into deeper experiences of Christianity, Hinduism, Islam, and Judaism.

Remember the verse from the Bible about God's presence being amplified "where two or there are gathered in my name"?*

---

* Matthew 18:20, "For where two or three come together in my name, I am there with them."

This truth comes alive for a spiritual empath because God has many names, hundreds of them. Call upon any holy name you choose, open your Spiritual Oneness, gather with friends, and feel That presence.

Some people vacation at Disney World. *You* can vacation in the celestial realms. Spiritual Oneness is your free pass to visit God's many names, forms, mansions, and presences.

Rare Forms of Empathy

Our introduction to the six main forms of empathy wouldn't be complete without surveying other empathic gifts.* Maybe you'll recognize them in people you know— in which case, please do them the favor of telling them so. (Most empaths don't know they are empaths.) And maybe you have one or more of these unusual talents.

MOLECULAR EMPATHY is the deepest type of empathy I've encountered so far, and I learned about it first from one of my spiritual mentors, Tantra Maat. The very substance of her aura consists of superfine particles of energy which easily blend into the auras of others at an equally superfine level. She Holds a Space with clients at the molecular level. Then, being skilled as an empath, Tantra can describe what she notices, to validate experience. And like all who have this gift, skilled or not, she effortlessly moves others forward in their spiritual evolution.

Personally I have met just eight Molecular Empaths so far. One knew nothing about her gift. I had been hired to give readings at a Christmas party. Leslie was the last to approach my table. When I described her gift and ways she could use it, her entire being lit up. Eureka!

---

* Here, as with the previous descriptions of more common forms of empathy, I follow in the tradition of Abraham Maslow, who pioneered descriptions of "peak experiences." In surveying the territory, he wrote this footnote in *Toward a Psychology of Being*, John Wiley & Sons, 1968, 1999: "I realize that I am using language which 'points' to the experience, i.e., it will communicate meaning only to those who themselves have not repressed, suppressed, denied, rejected or feared their own peak-experiences. It is possible, I believe to communicate meaningfully with 'non-peakers' also, but this is very laborious and lengthy."

"I work on Capitol Hill," she said. "And what you've told me explains something. Newt Gingrich (then Speaker of the House of Representatives) has told me that I'm the only person he's ever met who frightens him."

Watch out, Speakers, wherever you are! Now Leslie isn't just a natural empath; she has started to use her gift on purpose. If you give her permission, she'll jump-start your spiritual growth.

On a practical level, results may show even more dramatically from the gift of Animal Empathy, witness the success of horse whisperer Monty Roberts, who has worked with more than 10,000 four-legged clients. Part of the inspiration for the novel *The Horse Whisperer* by Nicholas Evans, Roberts has developed Join-Up, a nonviolent method of "starting" horses rather than "breaking" them. "Join-Up" could be considered a systematic use of Animal Empathy.

Roberts calls the silent language of horses *Equus*; he teaches how to speak it through eye contact and body language. Yet I suspect that the power of his teaching comes primarily from the empathy fine-tuned by speaking Equus. Roberts has trained hundreds of other horse whisperers.

If you're an Animal Empath, you may prefer whispering to cats or dogs or pigs. Whatever your creature of choice, you understand how it is to be that animal. Perhaps you commune telepathically or stretch the limits of your human system to feel some of its perceptions. Clearly, however, you appreciate what Animal Empathy is *not*. It is *not* dressing your poodle, Queenie, in a white lace ensemble and feeding her sirloin on a silver platter. It is *not* imagining that your pet has feelings like your own.

No, Animal Empathy is a wilder and freer kind of knowing. You join with the animal's intelligence. You know its fears, its curiosities. Beyond anything else, you explore a non-human form of consciousness. More power to you! Power, incidentally, is where Roberts' aura shows its greatest distinctiveness. From what I've seen in photos, he merges his aura with that of the horse he works with, until they can come to a friendly understanding about power.

The equivalent for those who work with humans is MEDICAL EMPATHY, the ability to join with others at the level of physical awareness—with a mind-boggling result. The empath diagnoses illnesses by means of personal experience.

For those who have heard of Caroline Myss, Edgar Cayce, or other Medical Intuitives, it's worthwhile to make a distinction between their specialty versus being a Medical Empath. MEDICAL INTUITIVES are psychics who specialize in receiving health-related information. With an objective understanding, they read the client's problems. Energetically they stay within their own personal boundaries. Take Myss as an example. I've read her aura from photos and videotape; her energetic boundaries are as crisp as her no-nonsense delivery as a speaker.

Delightful as this is, it's a complete contrast to the modus operandi of Medical Empaths, who energetically merge into their clients. They, too, impart diagnostic information. But their means of gaining knowledge is more personal. It's more likely you've heard of Myss or Cayce than Dr. Brihaspati Dev Triguna. . . unless you're involved in Ayurvedic medicine, in which case you consider him a major celebrity. Triguna been trained to do *nadivigyan*, the ancient science of pulse diagnosis. During this procedure, the Ayurvedic physician's consciousness "walks around" in the patient's body. Talk about inside information!

Of course, learning to do pulse diagnosis doesn't necessarily confer Triguna's personal empathic gift. Reading his aura from photographs, I'm awed by the softness and devotional quality of his energy field. He also shows the other signs of a Medical Empath. Be they trained as pulse readers, doctors, nurses, computer programmers, or Frisbee throwers, Medical Empaths show certain distinctive abilities in their auras: Physical Intuition; the soul-level choice to be a healer; mechanical ability; plus the kind of intelligence that can soak up information about how the physical body works. Sound great? Don't envy them too much. Medical Empathy isn't necessarily convenient.

Olivia, one of my students, told me about her checkered path as a Medical Empath. "By training, I'm a nurse. Soon after my training I discovered something they never covered in Nursing School. I could tell when people were ill. It was as if I could feel what was going on in their bodies. This took no effort at all. It kind of hit me over the head.

"I'd walk by a patient and smell something at the throat or belly or feet. It would tell me which part of the patient was sick. Immediately I'd know who was getting better and who wasn't. It was uncanny. I was right every time. The lab tests would prove it.

"Eventually I started to tell other nurses and doctors about what I knew. Big mistake! They weren't prepared to receive my help. In fact, they convinced me I was crazy. I even spent time in a mental hospital. Afterwards I got out of nursing. And for so many years, I've struggled to seem normal."

For Olivia, becoming a skilled empath meant finding a way to make it safe for herself to know what she already knew.

Another one of my students, Jack, is an oncologist. Knowledge about Medical Empathy wasn't included in his medical training, either. Yet he has the gift, so he knows which patients have cancer, where it is, when it has gone, and when it returns. "I've stopped telling my colleagues what I know," Jack confided, "because they think it's weird. It's a shame, because knowing what I know really makes me a better doctor."

It's very flashy to be able to join your consciousness with someone in order to come up with a medical diagnosis. And Jack's right, the opportunities for service are great. However, it's important to understand that Medical Empathy is just one specialty. It is *not* required that you have it in order to be good at Physical Intuition or Physical Oneness. Also, empaths do *not* have to be medical healers. What if the sight of blood makes you hurl? What if you lack enough mechanical ability to put together a broken clothespin? Not to worry. This book can help you to find alternative ways to use your gifts that are just as valuable (if not as trendy) as being a Medical Empath.

Some hands aren't healing at all, but they're green—at least the thumbs. Among gardeners, a small but fascinating minority have GARDENING EMPATHY. You can have it exclusively with one type of growing thing, like corn or roses; or maybe you have it with every plant on God's green earth. Either way, having the gift means that you can join in consciousness with things that grow. Through consciousness, you enter into their slowly throbbing bodies and ask, "What do I need?"

After you return to human consciousness, you can use that information to serve as a plant co-creator, a.k.a., gardener.

Luther Burbank, the horticultural genius who developed the Burbank potato, the Burbank tomato, and more, had a less known accomplishment that is equally remarkable. He developed an edible form of cactus, one without thorns. "I often talked to the plants to create a vibration of love," he told Paramahansa Yogananda, as described in *Autobiography of a Yogi.* Because Burbank could connect with the plants on their frequency of consciousness, they listened when he told them, "You don't need your defensive thorns. I will protect you."

Of course, you don't necessarily have to undertake such ambitious projects to qualify as a Gardening Empath. Also note: this gift is *not* the same as merely talking to your plants, commendable though that may be. Can you feel from the inside out what it is to *be* a particular plant? That's the requirement for your being able to call yourself a Gardening Empath.

Moving on from vegetable and animal matters, yes, it's possible to be an empath for the mineral kingdom, too. CRYSTAL EMPATHS, like author Katrina Raphaell, can travel into the consciousness of semi-precious and precious stones, polished gems, and crystals. Like all empathic gifts, this can come as a big surprise. I'll never forget the first time I picked up a crystal and held it in my hand. Instantly it took me on a journey into its vibration. Wow, and I thought I was just holding a rock! Only later did I learn that crystals are used for healing because of their lively vibrational qualities.

---

* Paramahansa Yogananda, *Autobiography of a Yogi* (Los Angeles: Self-Realization Fellowship, 1972) p. 411

Attuning to precious stones through empathy is *not* the same as good taste in jewelry... or the kind of bad taste that demands wearing no fewer than 20 rings, earrings, necklaces, and bracelets at every opportunity. Sheer quantity of self-decoration bears no relationship to being a Crystal Empath, nor does enthusiasm for body piercing. Crystal Empathy involves a particular knack for travel into the consciousness of the mineral kingdom.

Consider the saying, "diamonds are forever." To a jewelry collector, this may work on a sentimental level. But, to this Crystal Empath at least, the experience of being a diamond is not about eternity. Faceted diamonds have a here-and-now, multi-level intelligence, with a transformative quickness. Beyond that, every individual diamond you meet will have its own quirks.

Ask to join with a diamond empathically. You, too, may be in for a surprise. Then go on to sample quartz crystals, calcites, pearls, amethysts. Have an empathy party and jewelry festival wrapped up into one!

Next, consider Elemental Empathy, a gift for linking with nature spirits, whether elves, devas, fairies, or angels who specialize in protecting Mother Earth. Marko Pogacnik is a leader in this little-known specialty. As recounted in *Healing the Heart of the Earth*, he has joined in spirit with the Angel of Earth Healing to bring light to hideous cities, battlefields, even an invisible structure remaining at the site of the Berlin Wall. Here is a man who knows pain, but he's also so deeply steeped in joy that his aura positively twinkles.

More commonly earth healers use Environmental Empathy, a gift for linking their consciousness with the body of Mother Earth. One way to tell if you have this gift is to remember what happens when you walk in nature. Do you find that you connect in a powerful way with the different patterns of forest, ocean, mountain, or desert? As you hike, does it thrill you to move from one ecological system, or neighborhood, to another? Do the smells, the plants, the animals stop you in your tracks, making you a captive to wonder?

That's the upside and the inside. There's also a downside. When a glade of trees near you is cut down to make way for yet another shopping center, it hurts. Likewise, you may suffer because of the destruction of rainforests on another continent entirely. Far fetched? All on earth are connected in consciousness. Joanna Macy, one of the most gifted and skilled Environmental Empaths of our time, encourages the practice of "despair work" to cope with these feelings in *World As Lover, World As Self.* "To experience anguish and anxiety in the face of the perils that threaten us is a healthy reaction." she writes. "Far from being crazy, this pain is a testimony to the unity of life, the deep interconnections that relate us to all beings." *

As a natural Environmental Empath, you may suffer psychologically or physically without even knowing why. So techniques for switching empathy off or on at will can help you greatly. Afterwards, as a skilled empath, despair work still can be done, but on your own schedule. Also, you'll be able to taste nature's flavors of joy with greater awareness than before.

Environmental, Elemental, Animal, Garden, Crystal, Molecular—these are just some of your possible empathic gifts. The most talented actors, artists, writers, musicians, scientists, lovers all have a gifts for empathy (and a drive to use their gifts that won't quit).

Like a poet, you can delight in naming varieties of empathy. NAMING can be an invocation. It invites a showing forth of the truth about what has been named. Never underestimate the quickening power of naming. By naming your gifts in this chapter you have taken an important step in becoming a skilled empath. Use the next page to make notes about your own gifts. Then our next step together is to explore what makes empathy work.

---

* Joanna Macy, *World As Lover, World As Self* (Berkeley: Parallax Press, 1991), p. 21

Personal Notes

What have I noticed about my gifts for empathy?

How about other people I know? Which gifts are strong in them?

What have been my biggest Aha!s from this book so far?

4. Service with a Smile— or a Frown

"What was the trauma?" the doctor asked. It was 3:00 a.m. at Reston Hospital. Excruciating pain in my right foot, which had been building for days, woke me out of a sound sleep. Finally, I had driven myself to the hospital and limped my way to the Emergency Room.

All I could tell the doctor was, "The pain just happened. I can't tell you why."

My foot was bandaged. Days later, I saw a specialist, received more treatment. Still I had no clue about what caused the pain in my foot until I received unexpected help from an empath. My mentor, Tantra Maat, sponsored an Irish healer named Penelope to give a talk. I attended, hoping to cheer myself up. Although Penelope had come well recommended, I didn't enjoy her talk. No doubt my cranky questions made this clear.

Eventually Penelope suggested (with remarkable tact) that perhaps I might prefer to go home. I limped out of the room. Layne Ferguson left, too. She was someone I had met casually a couple of times; we hardly knew each other.

"What's wrong?" she asked.

I didn't like that woman from Ireland." I said. "I guess I shouldn't have come."

"Let's sit for a while," Layne suggested.

Together we sat on a couch. I could feel her inquiring presence, but she didn't say a word. Slowly she began to cry, then to sob. It was my pain. She sobbed out my sorrow about becoming a mother for the first time, so late and so scared, at 43; about loneliness and fear mixed with a new enormous kind of love I could hardly hold. She cried about hormones out of control, about being humbled by a mountain of maternal not-knowing. How could I carry on?

It was the deepest pain I had ever known, inconvenient and shockingly ungrateful. Wasn't motherhood supposed to be like apple pie, utterly delicious? My husband was so supportive; we were in love and now we had this exquisite baby.

So I had pushed the ungrateful pain down until nobody could notice it—except for that inconvenient foot and, now, Layne.

As she cried, the truth came back to me. Layne's service to me was the starting point in a healing that took many years to complete. I'll never forget how she gave her gift, either: the simplicity, the total honesty. In her unassuming way, Layne put together a puzzle out of the full set of pieces of me, including pieces I had disowned.

Many years later, I have put together a different puzzle: how empathy works. This model has served as the basis of my life-changing work with clients over the last eight years. Here are the pieces I've put together:

Mostly Consciousness

Empathy works because, more than anything else, you are mostly CONSCIOUSNESS. Your name, your job, your religion, nothing about your life, matters as much from a spiritual perspective as the way you radiate life force energy—your consciousness.

Prove it? Ask your friendly neighborhood quantum physicist. She'll tell you that physical matter, as we know it, is composed of atoms. When you investigate what's inside those atoms, you find elementary particles like quarks. Go deeper still and you'll find that particles can be waves, and that the mere act of investigating them changes their properties. This implies that consciousness has power over it. Subjectively, experience goes one step further: Matter is made out of consciousness.

Without a Ph.D. or a lab, you can research consciousness on your own—so long as you have an open mind. Empathic travel through any of the techniques in this book can be considered research. After you're back, having traveled in consciousness, consider how you have journeyed beyond your everyday personality.

The physical part of you is small compared to this consciousness of yours. Consider the concept that your physical body is relatively small. Like the tip of an iceberg, the part that shows is just the beginning. In fact, your body is teensy by comparison with your full grandeur as an energy presence.

One dramatic way to experience the hugeness of your consciousness compared to your body is to have OUT-OF-BODY EXPERIENCES (OBEs). According to the American Society for Psychical Research, they're fairly common. As many 1 in 10 Americans has gone through a full-blown OBE, whether a near death experience, seeing your body from outside, or some other dramatic spiritual awakening.

In an OBE your consciousness seems to expand beyond your body, enabling you to observe the world from a point of view other than that of your physical self. Even your perception alters, so that you are no longer limited to your everyday physical senses.* A one-minute experience forever changes how you understand reality.

Compared to an OBE, empathic travel lacks drama. It's a natural, subtle shift of consciousness. Techniques in this book, for instance, won't seem flashy to an outside observer. The picture on the cover of this book shows an imaginative version of the technique called I Want to Hold Your Hand. In real life, when you do the technique, it only looks like a very slow motion handshake—no big deal.

---

* Definition courtesy of Jouni A. Smed's FAQ on Out of Body Experience, www.spiritweb.org/Spirit/obe-faq: html.

Yet right after you finish the technique, if you pay attention on the level of your consciousness, yes, you'll notice that you have Flown in Spirit.

Personally I have experienced both empathic travel and OBE. I believe the latter is an extreme and dramatic form of an experience that happens to empaths many times a day.

When your skill as an empath grows, perhaps you'll agree. Certainly you'll know directly from your own experience that you are mostly consciousness.

Exploring consciousness will put you in the forefront of spiritual exploration in America today. Most Americans are uninformed on the subject, at best. Some are belligerent non-believers. Yet growing numbers of skeptics benefit from energy-based healing methods. They work because—know it or not—people are mostly consciousness. Even though healers don't trumpet the fact, their work primarily alters their patients' auras. Physical healing comes as a side effect.

Yes, energy moving techniques have grown wildly in popularity over this last decade. They include acupuncture, shiatsu, Reiki, Healing Touch, Therapeutic Touch, Tai Chi, Chi Gong, homeopathy. All these forms of medicine work precisely because the real you is consciousness.

(Funny how they're called "alternative" medicine. Maybe that term should be swapped with what's now considered mainstream medicine since research in the *Journal of the American Medical Association* has shown that by 1997, visits to so-called "alternative" healers began to outnumber visits to primary care physicians.)*

However great your enthusiasm may be for these mighty technologies, movers of chi and ki and aura, don't overlook what you've been doing all along with no formal training at all. Ever since birth, you've had consciousness. You have also been moving consciousness. Yes, that's right.

---

* This same year, acupuncture received its first official endorsement from the American medical establishment, courtesy of a panel at the National Institutes of Health.

Moving Consciousness

You don't just have consciousness, you *move* consciousness. Huh? So you're not aware of this yet? To give credit where credit is due, first let's try some consciousness-raising about your consciousness.

One thought experiment could be enough to raise that consciousness permanently. Take yourself to the movies. At least, *imagine* yourself in your favorite theater. You've arrived early, before the show starts. Soon, the big blank screen will show ads, previews, and eventually even the movie you paid for(!) but for now, that naked screen is a symbol of your own human consciousness.

When stuff projects onto that screen, you lose yourself in the movie. This isn't only the mark of a good film, it's the story of your life. Friends engage you in conversation. Dessert makes your drool. Your cell phone chirps. All your senses enhance the illusion that what's outside you is the show, rather than the truth that you, the viewer, are the basis for any show whatsoever. Metaphysically, your screen—your consciousness—is the most important part of your experience in the theater of life.

Here's a direct way to explore this. After you try it, keep reading and (as you'll be doing with every technique in this book) join my virtual classroom for a session of Questions & Answers:

Wake-up Call

Who are you, really? And what does it mean to wake up to who you are? Here's a second experiment to become aware of your consciousness.

1. Sit comfortably and close your eyes to *direct your attention within*.
2. To settle down to a deeper state of functioning, *take a few deep breaths*.
3. Be still for a while. Question, *"What do I notice?"* Thoughts are

there and maybe, too, some physical sensations.

4. *Stay with your experience* for about one minute, whatever your experience, and whether it changes or not.

5. Direct your awareness outward. *Open your eyes.* Find your own words to describe your experience.

 ▫ To some, it is silence.

 ▫ To some, it is a new sound in the silence.

 ▫ To some, it is darkness.

 ▫ To some, it is light.

 ▫ To some, it is the discovery that you, the real you deep inside, are a kind of dancing light.

6. How does the self inside seem to you? *Language it*.

Wake-up Call—Q&A

Q: TRYING TO PUT THIS CONSCIOUSNESS THING INTO WORDS MAKES ME FEEL STUPID. WHY CAN'T I JUST CALL IT "STUFF"?

A: Languaging your experience will enhance it in the long run. Stretch yourself.

Q: BUT WHAT IF ALL I HAVE TO SAY IS "BORING"? I'M NOT A "DANCING LIGHT" PERSON. ALL I GOT WAS A QUIET KIND OF STATE. FOR ALL I KNOW, I WAS ASLEEP.

A: Were you drooling on your knee? If not, don't call it sleep. "A quiet kind of state" is more accurate. The point is, you've described finding the screen. Without the movie, of course it's quiet. Don't let that quietness fool you into belittling a major spiritual discovery.

Deep down, you are consciousness. Maybe others in the class have had flashier ways of describing it, but so what? Whether your mind is boggled or soothed, it still counts that you have made contact with consciousness.

Q: WHAT DO WE ACTUALLY <u>DO</u> WITH THIS CONSCIOUSNESS, WHEN WE'RE NOT PAYING CLOSE ATTENTION TO IT LIKE JUST NOW?

A: Our consciousness travels to classrooms and offices and bedrooms, breakfast and dinner, play and work. Everything we do when awake could be considered going to movies with our consciousness. The one thing that does *not* go on is clear, crisp labeling. Without a word of warning, your consciousness can shift from your inner theater to somebody else's, then shift back again. That's why part of your training as an empath will include learning to do the labeling for yourself.

Flying

Name me a kid who doesn't wish he could fly. Name me a grownup, for that matter. Everyone I've asked has a great longing for the freedom, the weightlessness. Don't you?

Actually, you *can* fly. You do it often every day. But here's the trick. You don't do this flying with your physical body, just with the part of you that is consciousness. You FLY IN SPIRIT by means of this consciousness.* Of course, most of us could use some consciousness raising about our own consciousness.

Sex is a fine example of how people travel in consciousness. Don't necessarily tell your lover if that is the best part for you. Your lover may happen to think the whole dance is about raw physical pleasure. Nevertheless, human body-mind-spirit systems are set up to enjoy a wide range of enjoyment. An orgasm, for instance, isn't just a moment of physical

---

*This is not ASTRAL TRAVEL or ASTRAL PROJECTION, where you experience yourself in a light body that seems as real as your regular physical body and you travel in parallel but different worlds. Flying in Spirit is a much more common experience. A sensation, like floating or soaring, may be present or you may simply notice that you are tuning into a different frequency of information, but you are still in this world.

By analogy, Flying in Spirit is like listening to a different station on your regular bedroom radio, whereas astral travel is like finding a new type of radio that behaves altogether differently—e.g., You can move it around the room just by sending out a thought. The American Society for Psychical Research (www.aspr.com/index.htm) suggests that astral projection is very different from out-of-body experiences.

release. It's a moment when you completely let go of the familiar way your consciousness is stuck in your body. Beyond this, as an empath you may notice other nuances during sex when you merge your consciousness with your partner:

- Ever share in your partner's sexual pleasure as though it were your own?
- Ever feel as though that person has become a piece of your heart?
- Ever feel your breath has merged, or changed into, the breath of your partner?

Sex doesn't have to make the earth literally move to be a trip for your consciousness. Sex has moved your energy if it has taken you beyond the usual sense of self that climbs stairs and does laundry.

Sex lets your consciousness fly. It's freedom. Specifically, it's weight-lessness alternating with being very physical. Sex is just one of dozens of ways available to you to fly in consciousness.

For instance, speaking of wake-up calls, when was the last time you visited somebody over the telephone? No, not that telemarketer who called in the middle of dinner—think of a voluntary conversation, a meeting of minds.

Picture yourself. Maybe you're in the kitchen, multi-tasking at your usual frantic new millennium pace. So you call your best friend on the cordless phone. Your hands are doing the dinner dishes, moving like a secular version of one of those Hindu gods with the multiple sets of arms. Your physical body packs the dishwasher, stores the leftovers, crams them into the fridge, cradles the telephone; maybe you scratch or sling a stray kid over your hip or take one of those food containers back out to toss a few more bites into your mouth, then angle the food and head position so your friend won't know you are noshing.

In short, you do your whatever.

Meanwhile, though, you and your friend are in a mind meld. You have met each other in consciousness, through the medium of the telephone.

Mere chit-chat on the phone is different. You realize this at once if you are in the position of teaching your child how to conduct a telephone conversation. Three-year old Matthew holds up the receiver with its funny little holes and babbles into it with a puzzled expression. He talks. You coach him, "Now hold it next to your ear and listen." He shrugs, throws down the receiver, and goes off to play with another toy.

Eventually your kid picks up the mechanical part of phone manners, but that can be years away from holding a person's energetic presence over the phone, which is what *you* do and take for granted.

As an experienced telephone talker, you are traveling in consciousness. Non-physically, you visit your partner whose body is at the other end of the line. How? By switching off awareness of your physical senses, you amplify whatever part of you does the visiting. That's moving in your consciousness!

If you feel comfortable leaving voice mail messages, you've taken this form of travel one step further. Without here-and-now verbal cues from the person you're calling, you imaginatively join with that person's energy presence and talk to it.

Not all adults have mastered this more advanced form of telephone talk, however. Can you tell the difference when you play back the messages on your voice mail? Do you hear a speech or a connection? A trained empath can tell the difference. And any empath, skilled or not, has a natural knack for connecting over the telephone. The prosaic name for this is "talking on the phone." The metaphysical name is "Flying in Spirit."

Very, Very Good

Why don't we usually notice our frequent non-physical travel through telephones, or sex, or dozens of other everyday situations?

Once we learn how, we're so very good at it. No special effort is required. Assembly and battery have been included in the original purchase price because you have been made in the image of God, the ultimate traveler.

Skill that good is easy to take for granted. The same could be said of your heartbeat. You take a healthy heart for granted, so effortlessly does it beat. When it comes to your physical equipment, not being conscious that it works can be a good sign.

But let's make an important distinction between your heart, your breath, in fact the whole of your autonomic nervous system, and your spiritual consciousness. When you use your spiritual consciousness consciously, it works *better*.

The human ability to be conscious is tremendously important. We're told that homo sapiens differ from earth's other animals just because we think. Well, dogs and cats think, too, or they wouldn't interest us much as pets. "Thinking animal" really means having a distinctive, individualized form of consciousness. What happens when we gain greater skill at flying with that consciousness? We sapiens move up another notch on the evolutionary scale. Sapiens turn into enlightened ones.

Interconnected? It's Automatic

Want to break through one of the greatest illusions of life on earth? You only *seem* to be separate from others. Spiritual life is about learning that you aren't.

This illusion of a body you're in, circled with skin and filled up with all sorts of stuff—sure it seems to be separate but really it's just a house for your consciousness. Anyone can visit; the truth of what's going on there can't be hidden. Likewise, you can easily enter and explore any other house. In consciousness, unlike real estate, there's no such thing as a detached, single family home.

Cosmic joke? Sure is.

As part of the joke, society teaches you just the opposite. To be an American at this time in history is to celebrate individualism to the max. Have any people, at any time on the planet, made more of their seeming independence? Nonetheless we're more interconnected than not, and not merely by virtue of our Internet, our car-clogged highways, and chain stores linked across the nation, each so interchangeable that physical travel across America has become an exercise in déjà vu.

Human beings are interconnected spiritually, emotionally, mentally, even physically.

Everyone remembers this occasionally, with a little shock of recognition. Take breathing, for example. What could seem more personal than your breath? Yet humans all over the world share your air. As songwriter Tom Chapin sings about recycling, "Someone's going to use it after you. Someone's gonna need it when you're through."

Our physical swapping doesn't stop with the nostril stuff, either. It's mind boggling to realize that Planet Earth uses, and always has used, the same water supply. Dinosaurs drank from pools that, many weather cycles later, have filled up bottles at your local convenience store, bottles that bear the mystical label *Coca-Cola*. In fine print those labels should read, "Recycled over the eons from mountain lakes, jungles, and city sewers; distilled from the sweat, blood, and tears of every race that has lived on this earth."

Vital though environmentalism is, all too often it emphasizes the aspect of pollution when considering oneness. Why not give equal time to the good in our shared air? *Possibly* what you're breathing right now is tinged with toxins, for sure—*guaranteed*—every communal inhale's a miracle.

Most of what we recycle works for us. Inspire yourself (literally, "breathe in") with this thought. You share the same air and water used by Jesus, Buddha, Krishna, Moses, and Mohammed. And just as people are mostly unconscious about this magnificent sharing, we foolishly ignore how interconnected we are on the level of our consciousness.

Can Do

Not only *can* you fly, you already *do*. Being interconnected with others, you travel to them by means of consciousness countless times each day. So how come this may be news to you? Two reasons: Travel through space and time occurs with the utmost effortlessness. It's just not restricted to your physical body.

Do your flights of fancy, consciousness, and subtle bodies count, even though they don't involve your outermost layer, the physical body? The answer depends on you, and whether you are ready to use your gifts of consciousness. Here's one experiment to help you find out. (Remember to read the Q&A section only *after* you do the experiment.)

Time Travel, Instantly

1. *Choose a destination.* The following list of travel ideas gives you a selection of places to think about. As you read through the list, stop as soon as an idea jumps out at you.
2. Close your eyes and *connect with a memory* for at least one minute:
   - What is one of the best presents anyone has ever given you? What were the circumstances?
   - When was the last special occasion where you ate cake?
   - When was the last time someone you loved held your hand?
   - Have you ever had a haircut that was so good (or so terrible or just plain strange) that you'll always remember it?
   - When was the last time you bought yourself something you really wanted?
   - Place yourself outdoors in a memory connected with intense weather.
   - Who is one of the best teachers you've ever had? When did you realize this person had something special to give you?

3. *Return to the here and now.* Open your eyes and connect with one item from the following list:
   - Pick out at least one sound from your present surroundings.
   - Look at whatever lies directly in front of your eyes.
   - Wiggle your toes.
   - Notice how something smells.
4. Time to travel again. Choose a topic, *close your eyes, and reminisce* for a minute on one of the following topics:
   - Think about a dear friend whom you don't see much any more.
   - Touch on a memory of your friendship that brings up warm feelings.
   - Recall one of the proudest moments of your life.
5. Return to the here and now. (See Step #3.)
6. Close your eyes and *fantasize about a future vacation.* If money were no object and responsibilities didn't limit you in any way, where would you go? With whom? Which part of your vacation would be the most fun?
7. Return to the here and now. (See Step #3.)

Time Travel, Instantly—Q&A

Q: I COULD HAVE DONE THAT FOR HOURS, EXCEPT I HATE THE COMING BACK PART. IT MADE ME FEEL LIKE A YO-YO. WHY DID WE HAVE TO DO IT THAT WAY?

A: The purpose was to wake up both parts of the travel process: going out and coming back. For you, the travel part came easier. For others, it was the opposite. But one way or another, you've demonstrated that you can travel by means of your consciousness, round trip.

Q: TO ME, ALL THAT CAME EASY WAS WORRY, WORRY, WORRY. EVEN ON THE "VACATION," I COULDN'T ENJOY MYSELF. DO YOU THINK SOMETHING COULD BE WRONG WITH ME?

A: Right now your consciousness—or body, or life situation—is emphasizing worry. Tomorrow or next week it could be different.

Q: Nah, for me, worry is a way of life. So?

A: Then that's how your consciousness travels most easily. Consider the possibility that you're a problem solver. When you find yourself traveling to a worry zone, ask yourself, "How can I solve this problem?" Stick around for the answer before you leave. That will be important for you.

And remember, whatever the emotional tinge, all journeys count. Travel could be in terms of smiles or smells, music or noise, bread or circuses. Go the way that you go.

Q: I hate to break this to you, but there's another word for what we were doing. Thinking. Why do you have to call it something grand and glorious when it's plain ordinary thinking?

A: Thinking means mental activity. But just because you're experiencing something *through* your mind, that doesn't necessarily make it a limited kind of thinking.

Thinking can be defined many ways. For Empathy 101, thinking sometimes means the use of your MIND to pay attention to people, things, and situations in the here and now. Children develop this kind of mental skill when they're in the developmental stage that psychologist Jean Piaget called *concrete operations*, e.g., when you count by handling blocks. This is focused, purposeful thinking, done with your mind.

A different sort of mental operation, that also could be called thinking, involves your INTELLECT. At this level you sort through ideas, work with concepts and categories. Although using your intellect is very different from using your mind, it still expresses itself in thoughts. What else can it do, tap dance?

Yet one more entirely different kind of mental operation, also expressed through thinking, involves using your consciousness. Consciousness means your ability to be aware, whether you focus on a particular thought or leave your mind big and expanded. Yes, your consciousness can dress up as plain, ordinary thinking. Or it can be grand and glorious—up to you.

Q: To me, the exercise we did wasn't about any of that. It was just imagination. How about defining that, too?

A: IMAGINATION means creative exploration by means of thought. Everyone has a vivid imagination, by the way, provided you let yourself to use it freely. As you become a skilled empath, imagination will play a big part in your discovery process.

Q: JUST IMAGINATION? AS IN, "THAT DIDN'T REALLY HAPPEN, IT WAS JUST MY IMAGINATION"?

A: Trust "just my imagination." You'll be way ahead of most people, for whom imagination is a dirty word, which is a shame. Because this word has such a bad connotation, some people are more comfortable calling it something else, like *creative visualization*, *daydreaming*, or *fantasizing*. Call it *Gregory*. Who cares, so long as you give yourself permission to use your imagination.

Q. IMAGINATION IS ALL WELL AND GOOD, BUT I PUT IT IN THE CATEGORY OF JELLY BEANS OR THE FRILLY PINK TUTUS I USED TO WEAR WHEN I WAS A GIRL. NOW I'M A GROWNUP. IS IMAGINATION GOING TO HAVE TO BE A BIG DEAL WHEN I'M DEVELOPING EMPATHY? BECAUSE IF IT IS, I'M NOT SURE I WANT TO PLAY.

A. Aha, so you're a grownup! For many of us, imagination is permissible only when sharing in someone else's creativity. It's okay to enjoy animated films and the big-buck movies with Titanic budgets for special effects. In your real life, if you can't touch your experience, weigh it like a slab of dead meat on a butcher's block, and convince all the world's skeptics to hold exactly the same reality, you're not being "sensible" enough. Imagination, your power to create reality out of thought, doesn't count.

As if! You'll find it's a relief to connect—or reconnect—with your capacity for imagination. It resonates with your most delicate, intimate ways of experiencing life. Admittedly, some people will always label imagination as childish, and so forth, but these are people who have buried their souls in the sand. As empaths, we not only have imagination, we need it. Part of an empath's development is to trust and nurture imagination, so I hope you'll give yourself permission to do that.

Q: WELL, MAYBE. BUT ONE MORE QUESTION ABOUT THIS. FOR AN ADULT, CAN'T IMAGINATION BE A WASTE OF TIME?

A: For adults to spend hours a day on imagination, yes, that could be considered a hideous waste. But spending time to be aware of your consciousness and how it works—or other balanced use of imagination—will not make you one whit less successful at everyday life.

Imagination remains a precious spiritual faculty, regardless of the degree to which you have been taught to value it. Moments of travel, via imagination, are a human birthright.

Children, coming to us fresh from God, start off very good at this. But in America today, even children seldom have time for the luxury of imagination. They must settle for entertainment provided by others because they have forgotten that they can travel through their own imaginations. So they hitchhike in front of the TV or the Internet.

Q: GUILTY AS CHARGED. APART FROM MOVIES, I HAVE ZILCH IMAGINATION. DO YOU REALLY THINK I CAN BRING IT BACK?

A: Imagination can always be recaptured, full force and better than ever. For starters, give yourself permission to play every day, to dream, to have fun. Even if there were no other reason, you'd want to activate imagination so you can become a skilled empath.

Empathy Means Flying

Spiritually you are made up of energy bodies. They are layers of your aura, or energy field. Contrary to what you may have been told, auras are not simply blobs of color with assigned meanings. Auras are three-dimensional bodies, made of electro-magnetic energy and packed with information. (See my earlier book, *Aura Reading Through All Your Senses*.)

The topic of auras relates directly to the mechanics of empathy. Your body isn't just physical. It includes a set of overlapping energy bodies. Each of these subtle-body layers specializes in a different aspect of life: physical life force, mental functioning, emotions, spirituality, and more.

Why Empaths Need to Read Auras

Given the time in which we live, it's important to remind you that auras DO have a legitimate place in the practice of empathy. Reading them need not brand you as "New Age."

Are you Christian, Hindu, or Buddhist? All your life you've been seeing haloes on pictures of the beings you worship. Of course God in human form should be painted with an aura. So should every creation God has made. When we look deeper into reality, the presence of this level of life hits us like a ton of bricks. It's that true (if not that heavy).

What if you've been raised in a religion that says "Don't worship idols" like Judaism or Islam? Then you haven't grown up with pictures of saints or angels or Masters. But anyone who prays to God has the right to receive an answer to prayer. The clearest answers come on the level of Celestial Perception, which is also the level of auras.

So, whatever your religious background, the decision is yours. Do you choose to fully appreciate God's living presence in people? Then it would be tragic to settle for just the outermost covering of life. Even if nobody from your family—or your church—talks about auras, you have every right to explore them.

Celestial Perception is yours for the asking, but you must claim it. The same goes for literacy, making money, or enjoying sex. For these gifts to enter your life full force, you must give permission.

Because you're set up as an empath, your whole life long a spiritual part of you has been giving service on the Celestial level. Unskilled empaths don't notice. Becoming skilled, you'll need to cast off unnecessary humility. Of course you deserve to understand what's going on! And you can't do that without being willing to read auras.

As an empath, your skill and service, both, will involve working at the Celestial level. If, in the past, you've heard things that turned you off, most likely what you heard wasn't true. Popular ideas about auras in America are often pathetically limiting. Read with an open mind and you'll discover the truth for yourself.

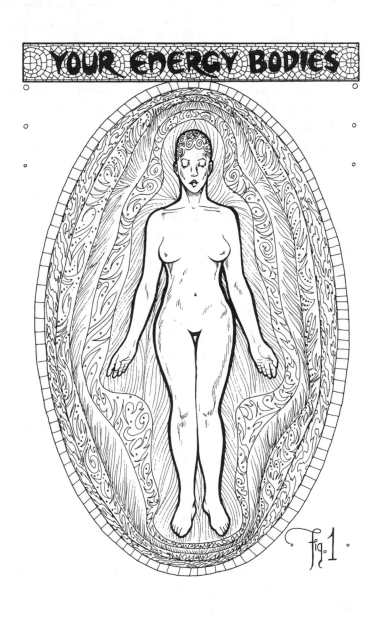

YOUR ENERGY BODIES

fig.1

Each of these subtle-body layers specializes in a different aspect of life: physical life force, mental functioning, emotions, spirituality, and more.

Different aura readers understand these subtle bodies differently. If you want to give yourself a headache sometime, compare pictures in books by Leadbeatter, Rosalynn Bruyere, Ann Meyer, etc. If you don't want to give yourself a headache, study just one person's system at a time or, even better, develop your own.

Why do so many professionals have conflicting ways of understanding auras? Aura reading is a spiritual gift.

Hold that thought for a moment. Chew it around. Savor it as though you were tasting your favorite chocolate. *Aura reading is a spiritual gift.*

Knowledge of auras is different from knowledge of physical life on earth, which is a relatively one-size-fits-all reality. Science works best on that physical level, with objective measurements and linear causation—although even science, when delving deeply into such matters as elementary particles, opens into the shifting spiritual field of consciousness. Ultimately even the physical level of life is spiritual.

Which leads to an operational definition of empathy. Empathy means you Fly in Spirit into someone else's aura. Physically, it can't be perceived, but spiritually it can. Which is why perception of aura reading is so important for becoming conscious about your empathy.

Perception of auras is shaped by the perceiver's spiritual specialties. Some of us, for instance, do most of our spiritual learning and service on the level of the intellect; others work more with feelings. Depending on your specialties, a diagram of how *you* perceive auras is going to put some levels ahead of others. Here is the model that works for me. (See figure 1.)

Another way to understand these bodies is that each one corresponds to a major energy center. These are called CHAKRAS. Don't let the ancient Sanskrit name (pronounced CHA-kras)intimidate you any more than a term about physical anatomy, like "belly button." Chakras can give you

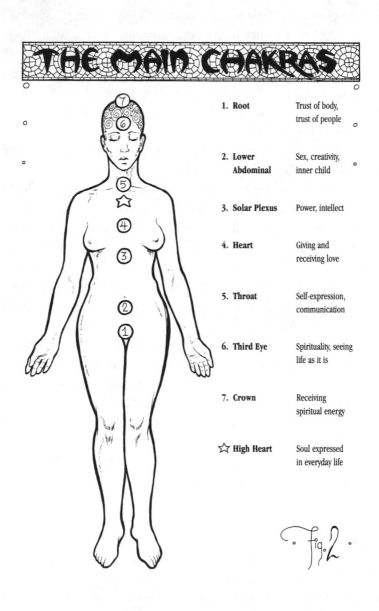

THE MAIN CHAKRAS

1. **Root** — Trust of body, trust of people

2. **Lower Abdominal** — Sex, creativity, inner child

3. **Solar Plexus** — Power, intellect

4. **Heart** — Giving and receiving love

5. **Throat** — Self-expression, communication

6. **Third Eye** — Spirituality, seeing life as it is

7. **Crown** — Receiving spiritual energy

☆ **High Heart** — Soul expressed in everyday life

Fig. 2

very practical knowledge about everyday matters. Figure 2 shows a diagram of these energy centers.

In many of the techniques for empathy you PLUG INTO A CHAKRA to obtain information about it.

That's right, I've discovered that you can plug into different chakras as though they were electrical sockets... except that you don't light up a lamp. You light up knowledge.

By paying attention to a particular chakra, you direct one of your energy bodies to merge with someone else's. And the merging takes place right at that level of subtle body. For instance, the Heart's Journey Technique you'll learn later sets up a situation where you plug into a partner's heart chakra, which relates to that person's emotions. Zap, you'll merge your emotional energy body to your partner's body on that level.

After your consciousness has traveled in this way, you'll be able to experience directly what is going on with your partner's *emotions*. Some of the information may be specific, since qualities like love, pain, and fear have distinctive patterns that you'll learn to recognize in your own terms. Equally fascinating, you will be able to learn about the other person's *way of having emotions*. As a skilled empath, it will be your privilege to access this profound kind of knowledge.

Even before becoming skilled as an empath, you travel in consciousness to the auras of others—and do it countless times daily. That's right, you merge one or more of your energy bodies with its counterpart in another person.

Sound sexy? Hmm, I suppose it is, except that your physical body isn't involved. And no physical body means no physical pleasure. Also, before becoming a skilled empath, you may be unconscious that these mergings of energy bodies even take place.

Neither of these conditions makes for what most people would consider great sex.

Flying as a Form of Spiritual Service

"Why bother with empathic travel?" you may be asking by now. Unless conscious that you're traveling empathically, you can't learn much from what you're doing. Even worse, as we've seen right from the first chapter, unskilled empathy comes with certain built-in problems. So why do it in the first place?

Empathy is a way to give spiritual service. Before birth, we empaths have volunteered. Consequently service comes to us as naturally as breathing. Sometimes we give service with a smile; sometimes we give service with a frown. Whenever we share another person's emotion, we lift a burden. One shining example of a skilled empath is John Gray, author of *Men Are From Mars, Women Are From Venus*. He has lifted burdens for millions through his empathic understanding of differences between the sexes.

Although Gray doesn't explicitly describe people as traveling and merging in their subtle bodies, he has helped couples to understand how deeply they link after committing to a relationship. "What you suppress, your partner will expresses," he explains in *What You Feel, You Can Heal*, drawing a diagram of two tanks that become linked through a connecting tube.* (As I remember Gray's seminars from this early period, when talking about this form of sharing he didn't use the polite term "tanks." He actually called it merging each other's garbage pails—because of the way it can feel.)

An everyday example of sharing garbage pails (a.k.a. the shadow self) is a husband who worries that his wife is going crazy because she acts hyper-emotional. Really, she's fine. Except she has taken on the burden of acting out an extra load of feelings belonging to her under-emotional husband, who denies his emotions and keeps them stuffed in his unconscious garbage pail.

---

* In this early self-published work, Gray explains, "The more connected you are to another person, the more you are able to share and experience... feelings." p. 116

Because empaths can take on emotional baggage for so many people other than spouses, I like to broaden Gray's garbage pail concept to a more general term, EMPATHIC SHARING. This means connecting at a subtle body level to any living being. Once connected, you can share any experience, positive or negative. Because empaths can connect on the level of *any* of our subtle bodies, empathic sharing may involve taking on stuff that is physical, mental, spiritual, or emotional.

What makes that service? *When we take on someone else's burden, we lift the burden.*

The service can be for ourselves as well. If we share someone else's joy, we discover (or remember) how to create that kind of joy.

Mostly, though, since so little is widely known about being a skilled empath, empathic sharing has mostly been noticed in the context of problems. For instance, emotional interconnectedness is familiar to family therapists. They look with a skeptical eye at the "identified patient" in the family, knowing that the problem child (or father or mother) is usually not the family's sole problem. Instead the identified patient expresses serious problems that involve everyone in the family to some degree. The apparent troublemaker is usually the most sensitive person in the family, not necessarily the one who is the most troubled.

The sacrificing kind of service performed by identified patients may be familiar to you in a less extreme form, social embarrassment. Have you sometimes been bothered by behavior that nobody else seemed to notice? Did your reaction cause you to act in a way that seemed inappropriate? For instance, think back to a time when people around you were rigidly in control (and hiding their feelings). You laughed or yelled, out of control, then felt humiliated to be acting this way.

If inappropriate behavior is not your usual mode, consider reframing those "shameful" episodes. Could you have been acting as an emotional releaser for one very stuck person? Was an entire group of people in an unbearably awkward situation before you burst into laughter? Maybe other people's denied feelings exploded out of you like air from an overfilled balloon?

Rather than blaming yourself for being "immature," consider the possibility that you were performing service. Maybe it wasn't the highest level of empathic service. Maybe it was pathetically not-yet-skilled. Service it remained nonetheless.

The first step in claiming greater skill now is to start recognizing the signs of empathic volunteer work. As you become more skilled, you'll become aware of what's going on. You'll be able to help others *without* going out of control. Eventually, you'll be able to stop linking emotionally (by choice) and simply speak words that reflect your insight. And you'll be able to enjoy watching people heal as a result. Then they'll be the ones who react in intense and surprising ways.

I'll never forget what happened when I gave some feedback to a woman at one of my book signings for *Aura Reading Through All Your Senses*. Along with autographs, I gave mini-readings. Usually I could find something nice—and public—to say. But one woman, Geraldine, was overwhelmingly brokenhearted. I told her so, delicately and discretely.

"You can tell that?" She practically sang. "You mean it shows? It's true. We broke up only yesterday. I *am* heartbroken. We were together seven years, you know. I *am* heartbroken. Gee, it shows!" An enormous grin lit up her face. She sat down in the front row, laughing her head off for the rest of the evening.

Acknowledgment does heal—not that it will necessarily remove all pain. Still, the worst aspect of personal suffering may be the feeling that we face it alone. Did you ever fear that your isolation in pain would last forever? When an empath shares the precise quality of your experience (even more if she can also language it for you) this illusion shatters.

As an *unskilled empath* I would have absorbed some of Geraldine's sadness as my own, rather than realizing clearly that it was her problem. As a *non-empath*, I wouldn't have felt her sadness at all. But as a *skilled empath*, I could share the experience, then help change it. And in the healing process, laughter like Geraldine's definitely counts.

Laughter or tears, even outrageous bragging on the part of your client, counts as a sign of success. With the discernment of a skilled empath, you'll come to recognize successful service in its many forms. Provided that you have made a genuine connection, then acted with a worthy intention, you will feel an inner glow. Quiet though the blessing may be, you'll feel it shine, pure as candle light.

Terrible Waste

When we ignore our spiritual calls to action, we pay an inner price. Our gifts won't quit, they won't go away. Their call can even turn to pain, if need be, until we're forced to acknowledge that empathy is a terrible thing to waste.

Why? Imagine that the SOUL you've been given, your distinctive human identity, is like a robe. Woven into the finest threads of its fabric, spun from the finest gold thread, are your patterns of talent. To wear your soul is to wear that golden thread. No matter how it's ignored or overlooked, gold has a way of shining. Should you ignore it too long, your soul will force you to notice—usually in pesky little ways. But if it takes big drama to get your attention, guess what? Big drama is what you'll get.

No doubt you have known people like Bradley, a friend of mine at college. Playing the cello was his passion. But the thought of doing it professionally scared him to death. Bradley was smart, studious, and very responsible. His parents had brought him up to be a doctor or lawyer, not some dreamy-eyed musician. Accordingly he studied anything but music—and flunked course after course. Finally the Dean called him in for a final warning, one last chance before he flunked out of school.

Bradley couldn't understand why he seemed to be sabotaging his academic career. He studied so hard. Besides, he knew he was smart. We fell into a conversation over this scary turn of events. He asked, "Why does this keep happening to me? I don't understand."

Joining with his musician's consciousness, the solution seemed obvious to me. Out popped these words: "When are you going to let yourself major in music? Maybe your soul won't let you succeed at a career that would waste your gifts." Amazingly, nobody else had suggested this. Bradley's face lit up. He decided to give music a try. Of course, his grades (and life) improved immensely.

Why had someone as smart as Bradley landed in such a predicament? Maybe he had two things in common with you:

- Conscientiousness: Bradley was conscientious, so it took great courage to consider a chancy profession like music. Similarly, you may be very conscientious about fitting into a society that does not honor empaths. "Squelch that talent. It makes you too weird." Thus speaks your tribe. You may be tempted to hear and obey.
- Talent: If Bradley's talent hadn't been so overwhelming, his soul might have let him keep music a hobby. Similarly if you are set up to be a majorly talented empath, saying no won't work. Eventually not using your gift will become so unbearable that all the good reasons in the world to say no just won't work any more.

Another possibility is that you're *not* like Bradley. A talent for empathy doesn't dominate your life. Maybe you're put together with so many other gifts that you'll do fine as an unskilled empath. In that case, you are free to use your empathy consciously and fully or not. Either way, your life will work fine. Still, for the sake of yourself as well as for others, your empathy would be a terrible thing to waste.

Service Defines an Individual

Does the idea of service make you think of some faceless, downtrodden worker, like a butler whose boss calls him George even though that isn't his name? Unfortunately some employers are like that; every butler is going to be called "George" as a matter of convenience. Even when service jobs aren't that bad, they often squelch a servant's individuality. Volunteer work as a *spiritual* servant does just the opposite, however. When you decide to use your God-given gifts for empathy, it brings a delectable clarity to your awareness of who you are. Then your work can become as distinctive as your gifts.

Johanna Macy, for instance, has made a fascinating career of service as an Environmental Empath. In *World as Lover, World as Self* she writes, "The way we define and delimit the self is arbitrary. We can place it between our ears and have it looking out from our eyes, or we can widen it to include the air we breathe, or, at other moments, we can cast its boundaries farther to include the oxygen-giving trees and plankton, our external lungs, and beyond them with the web of life in which they are sustained."*

In expanding empathically, which she calls "dependent co-arising," Macy allows her personal flow-through to include an intensity of suffering that many people (myself included) would never volunteer to handle. But she is energetically designed to do this, and thus she succeeds in bringing alive one of the most fundamental concepts of Buddhism.

Dr. Bill Bauman, my mentor and the author of *Oneness: Our Heritage, Our Path, Our Destiny*, is a master of spiritual, emotional, physical, and intellectual oneness. His clarity about spiritual service is illustrated by the experience of my friend Sam, during one of Bill's seminars. Right before a break, Sam approached Bill, asking for advice about a chronic health problem. "I was just on my way to the bathroom," Bill told him. "But I'll keep you in mind and see what we can do."

Within minutes, Sam felt an energetic shift. The nagging pain was gone. "I see why people might want to put you on a pedestal," he joked with Bill. "I'd never permit that to happen." he said. "I'll knock us both off." Although Bill's sense of service doesn't permit pedestal-ism, he and his wife Donna model how empathy can create miracles. Theirs can. Yours can.

Dr. Elaine N. Aron maintains psychotherapy practices in San Francisco and New York. Her book, *The Highly Sensitive Person*, demonstrates her

---

* Joanna Macy, *World As Lover, World As Self* (Berkeley: Parallax Press, 1991), p. 12

intellectual giftedness. But her greatest strength jumps right out at you from her photo at the back of her book. The woman's aura reveals an off-the-chart emotional empath.

Fame and wealth are possible results of using your gifts, but let's not kid ourselves. For most of us, spiritual service is rewarded mostly *spiritually*—in denominations you can't take to the bank, such as delight and friendship. The greater your skill, the more richly you'll be rewarded.

Working personally with clients, I've found that, conscious of it or not, empaths continually perform spiritual service. But the catch is, if they're not conscious about it, their personality misses the whole show.

It's like a distant father who ignores his child. The child's life goes on, even without playing with his father. Both survive but they suffer a loss of joy. Don't be an absentee parent to your own empathic Inner Child. Revive the joy you have been given all along.

5. How to Switch Empathy OFF

What happens when you switch empathy off? Besides developing your skill as an empath, it's fun, as you'll discover with the techniques in this chapter. By exploring, you'll lift this book right off the page and into your multiple-dimensional reality. So join our virtual classroom, first by trying each technique, then reading the Q&A section that follows it.

I Like

This technique helps you to pay attention to things you like. Yes, it's all about ME ME ME. Liberate yourself temporarily from concern about anyone but yourself.

1. Sit or stand somewhere you can *be alone*, or at least uninterrupted, for a minute or two. (Actually, this technique is excellent for times like being stuck in a long line at the supermarket, provided you do it discretely.)
2. Look at your surroundings. *Find the color you like most.* Is it the blue upholstery on your chair, bright pink lettering on a poster near your bus stop, a fascinating and colorful food stain on your shirt? Go for likability, pure and simple.

3. *Say why you like it* out loud. "I like the color of the _____ because _____."

4. Now it's sound time. Close your eyes. Question, *"What sound do I like most*, here and now?" Listen a while to the variety of sounds audible wherever you are. Choose your favorite.

5. Open your eyes and *say why you like it* out loud, "I like the sound of _____ because _____."

6. For the final touch, close your eyes again. Seek out and touch different textures, such as the fabric of your clothing, the surface of the furniture near you. Parents, did you ever see a toddler absorbed in fondling a lovey? As adults we can retain the comfort of pure touch long after we have relinquished our teddy bears. Take a couple of fingers and explore your near environment until you *find a texture that especially delights you.*

7. Open your eyes and *say why you like it* out loud, "I like the way _____ feels because _____."

I Like–Q&A

Q: You'd be amazed how hard it was for me to do this exercise. Why?

A: "I Like" is a technique of pure selfishness and sensuality. You cease looking out for other people. You jump into your own here and now. Of course, that can be hard in the beginning.

Q: What if I keep thinking, "Who cares what I like? What does it matter?"

A: It thrills your soul to find pleasure through your senses. If you have ever hungered to be in closer contact with your soul, guess what? It will help to pay attention to what you, personally, like. Ignore the inner grumbles and keep on exploring.

Q: I had no trouble finding a color I liked, etc. But what was the point?

A: Beyond giving yourself a vacation *from* empathy, you were giving *to* yourself. You reminded yourself that, at will, you can take delight in your senses. Ask your Inner Child how it likes this technique. Probably it's jumping for joy.

Q: How often would you recommend playing the "I Like" game?

A: Do it three times a day for a week, at the minimum. You're right, it *is* a game. And the more often you play it, the more you'll enjoy it.

Q: What is the purpose of the "because" part of the game? Why isn't it enough to choose something I like?

A: When you push yourself to express why you like something, you're challenged in several ways, all beneficial.

1. You probe into a non-verbal, non-rational part of yourself, which connects you to deeper aspects of who you are. Every time you probe for words, you strengthen coordination between your conscious mind and this deeper self.
2. Expressing experience in your own words can exercise the same languaging ability you will use later to refine empathic insights.
3. Answers you come up with may be very childlike and simple, such as "I like the purple color of my calendar because it makes me feel happy." It's good practice for you, as an adult, to speak with such simplicity. From childhood we've been trained to make ourselves sound educated, complex, sophisticated, important. But often the truth of our deep experience *is* childlike.
4. After you say your answers out loud, you have the chance to practice nonjudgment. "I like the carpet because it's soft." "The sound of the wind in the trees feels dark brown and soothes my forehead." Whatever words come out of your mouth, strive to accept them without judgment or criticism.

Q: I happen to have a major challenge about making decisions. This sounds stupid, but what if it takes me a really long time to choose?

A: Keep at it. Eventually you'll improve your decision-making, especially if you add one simple rule: When you're hunting for your favorite color, sound, or texture *give yourself no longer than two minutes*. Set a timer—not to pressure you but so that, if you have picked nothing by the time the buzzer sounds, whatever you are noticing at that time will count as your choice. With practice you'll eagerly choose your favorite.

Also, remember, this technique can be lighthearted and fun. You're not on the witness stand in some murder trial. Just pick something. Pick anything. With repetition, you'll lighten up enough to enjoy yourself.

Q: But what if I don't have any strong likes or dislikes?

A: Deep down you must. Watch any two-year old. You were that willful once, until somebody taught you to be so polite, so thoughtful. Well, phooey on that! "I Like" will put you in touch with the best part of your Inner Child, as will the next technique.

Coming Home

Here's a way to become more aware of what's happening with your energy bodies, those layers of deeper self within you. Read through the complete instructions. Then go through step-by step (open one eye and peek at the printed page as needed).

Since this technique is by far the longest one in this book, you might wish to tape record it, allowing 30 seconds per step. After you've done the technique once or twice, you can peek at the summary that follows the technique.

Even though Coming Home has a lot of steps, it's simple. Your purpose is to notice things without trying to change them.

1. *Sit* somewhere comfortable where you can be alone for 10-15 minutes.
2. Close your eyes and *breathe*: take at least seven Vibe-raising Breaths—inhaling through the nose and exhaling through the

mouth. Why breathe this way? Inhaling through the nose, combined with the intention to raise your vibrations, will do just that. You'll become more awake inside. Exhaling through the mouth, combined with the intention to release fatigue, doubts, and worry, will do just that. Although a lifetime's worth of troubles won't instantly vanish with Vibe-raising Breaths, you can *peel off surface stress* as if pulling the skin off a banana. Vibe-raising Breaths also make you more *aware* of your own consciousness, so breathe this way any time you want to be more awake inside. And when you choose to *travel* with your consciousness, Vibe-raising Breaths can help take you where you want to go.

3. Be aware at the level of your breath. Ask, *Breath, what do you have to tell me right now?* Allow your attention to shift to the level of breath, where you'll find yourself noticing tender nuances like the quality of in-breath vs. out-breath; timing; depth; which nostril is more active; which feels juicier, in-breath or out-breath. Automatic BREATH is the grace of God taken for granted. CONSCIOUS BREATH is an entryway to the presence of God.

4. Take a Vibe-raising Breath. Be aware at the level of your physical body. Ask, *Body, what do you have to tell me right now?* Inwardly explore the soles of your feet, the floor, the soles of your feet again. Move upward all the way to the hair on top of your head (or the ripe baldness of your pate). Your BODY is your temple, your playroom, your kitchen—it's every room in the house. That body works so hard to fulfill you. Don't ignore it until it must get sick to grab your attention. Offer attention now, as a gift, free and clear.

5. Take a Vibe-raising Breath. Now be aware at the level of your mind. Ask, *Mind, how are you doing right now? What would you like me to know about you?* MIND is separate from intellect. It is your faculty for paying attention in the here and now, bridging your physical senses with deeper forms of knowing. How rejuvenating to mind the mind!

6. Take a Vibe-raising Breath. Now be aware at the level of your intel-

lect. Ask, *Intellect, what is happening with you? What can you teach me right now?* INTELLECT discriminates, forms new concepts, works at the subtlest levels you have attained for understanding life. Being the most sophisticated part of you, your intellect will have charming ways to reward your paying attention.

7. Take a Vibe-raising Breath. Be aware at the level of EMOTIONS, which goes the full range from raw, gut-level feelings to the highly abstract emotions that could be termed "unconscious." In Freud's day, apparently, clients were terribly cut off from their deep feelings, requiring lengthy analysis to penetrate the mystery. But the consciousness of humanity has evolved a great deal since then. Today we can explore even our innermost feelings without great effort. Just sit quietly and ask, *What deep, underlying emotion do I have right now?* Then drop the question, taking a few Vibe-raising Breaths. An answer will come to you.

8. Take a Vibe-raising Breath. Be aware at the level of your soul, a silent witness to your human experience. Ask, *Soul, teach me now. Tell me about the wholeness of my life.* Realize, your SOUL is a part of you that expresses your spirit in its complete human form, hidden like the roots of a tree but nonetheless knowable. Yes, soul is like roots, being earthy, tangled, contradictory, complex, and rich. Sometimes the language of your soul will shock you with its earthiness. Then be shocked! It's your soul, ain't it? Travel into your soul with your awareness and it will impart what you most need to know, here and now.*

---

* Soul includes aspects of you that are more animal-like than your usual conscious identity but also includes aspects that are more spiritual. Indeed, one of the most important aspects of soul is its ability to recognize and validate choices that move you forward most rapidly along the path of spiritual evolution. (See my video, *Thrill Your Soul, Inspiration for Choosing Your Work and Relationships*.)

9. Take a Vibe-raising Breath. Be aware at the level of your SPIRIT, the individual spark of God that makes you YOU. Ask, *Spirit, breathe more truth into me. I am ready to accept the truth of who I am. Help me to awaken more than ever before to the Divine truth of who I am.* Breathe and be. Information may come to you in words or images. Or maybe you will simply feel a presence. Rest assured, that is your presence as spirit.

10. Be aware at the level of your AURA, the energy bodies that surround your physical body, layer upon layer. Ask, *Aura, what is the energy like in and around my body?* Explore from head to foot, around you in every direction, how your aura pulsates in the form of subtle sound and light. It is information. It is electromagnetic energy. Later you may learn more about it intellectually. However much you know about auras already, don't push yourself to visualize colors into yours, or otherwise change a precious particle. Simply enjoy what is there.

11. Before finishing, *ground* your energy. Imagine a cord starting at the base of your spine. Run it downward. And don't be overly modest about how deep you it can go. Run that cord all the way to the hot, compact core of planet Earth.

12. Give yourself the benefit of seven or more GROUNDING BREATHS. These are quick, shallow breaths, out and in, through the mouth—half a blow, half a whistle. Pucker up! Combined with the intention to ground your energy, this breathing pattern helps you to integrate spiritual experience into your physical body.

13. *Shift attention outward,* toward your body and environment. Take a few seconds to stretch before opening your eyes.

14. When you feel ready, *open your eyes.* You have completed the technique for Coming Home. Even with your eyes open and attention moving outward again, you'll find yourself more in touch with the totality of who you are.

Coming Home–Quick Version

1. Prepare to pay attention to yourself.
2. Take seven Vibe-raising Breaths.
3. Pay attention to your breath.
4. Pay attention to your physical body.
5. Pay attention to your conscious mind.
6. Pay attention to your intellect.
7. Pay attention to your emotions.
8. Pay attention to your soul.
9. Pay attention to your spirit.
10. Pay attention to your aura.
11. Put down a grounding cord.
12. Take seven Grounding Breaths.
13. Shift attention outward, toward your environment.
14. Open your eyes.

Coming Home–Q&A

Q: WAS THIS SUPPOSED TO BE HARD AND GIVE ME A HEADACHE?

A: No! When you're studying *any* technique related to empathy, take it easy. And keep breathing.

Q: YOU MAY AS WELL KNOW, I'M A WORKAHOLIC PERFECTIONIST. ANY OTHER ADVICE FOR PEOPLE LIKE ME?

A: When you do things in MATERIAL LIFE, where success is measured in physical terms like money, being a perfectionist can pay off. "We try harder" once helped bring mega-business to the Avis car rental company. Maybe it's your slogan, too.

Here, though, we're concerned with your SPIRITUAL LIFE, where even something as physical as your body can be approached as a form of consciousness. Trying harder with spiritual life won't make you succeed more. If anything, you'll create "benefits" like a headache, a stiff neck, or a general sense of frustration. Luckily, you don't need to push. Ideally, Coming Home is as comfortable as taking off your tie, un-squeezing your feet from tight shoes, or plopping down in your favorite armchair with a refreshing drink.

Q: I LIKED EXPLORING WITH YOUR TECHNIQUE, EXCEPT DOESN'T IT TAKE AN AWFULLY LONG TIME?

A: At first it may, much like driving somewhere unfamiliar in your car. Coming back home is faster. Ever notice? With more experience at this technique, you'll cruise through levels of yourself as if driving back home.

Q: WHAT IF ALL THE TIME YOU'RE SUPPOSED TO BE COMING HOME YOU KEEP THINKING ABOUT OTHER PEOPLE?

A: Many empaths do that habitually. But remember now, you're switching your empathy off. And no matter which way your stream of consciousness drifts, eventually a choice will become available. *You'll realize that you're thinking.* In that moment lies your choice. Just then, choose to pay attention to part of your physical body. By searching gently for information, you'll shift away from the habit of always putting others first. Your inner life *is* fascinating. The more you're in touch with it, the better you'll do as an empath.

Q: THAT THREE-RING CIRCUS WAS THE REAL ME? SCARY.

A: Going within can be a shock, especially if you haven't had much practice. So much is going on. Nonstop motion is an illusion, though. With repeated experience, you'll release the superficial stress that makes for apparent chaos. Meanwhile the practical point is simple: Whenever you have a choice between racing thoughts and gentle awareness of your body, go back to your body. When you have a choice between racing thoughts and gentle awareness of your mind, go back to your mind, etc.

Q: Couldn't you be a talented empath but a klutz at being self-aware?

A: Talented *natural* empath, yes; *skilled* empath, no. Self-awareness is vital for becoming skilled. So count yourself successful every time you do the technique for Coming Home. Regardless of your particular experience, the process will strengthen a coordination between your spiritual life and material life—which can lead to a higher state of consciousness.

Q: My problem was just the opposite of his. How can I keep from boring myself to death?

A: Lightly pay attention during your self-survey. When boredom strikes, take a few extra Vibe-raising Breaths. Ask if the boredom is connected to any part of your body. Automatically your mind may shift to discomfort in or around your body. Then keep your attention there until the sensation or pressure eases. Another possibility is that what you call "boredom" is simply discomfort with being left all alone all by yourself.

Q: You got that right. I hate it in there. So?

A: Ever see a romantic movie where the couple starts off sparring? Think of Coming Home as a kind of courtship between your conscious awareness and the rest of you. This friendship is worth the winning.

Q: What if I noticed something really weird, like the fact that my head didn't seem connected to my body?

A: Very important point about this technique: for best results don't try to fix a thing. Simply pay attention.

Q: I thought maybe if I sent myself a little healing energy....

A: Then you'd be doing a different technique. The power of this technique consists in your doing nothing except being aware of yourself at home. Think of it as a "Come as you are" party. Being willing to visit yourself, *as you are*, is a great gift of unconditional self-love.

Q: How does your technique for Coming Home in differ from cutting yourself off from people?

A: Context makes the difference. What you are doing here is waking up your consciousness and learning to travel with it. Plus you're doing this in the context of becoming more skilled as an empath. Realize, you're not trying to push people out, which would actually cause you to send some energy in their direction, due to the dynamics of resistance. Rather, you are drawing inward.

Q: WELL, HOW DOES THIS DIFFER FROM MINDFULNESS MEDITATION, OR YOGA?

A: In mindfulness meditation, there's an agenda of self-healing. In the time-honored techniques of yoga, there's a goal of spiritual expansion and/or physical healing. But with Coming Home, as the name suggests, your purpose is to engage with yourself, all the parts or rooms of you. Agenda has been cut to the minimum, aside from the purpose of your being you.

Breaking out of the Amusement Park

THE AMUSEMENT PARK is my name for the experience of unintentional empathy. A Disney World for your consciousness, it's the opposite of home. Whether your inclination runs more towards physical, intellectual, emotional, or spiritual forms of empathy, you'll find attractions galore at this fascinating playland.

The good news is, because this amusement park adventure happens in consciousness rather than physical reality, you don't have to pay for tickets or wait in line. No matter how many empaths are in the crowd, your turn comes instantly every time. And your rides are unlimited. The bad news is, unskilled empaths routinely ride to the point of exhaustion.

Think about it: Free rides, all day, all night. It's as easy to overdo as free food. To make matters worse, unskilled empaths miss the pleasure of taking these rides, unconscious that they're even riding. For instance, your best friend's emotional wavelength is not clearly visible, obvious as a clattering wooden roller coaster. So you may never have noticed that your consciousness goes riding on it every single time you meet. But whether or not you're aware of it, that trip has consequences that impact you afterwards, as you carry her consciousness with you.

The following awareness regimen will help you to Break out of the Amusement Park so you can return home at will. Eventually you'll be able to come and go as you please, on your own terms.

1. Schedule the timing of this technique so you can start it within 45 minutes of waking up. To begin, *do the technique for Coming Home.*

2. Gently monitor yourself as you go about your daily activities. *Three times that day, consciously Break out of the Amusement Park.* Remind yourself what you're like, just you, whatever the situation. It may take a trip to the bathroom to find privacy but you'll need only a few minutes to be alone. Pay attention to mood swings, new physical sensations, unusual thinking patterns. Observe without trying to change anything.

3. *Describe in words what it's like for you*, being in the Amusement Park right now. To help yourself find language, take a few Vibe-raising Breaths and ask, "What deep, underlying quality do I feel right now?" Allow yourself to receive an answer.

4. *Inwardly ask: "Who am I empathically connected to right now?"* Take a Vibe-raising Breath. Allow yourself to receive an answer. It could come as a thought, a name, a fragrance, an image. It could flicker by in a flash. (If you get nothing, don't worry. Go on to Step #6.)

5. *Cut the empathic connection.* Say to yourself (aloud if you can): "All that does not belong to me, please leave immediately." It will, because of the immense spiritual power of your free will.

6. Come Home. Pay attention to what it is like being YOU right now. *Describe it in words.* To find language, take a few Vibe-raising Breaths and ask: "What deep, underlying quality do I feel right now?" Allow yourself to receive an answer.

7. *Come out* of your session. Take a few seconds to stretch before

opening your eyes. Give yourself the benefit of seven or more Grounding Breaths, those quick, shallow breaths, in and out, through the mouth.

8. When you feel ready, *open your eyes*. Now you're ready for several more hours of spontaneous, natural activity where you enjoy yourself.

Breaking out of the Amusement Park—Q&A

Q: WHAT IF YOU KEEP THINKING ABOUT OTHER PEOPLE?

A: Sometimes that happens out of habit. This technique gives you the chance to explore a new habit.

Q: BUT HOW ABOUT DEALING WITH ALL THOSE THOUGHTS?

A: Eventually you'll become aware that you have been thinking about other people. Right in that instant you have a choice. Aim your attention at yourself: your physical body, your emotions, or some other aspect of what is happening with you in the here and now.

Q: IT'S NOT ENOUGH FOR ME TO SAY "STOP." MY EMPATHY KEEPS ON GOING. I DON'T MEAN TO BRAG, BUT COULD THIS BE BECAUSE MY GIFT IS TOO BIG TO SWITCH OFF?

A: No such thing—any gift can be switched off. I think of a conversation I had with Janet Mentgen, founder of Healing Touch. She said, "I tell my students to command whatever doesn't belong to them *to leave*. If it doesn't leave within 90 seconds, they need to find help for their own healing. Probably their problem has to do with a need to control others."

Q: CONTROL? WHAT COULD LACK OF CONTROL ABOUT EMPATHY HAVE TO DO WITH CONTROLLING OTHERS?

A: Think about it. When become a martyr to empathy, it can be a way to demand attention. Or sympathy. Even admiration. If the techniques in this chapter aren't enough to break you of the martyrdom habit, seek professional help. But probably all that's needed is perspective: You're in control of your empathy, not the other way around.

Q: Part of me resists switching off empathy because I'm afraid it's selfish. What if you've been taught that being self-absorbed is a sin?

A: Being interested in yourself is natural and healthy, maybe even a compliment to your Maker. Certainly a few minutes of focusing just on yourself need not keep you from being interested in other people, too.

Q: How about all the critics of "The Me Generation"?

A: Sure, critics of "The Me Generation" have lambasted Baby Boomers for supposedly being narcissistic. Pitiful! Sages from time immemorial have said "Know thyself."

Q: I guess it would be more honest to admit I'm scared. When I go inside myself, could there be someone disgusting in there? Or could it be like falling into some bottomless pit, and I'd never come out again?

A: Anticipation is the scary part, not what's inside. For comfort, you're welcome to find a buddy to be in the room with you during Coming Home or Breaking out of the Amusement Park. Do this a few times and you'll feel more comfortable soloing.

Q: It thrills me to be able to return to myself at will. What happens when you get good at this?

A: Security comes from being able to balance your empathy and non-empathy. Freedom is another result. Since you know that, afterwards, you will come back stronger and more stable than ever, when you decide to travel you feel safe about letting go completely.

For instance, the other day I was Flying in Spirit at the health club. Picture me there, on the stationary bike. To a casual observer, I'm just thumbing through a magazine as I work out. But for a skilled empath, there's more. I'm using a variation of Aura Rub (which you'll learn later) to plug into the photos that interest me. What a way to learn about the celebrities and fashion models of your choice! For example, here's what happens when I casually come to a picture of hockey player Cammi Granato just after she won a gold medal in the Olympics.

Cammi looks happy and wholesome and pretty but, frankly, I doubt that I'm in for anything very special as I connect my consciousness with her. Then zap! Tears start squirting out of my eyes and my gut is heaving with a mixture of primal scream and suppressed sob. The power of Cammi's triumph surges through me. Here, I realize, is a fierce warrior energy unlike anything that I, personally, have known. Her body is electric, not only with victory, but with a distinctively powerful way of being physical. The woman is like a force of nature.

Sure not my usual way to inhabit my body!.

When I've had enough of it, boom, I bring myself back to myself. I keep on cycling, then work my way through the magazine, researching some of the other amazing ways of being human.

Soon you'll have adventures like this, too. First you're making it safe by developing your skill at Breaking out of the Amusement Park. Keeping this in mind, let's acknowledge something awkward but necessary:

The Learning Dance

Your skill at switching empathy off will grow as you move from Empathy 101 to intermediate and advanced levels of skill. Be prepared. Every important new behavior has a non-glamorous learning dance. Your dance as an empath will probably include...

I. Pep talks AFTER you've goofed

Empaths typically carry shame and guilt over incidents about unskilled empathy from the past. When you wake up to empathy for the first time, you can start to reframe these incidents.

Personal history can be interpreted in dozens of ways—to justify selfishness, to make yourself feel guilty, and so forth. To grow in skill as an empath, *choose an interpretation that honors your empathy but does not tolerate inappropriate behavior or unnecessary suffering.*

□ Did you take on physical ailments that didn't belong to you? Stop blaming yourself. Maybe you were just a victim of misdirected, unskilled empathy that you can learn to use better.

□ Did you have friendship problems because you were living mostly in your head, a slave to Intellectual Shape Shifting? There's hope. Learn to use the ON-OFF switch and you'll be free to live in better balance.

□ Did your talent for emotional empathy cause you to label yourself as crazy, immature, a social mess? Not fair! Painful memories may involve lack of skill but genuine talent as an empath.

Personal confession here: Before learning how empathy works, I carried a guilty memory dating from when I was 12 years old. My aunt Elly, a not-very-good opera singer, was the guest of honor at a family party. Elly burst into mega-decibel song (just like in the musicals, except that Elly sang off key). I felt an urge to laugh and would have run out of the room if Elly had not positioned herself right in the doorway. Gesturing dramatically, she blocked the only exit.

I sweated. I covered up my mouth and turned red as a beet. Then the laughter burst out. Everyone heard, including my poor aunt. Elly's pale, round face and huge eyes shifted from her big on-stage persona to a small stricken look. No apology could undo that pain. When I bring back the memory, to this day, it tears at my heart.

Until I understood empathic sharing, however, it never occurred to me there could be more to this incident than bad manners or poor self-control. In retrospect, I get a very different picture: Fifty other people in that room had been stuffing their laughter to the point where it became unbearable. Somehow, it had to find release. By laughing, I acted like a steam valve for the entire boiling room.

No, of course, I don't recommend that you or I purposely act out for the sake of displaying how empathic we are. Instead I encourage us to reinterpret the guilty memories where, despite a lack of skill, we volunteered for empathic service.

Pep talks after you've goofed are a start. Resolve that in the future you'll be quicker to catch on. You'll meet the challenge more gracefully—either by choosing to switch your empathy OFF, detaching from the situation, or taking appropriate action on behalf of the group.

2. Catching yourself MID-GOOF

As you become more skilled at switching empathy OFF or ON, you'll catch your mistakes sooner... not necessarily before they happen but soon enough to give the situation a happy ending.

Here's another personal example. At a party where I was hired to give Face Readings, three boys sat at my table. The line of people waiting stretched before me, 20 people deep. One of them, being slightly drunk, started a rant about date rape at her college. Soon she was berating college boys as, "sex maniacs, every one of them." Everybody in the room could hear her, loud and clear.

The clients at my table were college boys. Although they tensed up visibly, they said nothing, presenting a solid, not-reacting front. Yet how could they not hear this diatribe?

Understandably, I didn't want to talk about it, either. In my case, the party host was paying hundreds of dollars for me to stay professionally focused. Tension mounted, minute by minute.

Ten minutes later, boom. I laughed so hard, tears streamed down my face. The college boys stared, as if to say "What's wrong with her?"

I judged my behavior equally harshly until, mid-goof, I realized what was happening—yet one more incident of slightly misguided empathy.

Why, I wondered, did these college boys have no reaction whereas my feelings couldn't be hidden? Answer: I had reacted so strongly *because* nobody else let their feelings show.

Then, since my polite stance of professional indifference hadn't worked, I decided to fully accept the situation. Whether or not I wished to act like a leader, nobody else was doing the job; my reactive outburst had nominated ME.

Soon as my breath came back, I walked over to the girl in line. She was still ranting away. Quietly I said, "Everyone in the room can hear you. Please stop. You're embarrassing us."

Yes, it would have been preferable to respond *before* my uncontrollable outburst. Next time, at least, I'd recognize the dance earlier, respond with more skill. Whatever your level of skill, however, knowledge about empathic sharing helps you to properly finish what you've started.

3. Catching yourself at the START of a goof

If there's one place empaths need self-control right from the start of a tough situation, it's on the road. You know about road rage, that increasingly dangerous trend where drivers act out their anger using their cars. Well, how do you handle empathy while you've Joined in Spirit with a thousand frustrated drivers, all part of the same traffic jam?

Without considering that empathy could be part of the picture, I used to congratulate myself for having good impulse control on the road. When one of those lane-weaving, non-signaling drivers would cut ahead of me, sure I'd be sorely tempted to bash into him, especially if I disliked his bumper stickers. But, I'd drive primly enough, except for the running verbal commentary in the privacy of my car.

Anyone within earshot could tell that "they" were getting to me. As an empath, though, I realized who had responsibility for the rage in my car— me, not "them." Forgetting to switch empathy off, I was soaking up rage that belonged to *other* drivers, though inside I still had the choice to decline the mission. If I let shared anger push my personal stored-up anger into gear, eventually my driving could turn dangerous.

After this Aha!, I developed the habit of Breaking out of the Amusement Park at the start of each drive; then I'll do it again at the first impulse to scream. Definitely an improvement!

4. Learn your early warning signals to become GOOF-PROOF

Wherever situations provoke you to take on feelings, symptoms, or thought patterns belonging to others, you can learn your early warning signals. For me, wisecracks on the road would escalate into muttering, grumbling, and the like. In a situation like the one with forced listening to the date-rape lecturer, uncontrollable laughter had early signals, too: mentally being startled, trying to push awareness away (Denial is never a good sign!), increasingly uncomfortable feelings in the gut.

How about you? Where do you feel your early warning signals? The faster you can recognize them, the better. And the beauty part of being a skilled empath is that you can stop unwanted reactions by temporarily switching empathy off, yet later you have full permission to switch empathy back on. Compare that to techniques of behavior modification, where you look at behavior from the outside in, maybe have great success at stopping what doesn't work for you, but squelch that yearning empath within.

Yes, you can mind your manners yet still Fly in Spirit. It's like having your cake and eating it. Contrary to proverbial wisdom, anyone can do both, just not at the same time. Similarly, as a skilled empath you can enjoy the serenity of your own self first, afterwards Fly in Spirit. And fly you will, starting with the next chapter.

*A*ffirmations

1. I am in control of my empathy. I choose when to switch it on and off.
2. My heart is a sanctuary. I visit my heart before I visit the hearts of others.
3. When I hear my inner truth, I honor the God within by following through.
4. It is safe for me to experience empathy fully. Through my breath, I release the fear of living too deeply. God protects me from harm, and so does my own common sense.
5. Body, I forgive you for having seemed to fail me. I feel the life and health in my body now.
6. I delight in my body. I release the false idea that anything about my body is not spiritual. Every particle of my body is made out of God-stuff.
7. I know my own mind. I stop neglecting my truth to please other people. I cast off false versions of myself from the past and wake up to who I am now.
8. I respect my intellect. Releasing the past, I live in the moment... brilliantly.
9. I choose to *know* the truth. I choose to *live* the truth. Never again will I lie to please others. I claim my spiritual courage now.
10. I release the belief that I am too sensitive. I balance my sensitivity with strength.

Part II

Switch on Empathy

"Many deaf people do "hear" the wind in the trees when they see the branches swaying. Some junction point in their minds converts a visual signal into an auditory one. Many blind people can likewise "see" faces by feeling them with their hands. A mental junction point has taken the signals of touch and converted them to sight."

—*Unconditional Life*
Deepak Chopra, MD

6. Naked and Glorious

Danny is a man I knew in college. A philosophy major and avid psych. student, he stumbled onto a highly courageous way to signal his willingness to have a *meaningful* conversation. In my mind's eye I can still see him at a college seminar we took in nonverbal communication. The seminar culminated in a weekend field trip off campus where, by definition, conversation consisted in waving our arms and staring into each others' faces. Often, Danny was seen to pause meaningfully during these discussions. Slowly, deliberately he would remove his shirt—then his sandals, his pants, his underwear. Nudism meant naked truth to Danny and, by Jove, was he ever sincere about it!

Nudism of a different variety was the specialty of Victor, in 1980 my fellow worshipper at the Madison Avenue Presbyterian Church in New York. Victor would approach even the most casual acquaintance with the following two questions:

"What's your name?" Then, "Would you mind telling me, what is your deepest religious conviction?"

Someone else might have hesitated to demand naked truth of strangers. Victor? Never. We pass this way but once. What if the stranger should die before Victor could reach her again? What would befall her immortal soul?

Both Victor and Danny have been fools for love. Their passion for truth has made them, in a way, ridiculous.

Many of us fear that if we look too deeply into life we, too, will seem foolish. Therefore, before jumping into this chapter's techniques for powerful empathy, let's acknowledge the fear of nakedness. What if, like these wacky guys from my past, you were to become naked, ridiculously naked?

Alas, no guarantees of dignity come in this world, whether we're naked or not. My Grandpa Hugo, a man who could have instructed Queen Victoria in proper behavior, once was arrested in Central Park for Indecent Exposure. Why? To beat the summer heat, Hugo had stripped down to his undershirt. Not exclusively, mind you—the man still wore his trousers, belt, shoes, and black wool socks. Standards just were different in the 1930's.

Spiritually, though, one thing hasn't changed. Making an outer show of your search for truth can always make you look foolish. An inner search for truth is different. Conducted in private as part of a balanced life, it won't show—except, perhaps, for an extra depth of light in your eyes. And if others recognize That, it's because when they look in the mirror, they see it too.

Holding a Space

HOLDING A SPACE means to join your consciousness with that of another person. It's the first step in turning empathy on. You give a person your full attention, but there's more to it—a subtle spiritual component that makes all of you, not just your mind, fully present. Depending on the situation, this spiritual component could show up as tranquillity, patience, openness, charity, or even wonder. (For a superb and thorough explanation of the psychological and social benefits of Holding a Space, see John Gray's *What Your Mother Couldn't Tell You & Your Father Didn't Know.*)*

---

* Don't let it confuse you that he refers to this as "paying attention." Gray is one of America's most gifted empaths. For him, I suspect, paying attention automatically means Holding a Space.

Here's an example. When you watch goldfish swim in a bowl, you can view them as swim objects. When you watch beautiful human physical specimens at the beach, you can view them as sex objects. In either case you'd be paying attention without Holding a Space. However, if you cared about these "objects" in a nurturing or deeply appreciative way, Bingo! They would become subjects, not objects. And you would be Holding a Space for them.

The purpose of the following technique is to show you how to make this mysterious shift of awareness, which is more profound than merely paying attention. Unlike John Gray's relationship techniques, Holding a Space is best undertaken without concern for pleasing a person or improving your relationship. It would be distracting even to wish that what you're doing be *recognized* by the person for whom you are holding the space.

Social benefits may come, indirectly, but the technique requires that you surrender to spiritual service and learning. Not to worry, though. Afterwards you are certain to benefit from this surrender since Holding a Space is the basis for all types of skilled empathy.

That's why you'll return to this technique again and again, as your skill develops. What won't change is the need to take it easy. Do this technique step by step, never trying to do a great job. This will help you simply be in the moment. Hey, you have official permission to be sloppy!

1. Stand or *sit near a person* for whom you wish to do spiritual service. For now let's refer to that person as your "client."
2. Quickly *do the technique for Coming Home*. That's your basis for comparison with what comes next.
3. *Ask inside (not out loud) to connect* with this client in order to be of service.
4. *Be there.* Remain awake and present to whatever you notice.
5. Conversation is optional. Let your client do most of the talking. When you respond, don't concern yourself with appearing clever or

sympathetic. *Emphasize enjoying the silence* more than paying attention to anyone's words.

6. *Conclude the session* of space holding. Unless you first told your client that you were going to Hold a Space for her, no formal announcement is necessary. Still you will need firm boundaries for yourself as an empath, so decide for yourself when this session of Holding a Space is over.

7. Take yourself out of earshot—admittedly, bathrooms are sometimes the best places we can find, lacking a designated Superman changing booth—and say: *"I now choose to disconnect from this client."*

8. Reflect for a moment on what happened when you Held the Space, however subtle. Review it mentally. Even better, write a summary in your personal journal.

Holding a Space—Q&A

Q: Duh, what was supposed to happen?

A: Holding a Space with your client was an opportunity to join empathically. To the degree that you were awake to your empathic gifts, in the here and now, you gained access to your client's experience. Physically, emotionally, mentally, and spiritually, what was it like to be that person? "Supposed to" doesn't enter into the picture, incidentally.

Q: Well, if you're not looking for a particular result, so you can find out how you measure up, what do you do? And how do you know if Holding a Space gives you access to anything meaningful?

A: Pay attention to your experience. As empaths, people fall into two categories, equally good, but different. Some of us tend toward the forms of empathy that unify, others tend more toward the forms of empathy that glorify.

First let's consider forms of empathy that glorify: Physical Intuition, Emotional Intuition, plus nuances of Intellectual Shape Shifting and Spiritual Oneness. Gifts like these reveal what it is like to be another person at a level far deeper than ordinary paying attention. You're seeing people more as if you were an angel.

By analogy, you can take a highlighter pen to underscore a sentence in a book. With or without the yellow glow, it's the same process of reading. But ink from the highlighter makes the words look special. When empathy glorifies a perception you might otherwise have, it's more special, too. The empathic glow can be switched on at will, through your spiritual intent to learn a deep truth. Then your perception slips into a kind of grace— subtle but it still counts.

Q: GLORIFIED PERCEPTION IS STARTING TO SOUND SO SERIOUS. IT ISN'T LIKE BEING IN CHURCH, IS IT?

A: No religious affiliation required! However, glorified perception is part of a higher state of consciousness that we'll discuss more fully after you've explored several more empathy techniques. A working definition of this state of consciousness is having a celestial *glow* to your experience. Depending on how your subtle senses operate, this extra dimension of spiritual truth could be experienced as a *resonance*, a *fragrance*, a *truth knowing*, a *presence*, a *remembering*.

Q: WOULD GLORIFIED EMPATHY BE REALLY DRAMATIC, LIKE SPECIAL EFFECTS IN A MOVIE?

A: Almost never. Your shift into this glorious kind of experience will probably not be dramatic at all. Sheer lack of drama means that you can miss the miracle of it. So stay awake.

Q: STAY AWAKE? THAT'S IT?

A: Language helps you wake up to conscious awareness of your experience. Later we'll explore in more depth how to use language to claim your fullest empowerment as an empath. For now, frankly, you're doing well if you can just stay awake. So much the better if, in addition, you can find words to describe your experience.

Q: CAN YOU GIVE A CONCRETE EXAMPLE OF HOLDING A SPACE WHERE YOU HAVE THE KIND OF EMPATHY THAT GLORIFIES?

A: Let's say you're Holding a Space with Anthony, your 80-something grandfather.

- With Physical Intuition, you know about what is going on with him physically. This is a different kind of knowing from watching and observing him (though you can't switch off your powers of observation and, actually, they may supplement your empathy.) Physical Intuition enables you to feel, as though you were inside Anthony's skin, the stiffness of his walk, the cascade of creaks when he sits down.
- Emotional Intuition reveals some of the truth of his feelings. At the beginner's level, you might simply notice that Anthony feels an overall depression. As a more advanced empath, you might be able to pick up more than one level of emotion. For instance, in the space-time of just one look, Anthony could move through curiosity, confusion, fear, and lethargy, all within the grayish haze of his chronic depression.
- Spiritual Oneness reveals details about how Anthony is "not all there." When a vacant look comes into his eyes, glorified perception shows you how 1/8 of his awareness stays within your conversation; 1/4 is mental sleep; the rest is spiritual travel outside his body. Like many who seem to fall into senility, Anthony is really lifting up, preparing for his transition from physical life.
- Intellectual Shape Shifting discloses a slowed-down thought process mixed with flashes of understanding. If Anthony's mind were a dessert, it would be bread pudding with a pretty stingy helping of raisins.

Q: ARE YOU SAYING THAT WE CAN READ ANOTHER PERSON'S THOUGHTS?

A: Definitely not. The intent to read someone else's mind is a form of trespass. Our minds are holy places. Even God doesn't enter without invitation.

So it would be a misuse of empathy to push yourself to read another person's mind. However, ethical use of empathy does empower you to move in phase with that person's mental process. Thus, you can experience *how*, not what, a person thinks.

Q: WHAT IF IMAGES OR IDEAS FLASH INTO YOUR MIND WITHOUT YOUR TRYING TO READ THEM?

A: That's TELEPATHY, gaining access to another person's thoughts without the need for speech. Ethically it's fine to have the telepathy that comes *without trying*. And if another person gives you *permission* to hold a telepathic conversation, that's fine, too. What wouldn't be fine? Don't break and enter into another person's mind. And don't speak to others about what comes to you telepathically, other than sharing with the person whose thought wave you've picked up.

Q: WHEN I HELD MY SPACE I THINK I HAD THE SECOND CATEGORY YOU MENTIONED, EMPATHY WHERE YOU UNIFY. WHAT'S THAT LIKE?

A: Forms of empathy that UNIFY are Physical Oneness and Emotional Oneness, plus nuances of Intellectual Shape Shifting and Spiritual Oneness. Here you experience a client in terms of your *own* body-mind-spirit.

Q: SO THE ANNOYING THINGS THAT HAPPENED TO ME WHILE I HELD A SPACE WITH MY DAUGHTER COULD ACTUALLY BE MEANINGFUL?

A: Could be. Let's hear what happened.

Q: FIRST OF ALL, I FELT ANTSY, AS IF I WANTED TO JIGGLE MY LEG ON THE FLOOR. IT FELT UNCOMFORTABLE—NORMALLY I NEVER DO THAT.

Then my mind started jumping around. You know, while I was holding the space with my daughter I became more visually oriented than usual. Well, my eyes kept roving around, staring at the furniture, the cracks in the walls. Usually I never notice that stuff. But *she* is very visual. Do you think?...

A: Once you start Holding a Space, for the entire time, everything counts. Even if something seems to be happening only to you, your client is probably having the same kind of experience.

Q: WOULD YOU COMPARE WHAT HAPPENS WHEN YOU UNIFY WITH WHAT HAPPENS WHEN YOU GLORIFY?

A: When Holding a Space, you stay *separate* from your client. Once you travel to this other person's consciousness, you maintain self-awareness. Deep down you know you are *you*—having an experience of the other person.

Q: AND IF YOU'RE A UNIFIER?

A: When Holding a Space, you *merge* with your client. Effortlessly. One minute you're listening or looking in the usual way. Then, whoosh. Temporarily you become part of that person.

Q: COULD YOU REPEAT THE EXAMPLE OF HOLDING A SPACE FOR THE OLD GUY, ONLY THIS TIME WITH UNIFIED FORMS OF EMPATHY?

A: Here goes:

□ With Physical Oneness, I feel tired and slightly woozy. The first clue, for me, is a strong craving for chocolate candy. (Hey, that's how my body-mind speaks to me. What can I say?) Still, I take a deep breath and keep paying attention. Next comes an angry thought that I feel so darned sleepy, and I start to spin off some self-blaming about not going to bed on time, chronic fatigue, blah blah blah. With another deep breath, I realize: a) All this mental chatter is about how sleepy I feel; b) I do feel sleepy; and c) that sleepiness is how it physically feels to be Anthony right now.

□ Emotional Oneness takes me on a trip through chronic depression, then curiosity, confusion, fear, and lethargy. Suddenly, pop! I wake up inside and realize this trip has been Anthony's, not mine.

□ Spiritual Oneness, from the unified angle, can be frustrating. Unlike the glorified form of empathy, I'm not privy to what's going on with Anthony in other realms. I simply feel the human part, which in this case is very boring, tinged with cynicism and fear. Whew, what a relief to slip out of holding that space and realize it's Anthony's form of hell on earth, not my personal spiritual state—which is, thank God, usually more like heaven on earth.

□ Intellectual Shape Shifting, from the unified angle, is really interesting because Anthony's thought process is so different from mine. Even though it's moving at 2% efficiency, I savor the quality of it—analytical, more sense-dependent, with a slow and steady pace. Altogether my experience of him is like walking through snow... that has mostly turned to slush. Granted this isn't snow at its best, still it is definitely snow. Whereas, in the climate of my usual mind, snow doesn't fall.

Q: YOUR EXPERIENCE SOUNDS POWERFUL. MINE WAS AMAZING, TOO, FOR A BEGINNER. HOW CAN I TAKE IT FURTHER. DO YOU HAVE ANY TECHNIQUES TO HOLD A SPACE MORE POWERFULLY?

A: Yes. Harness the power of intention.

How to Set a Clear Intention

Here's an investment proposition. How would you like to triple your effectiveness as an empath? All it takes is 10 minutes now to learn some basic concepts, then 30 seconds each time that you take an empathic journey.

This investment is called SETTING A CLEAR INTENTION. You say what you would like to have happen as a *result* of your empathic journey.

For the previous technique, Holding a Space, I supplied a generic intention in Step #3: "Ask inside to connect with this client in order to be of service." However, you can do better when you custom create your own intention.

1. Discern what you truly desire to happen as a result of using empathy. Take an honest look. Question, *"What is my highest and best intention for this empathy session?"*
2. *Take three Vibe-raising Breaths.* Don't concentrate on your breathing. Just shift attention so you can relax into it.
3. *Listen inside.* Whatever you hear, feel, or see in response to your question counts as your answer. Put it into words.
4. *Speak your intention mentally*, without moving your lips or making a sound. That's it! You're done.

How to Set a Clear Intention– Q&A

Q: WHY NOT SPEAK YOUR INTENTION OUT LOUD?

A: Intention falls in the same category as prayer, most powerful when kept inside.

Q: WHEN YOU SET AN INTENTION TO HELP SOMEONE HEAL, DOES THAT MEAN THAT WHEN YOU HOLD A SPACE YOU'LL BE GUIDED ABOUT THINGS TO THINK AT THE PERSON WHILE YOU ARE JOINED EMPATHICALLY?

A: Whoa! What do you mean by "think at" a person?

Q: TO HEAL SOMEONE, YOU HAVE TO DO SOMETHING SPECIFIC, DON'T YOU? I FIGURE THIS IS LIKE PRAYING FOR MY UNCLE MAX, WHO USED TO BE AN ALCOHOLIC. EVERYONE IN MY PRAYER GROUP AT CHURCH STARTED TO PRAY FOR HIM TO GO INTO TREATMENT, AND HE DID.

A: Thanks for raising an important issue. Healing when you Hold a Space is very different from wishing, thinking, or willing anything specific about a person.

Q: YOU DON'T SEND THOUGHTS?

A: Not one. Simply be with the person. As explained previously, empathy helps you to merge with the consciousness of your client. The real burdens that have been weighing on your client can be lifted best that way.

Q: HOW ABOUT SOMETHING MORE ABSTRACT, LIKE PUTTING COLORS INTO A PERSON? LIKE I'VE HEARD ABOUT AURAS THAT THE ROOT CHAKRA SHOULD BE RED; THE SECOND CHAKRA, ORANGE; AND SO FORTH. UNLESS I DO SOMETHING LIKE SEND THE RIGHT COLORS, HOW CAN I HELP ANYONE?

A: Unconditional love is the way of helping. Maybe it's not the case with you, but sometimes well meaning people panic inwardly when confronted with another person's problem. They want to solve it fast and solve it *their* way—which may mean applying a rigid system like the one you've described for pushing specific colors into a person's aura

I wonder, what gives a person the right to play God with someone else's energy field? Who authorizes people (or, for that matter, prayer groups) to decide what a client must do? However well intended, our personal solutions to other people's problems are often distorted by our own fears. Pushing our version of how to help people breaks the spiritual law of free will. It's coercive.

Holding a Space, in its simplicity, gives you a safer, kinder way to help. You can lend support without pushiness in any particular direction. Then, to make it even better, you can ask for spiritual help by setting an intention.

Q: I'M A SKEPTIC ABOUT INTENTION. HOW DO YOU KNOW IT REALLY MAKES A DIFFERENCE?

A: Here's a story from one of my classes. I led the class through a technique for touching auras. Everyone did great except for a middle-aged woman, Shirley. She complained that she had absolutely no experience whatsoever. Concerned, I did a reading of her third eye, the part of the energy field connected with conscious perception of spiritual experience. Shirley's was so closed down, it felt like a thick iron door, slammed shut and locked.

As tactfully as possible under the circumstances, I reported on my perception. Plenty of people walk around with third eyes like Shirley's, unfortunately, but usually they don't come to my classes. I asked her to comment on what my aura reading meant to her.

"You're right," she said. "I have no spiritual life. And this was a big problem when I was married to my ex-husband, the minister. He took me to all sorts of ministers and healers, but nobody had any success with me. I have no spiritual life."

Intuitively I felt that I would be able to help Shirley in a private session. I offered her one as a gift, which she accepted. I resigned myself to her not getting much from the rest of the class and proceeded to pay attention to the rest of the group.

We turned to a technique for seeing auras. After the class tried it, I asked to hear experiences. Guess who was waving her hand like crazy! Not only was Shirley unmistakably enthusiastic, her third eye had changed, popped open, pushed out a yard from her body. It was even sparkling with celestial light.

When I called on her, Shirley described in detail the auras of six class participants. "What changed for you?" I asked.

Shirley explained, "When we set our intention, I asked this: 'God, make me like I was before all this happened.'"

Shirley's story has a moral for every spiritual seeker. We have the right to ask for what we really want. When we dare to ask from the heart, we always receive an answer. It may even be a miracle. Intention is one way to request a miracle.

Intentions that Help

Here is a summary of what I've learned about setting intentions that are helpful for oneself and others.

I. Intention to help this person heal

Would you like to help lift this person's burdens, provided you can do it safely? Be sure to set this intention ONLY in conjunction with using the techniques that follow to Get Big and Set Personal Boundaries (or equivalent techniques).

2. Intention to learn from this person

Joining empathically can open the door to tremendous wisdom. How does this person think, feel, and so forth? Some of the most powerful teaching comes by example, and you receive that learning most clearly with a direct link to another person's consciousness.

3. Intention to explore possibilities

Sometimes people teach us by their *wrong* example. Be with them long enough to taste their reality. Then leave, clean yourself up, and continue moving in directions that are right for your body-mind-spirit. Better to experiment this way for five minutes than to live this way for five years! It's a form of spiritual vaccination. Caution: Don't fool around by merging with people who are really crazy or evil. Their vibes can be harder to shake off.

4. Intention to forgive

When someone has wronged you, a short empathic journey can help you to understand deeply how the mistake was made. Although you may never forget, at least you'll be able to understand—not by piecing together circumstantial evidence or other strained ways to manufacture a better attitude. Direct experience of another person's reality gives you a new perspective on emotions like fear, jealousy, and confusion, underlying causes that, unintentionally, lead to hurtful behavior.

5. Intention for spiritual service

Choosing to be of service is the quickest way to enhance the quality of your empathic experiences. Service means letting go of your personal agenda as an individual. Maybe you've heard it put this way: "Let go and let God."

6. "God, make me Your perfect instrument"

Here's a different sort of spiritual intention. You're asking to move into empathic experience to accelerate your personal learning as soul. This open-ended intention hastens the overcoming of personal limitations.

7. Intention to be strengthened as an empath

Maybe you don't have total confidence yet that you're really an empath. Unless you already have strong empathic gifts, however, I doubt that you'll feel an inward call to be strengthened as an empath. Therefore, this intention is probably unnecessary.

More likely, you're in a situation like Gwendolyn's. She told me her daily prayer to God was, "Please open my third eye." When I read Gwendolyn's aura, the third eye she considered "closed up" was already humongous, meaning that she had access to a vast amount of spiritual knowledge. All she had to do was use it.

Poor kid. She'd asked for it. She got it. She just didn't know she had it. Gwendolyn isn't the first spiritual seeker to be bogged down by too much humility.

Yes, there is such a thing. Besides, we often wait for God to come out of our hearts, out of creation entirely, and to show the Divine presence by whacking us over the head, as with a club. In a cartoon this might work. But life on earth doesn't operate this way. Ask for a spiritual gift and usually you will receive it bigger and faster and easier than you can humanly imagine. So you're probably plenty strong as an empath already. Use Intention #7 to bolster confidence.

8. Intention to grow in the way that will help me most

Fill in the blank. Request your heart's desire for your spiritual life. Automatically, you'll receive the empathic experiences that can help you. Some of the most valuable lessons you can request are spontaneity and the willingness to be vulnerable. Also important for empaths are self-love, the habit of choosing empowerment over victimhood, honesty, and confident intelligence. Learning any of these qualities can be easy. Find a role mode, then apply empathy techniques from the rest of this book to connect with that person. Zap, that person becomes your professor at Empathy School.

Intentions that Help—Q&A

Q: SPONTANEITY? THE WILLINGNESS TO BE VULNERABLE? YOU SLIPPED THEM INTO YOUR LIST OF INTENTIONS THAT HELP BUT, SO FAR AS I'M CONCERNED, THEY'RE SOME OF THE LAST THINGS I WOULD NEED AS AN EMPATH.

A: VULNERABILITY means that you are willing to open up, without protecting yourself. You don't know all the answers, nor do you demand to know them. Related to vulnerability are the spiritual gifts of humility and faith. However, I prefer to summarize all three as vulnerability because the deepest obstacle to faith or humility usually is the fear of vulnerability.

In case you have any doubt about the spiritual value of vulnerability, join empathically with a baby some time.

SPONTANEITY means that you flow—not trying to control your words or your actions. For one thing, talent as an empath has nothing to do with appearing dignified. For another, the qualities that you stand to lose by being spontaneous (guile, deception, and any related ego-pushing habits) are qualities that would block your empathy in any event. So clean 'em up.

To take an empathic journey, each of us must leave our ego at the door. Spontaneity and vulnerability make this easier.

Intentions that Hinder

Read this list to avoid problems. All eight of these intentions might be counterproductive or even harmful.

I. No intention

When you set no intention, spiritually you are left to your own devices. And given American society today, that means carrying over habits that help a person materially but are limiting spiritually, habits like "trying."

That's right, "We try harder" can make things harder. You can't surrender to a bigger part of you than your everyday personality—at least not when that personality is holding on tight to whatever has worked in the past. So consider yourself warned. Unless you choose your intention on purpose, the neediest part of your ego will do the choosing.

2. Intention to prove that "I can do this"

Empathy, being a spiritual gift, requires that we suspend our disbelief—at least for a while. Take it one day at a time, one technique at a time. Proving isn't just hard. It's irrelevant, since we can't measure ourselves by the same bootstraps we're using to pick ourselves up with....

Finally, asking for proof often carries a hidden agenda, which is "Prove that I *can't* do this, just as I've failed with so many other things." Who needs that?

3. Intention to make myself important

Let's use an example to figure this out: Kevin blows his ego up like a big balloon, then wonders why he can't get through the tiny door of another person's heart. Hmm, maybe there's a reason why most religious traditions teach humility.

Intellectually we all know that humility would be a good idea. Unless we set a specific intention, however, the need to be important can sneak up on anyone, even the most gifted empath. So Kevin might find his way into a client's consciousness clearly and sweetly, but then start bragging mentally about his great talent. Immediately his empathic lens will fog up. In this case, Kevin just needs to set a more worthy intention.

4. Intention to gain power over other people

Power hunger is the common denominator for many misuses of empathy. It underlies unworthy intentions like: "I want to learn about her so I can talk her into a date." or "How about some good gossip material?" or "Let me inside his head so I can make him buy what I'm selling."

However, laws of spirit keep this kind of intention from being fulfilled. Selfish motivations stop genuine empathy. God doesn't give away the candy store to gobblers.

5. Intention for sexual titillation or trespass

Would people who are hooked on pornography prefer to use empathy? Gee, could it be even cheaper than the Internet?

Too bad, there's a catch. Sure, it's possible to enter someone else's body-mind-spirit for a sexual thrill. But this form of recreation sets an empath back for a long, long time.

Why? Empathy is a spiritual practice and, although sex can be holy, sexual prying or snooping is not. One consequence is the loss of spiritual purity which, in turn, could affect every other aspect of life, including the gift of empathy. Even when a man has been given the key to unlock all the doors in a city, that key won't work properly if it is covered with mud.

So rather than giving in to temptation about using empathy for sexual thrills, a person is better off seeking out a flesh and blood partner—or, if that won't suffice, a psychotherapist. Please note, though: sometimes your practice of empathy will show you such intimacy, it's almost sexual. Don't feel guilty then. You're protected by the purity of your original intention.

6. Intention to escape from myself

When you're feeling out of sorts, go to the movies. Don't try empathy with real live people. First, your perceptions will be distorted. (Ever hear the psychological term "projection"?) Second, it's not fair to merge your consciousness with someone else when yours is all junked up. Instead, invite a friend to Hold a Space for *you*.

7. Intention to be as good an empath as somebody else

Does your friend Eric awe you with his abilities? Avoid the temptation to copy him. Empathy isn't a contest.

What works far better is to appreciate your own gifts. Develop them. Celebrate them.

Envy accomplishes zilch.

And since envy implies not being good enough, it's downright counter-productive. Spiritual gifts don't work their best when you insult them. And considering that spirituality means contacting the bit of God inside you, it is pretty insulting to complain that what you've been given isn't good enough!

8. Intention to become like somebody else

Oops, on the surface this seems better than envy. Actually, it might be worse. Empathy is a great way to learn from somebody else, but only when it can help you to be yourself better. Remember all the trouble you've gone through earlier with Coming Home, I Like, Breaking out of the Amusement Park? These techniques have helped you to love yourself. Genuine self-love will anchor you through empathic voyages and serve as a great protection.

Yet free will allows us to travel empathically unanchored, even to make a habit of losing ourselves in other people. Although this won't necessarily hurt others, it can slow down our own spiritual life to the point that rather than flying in spirit, we're limping.

All of us have moments of not liking who we are. However, if this is a chronic problem, it calls for a serious solution. Psychotherapy, exercise, better nutrition—expert assistance of some kind is needed, and often this will come from helpers *outside* the spiritual arena. For example, Dr. Bruce Rind, one of the nation's pioneering physicians in the cure of adrenal and thyroid dysfunction, has put together a profile of patients that correlates low adrenals with extreme empathy.* Consistently, patients who are cured report greater ease at turning empathy off.

In general, we must honor the fact that each of us combines three parts: spirit, mind, and body. When one part goes out of whack, it's time to approach healing from one of the other two possible directions. Holistic health is your birthright, so don't stop looking and praying for help until you find a solution that works. The better your balance, the easier it will be for you to harness the power of empathy.

---

* He told me, "When going through adrenal fatigue, your third eye opens up permanently. Fortunately, after the imbalance is healed, your third eye will stay open." That's a good reminder, in general, that spiritual growth sometimes happens in ways that involve suffering. More commonly, as we'll see later, it's the grounding of expansion that is experienced as suffering. (To learn about a physician near you who works holistically with cases of adrenal exhaustion ranging from sub-clinical to extreme and "incurable," call the Center for Holistic Medicine in Rockville Maryland, 301-816-3000.)

Get Big

By now you realize the mysterious requirement of empathic travel: to let go of your regular self. The urge to do good, the possible pushiness, the need to be right, all this has to go.

What makes empathy so powerful then? The sheer force of your consciousness merging with that of another person is a big deal, spiritually. And in case you would like to make your consciousness even bigger and better, you can voluntarily GET BIG. A ridiculously easy technique will connect your consciousness to a transpersonal source of huge joy, wisdom, and love.

1. *Place your attention inward* (closing your eyes helps) and take a few Vibe-raising Breaths.
2. *Ask inside to connect* your consciousness with a being whose consciousness is big, bright, and benevolent. For example, you may feel drawn to a spiritual helper like Mary, Buddha, Krishna, Jesus, or St. Germain. Each of us has at least one master teacher who can come to us inwardly, in a body of light. Call on someone you would like to be a teacher and helper for you right now. Ask in your own words, as directly as you might say, "Father, who is in heaven, here I am. Let me feel You here with me."
3. *Relax*. Whenever you ask, the connection is made in a twinkling.
4. Go ahead and *do an empathy technique*, such as Holding a Space. In your expanded state, you'll be far more successful than otherwise.
5. After you finish the technique, thank whomever you asked to join with you.

Get Big—Q&A

Q: What happens after you open your eyes at the end? Do you stay big?

A: Gradually your conscious mind will shrink back to its usual identity, much like a rubber band that has been stretched beyond its ordinary limits.

For jobs like driving to work, walking the dog, or cleaning the bathroom, we do fine with our everyday little minds. It might even be a strain to try keeping your workaday mind expanded full size (though this just might happen some day, when least expected). A big mind helps you to be most empowered when doing service as an empath.

Q: HOLD ON. WHY CAN'T I JUST ASK THE UNIVERSE?

A: You can. You won't get the same results, though. In my experience, miracles have a way of happening faster when you expand your individual self by connecting with an ascended master or archangel. Why not call on the highest first?

Q: HOW ABOUT CALLING ON YOUR GUARDIAN ANGEL OR SPIRIT GUIDES?

A: Is that inspiring? Yes. But your guides specialize in *you*. Empathy, by definition, takes you out of yourself. Therefore, empathy's best facilitated by a being whose consciousness is transpersonal. Archangels are executive angels. My favorites are Archangel Michael (whose specialty is removing what doesn't belong) and Archangel Raphael (whose name literally means, "The healing of God"). Another choice is to call on your favorite gods and goddesses from mythology, as described in Jean Shinoda Bolen's *Goddesses in Every Woman*.

Q. WHAT IF CALLING ON ANYONE GOES AGAINST YOUR RELIGION?

A. Then don't. Don't even go against your spiritual comfort zone. Choosing to Get Big is optional. The most important person to bring to your empathic travels will always be you.

Set Personal Boundaries

Have you ever had the experience where a person keeps weighing on your mind? Let's say that yesterday you had a short chat with a neighbor, Greg. Ever since, he keeps floating into your thoughts. Why? What's going on?

- Were you a character in *The Celestine Prophecy*, your answer would be simple. You're "supposed to" talk with Greg further. The very course of human destiny might depend on it.
- Were you in therapy, you might make a note to discuss the situation with your counselor. Perhaps Greg has come to represent some unresolved issues from your past.
- Were you into do-it-yourself self-criticism, you might come up with yet another interpretation. Guilt: "What's wrong with me that I keep thinking about Greg?"

However, there's an entirely different explanation. Recurring thoughts could signal a need to strengthen personal boundaries. Connecting with others can leave PSYCHIC TIES. Symbols of human bondage, they stretch like a telephone cord between another person's subtle body and your own.

How strong are these ties? Depends on three things: your involvement in the relationship; the other person's involvement; and whether your shared experience has been unusually intense. In a famous psychology experiment, Dr. Art Aron showed that if you have a conversation with a stranger on a bridge, you're more likely to fall in love if the bridge is shaking and you're both in danger of falling off.*

Love is one way to interpret psychic ties. Another is bonding. All that warm, fuzzy stuff is well and good... except when it gets in the way of your clear sense of who you are. Where do you draw the line between yourself and other people? That place is your PERSONAL BOUNDARIES. To gain control over your boundaries can be simple: remind yourself that you have 'em.

---

* Elaine Aron, *Highly Sensitive Person* (Secaucus, NJ: Carol Publishing), p. 146

Free will about spiritual matters can work instantaneously. Therefore, on a spiritual level, it is highly effective to affirm, "I have strong, clear personal boundaries." This command to your inner software will apply itself to every level of who you are. Supplement this spiritual upgrade by considering consciously what it means at each level to set boundaries.

- At the level of your *environment* (i.e., behavior with others) awareness of boundaries makes it easier to just say no. No, you won't do favors for others at your own expense. Yes, you will pay attention to your feelings about how much giving is appropriate, thereby avoiding excessive giving.* Should this understanding not be enough to keep interpersonal boundaries from causing serious problems in your life, consider psychotherapy.
- At the level of your *physical body*, awareness of boundaries makes it easier to make healthy choices apart from what others are doing. For instance, say you are at a party, having a great time but feeling increasingly sleepy. You decide to excuse yourself. Yet as you're trying to leave, your host says, "Sleepy? That's ridiculous. Have some more coffee." What will you do? When you choose to honor your body's message more than your friend's expectations, that's setting clear boundaries.
- At the level of your *mind*, personal boundaries help you to know your own opinion. Does the desire to please someone else make you vulnerable to psychic ties? Maybe it will help to remember the famous 12-Step Serenity Prayer. You know the punch line, asking for the wisdom to know the difference (be tween what can and can't be changed). In this case, you're ask

---

* For a facial tip-off about which people struggle with this challenge, look at smiles. When people smile so widely that the gums show, over-giving is likely; emotional generosity is certain. See my how-to, *The Power of Face Reading*.

ing to accept the things that come from your own mind but reject, or at least question, what comes from the minds of others.

□ At the level of *your intellect*, personal boundaries empower you to make the best decisions for yourself. Regardless of outside influences, ask for inner guidance. It will show you the truth—what you know deep down to be best. Make room within yourself for listening to guidance.

□ At the level of your *emotions*, personal boundaries help you to recognize who owns which problem—especially important in conflict situations, when emotions are flying like bullets. Strong boundaries help you to detach from others, hear *your* side of every story, and act accordingly.

□ At the level of your *soul*, personal boundaries help you to allow awareness of your shadow self along with the loftier aspects of yourself at your core. When your soul sends you a shadow-self message that is awkward or inconvenient, commit to paying attention—at least as much attention as you would give to another person you cared about. It's so easy to ignore these unattractive yearnings. Inescapably, though, your soul will express its needs one way or another. Many of us have mistakenly drawn boundaries around our souls that are too small. Right-sized, healthy boundaries will allow you to be who you are.

□ At the level of your *spirit*, personal boundaries keep you from being drained by others. You are in control of your empathy. Choose when to join with others, when to Come Home. Of all the levels of human life, free will is most powerful at the level of spirit. You can, for instance, choose to protect your spiritual boundaries by putting on an ENERGY SHIELD every morning, as routinely as brushing your teeth. To shield yourself, breathe deeply. Starting with an in-breath, imagine white light about two feet above your head. Send it spiraling down around you, to form a cocoon that reaches down to your feet. You'll feel the difference!

Yes, the art of setting boundaries has a lot to it, when you analyze in detail just *who* the boundary setter is. Going through the previous list can serve as a kind of initiation ritual. After one good Aha!, you won't need to constantly remind yourself about boundaries, just put on your Energy Shield in the morning and pay attention whenever your inner self sends a warning signal. For extra maintenance, it won't hurt to say an all-purpose affirmation like this aloud a few times a day: "I have strong, clear personal boundaries."

Set Personal Boundaries—Q&A

Q: AND IF AFFIRMATIONS DON'T SOLVE YOUR BOUNDARY PROBLEMS, WHAT THEN?

A: Take inventory. Is what's going on with you a matter of social behavior, an emotional imbalance, a habit of staying spiritually connected long after you meant to say goodbye? Different cases call for different remedies. Take action at the level where you have a problem.

Q: AS A COUNSELOR WHO WORKS WITH BEHAVIOR MODIFICATION, I'M CONCERNED THAT YOUR EMPATHY EXERCISES WILL WEAKEN PEOPLE'S BOUNDARIES.

A: Becoming a skilled empath actually strengthens boundaries. Granted, empaths sometimes strike non-empaths as having weak boundaries that need to be "fixed." But the secret to being well adjusted as an empath, I'm convinced, isn't toughening yourself up or numbing yourself so that you can meet someone else's standard. Some people are extra alive to life's nuances and their way of being healthy is different. So are their boundaries.

The same goes with INNER LANGUAGE, ways that your inner wisdom communicates itself to your intellect. As a born empath, you have unique language abilities, set up at the soul level. Until you become wise in the ways of your language, you can't consciously receive your full empathic experiences. So language is what we'll explore next.

Personal Notes

What fears do I carry about knowing too much about people?

Do I wish to keep these fears? If not, how can I release them?

What Aha!s did this chapter wake up in me about intention?

Which intentions are especially meaningful for me right now?

In the past, what have I believed about my personal boundaries?

What have my experiences with switching empathy OFF shown me so far about the strength of my personal boundaries?

How did this chapter move me forward in claiming strong, clear personal boundaries?

Am I ready to commit to an open, fearless exploration of otherness using my God-given gifts for empathy?

7. Speaking of Empathy

Just as you were born with at least one gift for empathy, you have been given at least one language channel for it. Since birth you've been speaking your language(s) fluently—and here comes the catch—fluently but probably unconsciously. For your Flights in Spirit to become conscious, you'll need to make language conscious. This requires coaching, much like English, Spanish, and other languages of the outer, material world. The first step is to say "Yes" to your imagination... and the inner languages that masquerade as fiction.

Imagination Alert

In the Time Travel technique, we've already defined imagination: It means creative exploration by means of thought. All empathy techniques work better with a sprinkling of imagination, like the pixie dust from Tinkerbell that helped Wendy, Michael, and John to fly with Peter Pan.

Now it's time to acknowledge that imagination facilitates language as well as travel. "Imagination is the faculty of the soul" wrote Thomas Moore in his masterpiece, *The Care of the Soul.* Accessed through imagination, our inner languages help us to become consciously aware of life experiences at every level: soul, body, mind, intellect, emotions, and spirit.

It's a stretch, an imaginative stretch, for most adult to acknowledge inner language. Despite some wobbly beginnings, however, finding language eventually becomes such a charming pursuit that you won't want to stop. You may even take a certain goofy pleasure in learning to trust your imagination, once you discover that often your deeper self can speak to you *only* through ways that seem fanciful, fictional, or outrageous.

So, yes, it can feel strange if your imagination leads you to one of the simplest forms of intuitive language, Truth Knowledge, so blunt that it makes itself known as a kind of inner blurting. A working definition of Truth Knowledge is that you don't know how you know, you just know—strictly no frills.

In fact, you may wonder if you "just imagined" it when words come to you in this language. Yet somehow you know things about people on a deep level. In situations where it's appropriate to check with those people and ask for feedback, most likely you'll find that your Truth Knowledge has been absolutely correct.

As intuitive languages go, Truth Knowledge is the most transparent. For this reason, at first it may seem like your usual sort of language for everyday experience. Yet words of Truth Knowledge are different because they carry a deeper resonance, as though they were written in gold or pure electricity.

Electricity? That sure was the consequence of a reading I did once in front of a large group. After I joined with a young woman named Jenny, the language of Truth Knowledge popped out with its usual spontaneity.

"You're quite an Intellectual Shape Shifter—one of the most gifted ones I've ever met. Hmm, there's something more, very unusual. You know, you would make a great spy!"

She looked at me then, eyeball to eyeball. Her face, even her eye gaze, froze into a kind of polite social mask. But deeper within her eyes, when I tried to make contact, it was as if she was running away from me, down a long tunnel that led to her inner being. Finally her eyes reached the very back of this tunnel and I heard her yell, "Oh, s___!"

All this happened in a split second. When that second closed up, I knew she really was a spy. Fortunately, I heard myself saying in a pleasant social voice, "So what do you really do for a living?"

"Oh," she said modestly. "People call me a scientist."

An even flashier variation on Truth Knowledge is Psychic Knowing, the inner language where imagination takes you across time or space or both. Quick as thought, you travel to a person's past or future. Perhaps your consciousness even connects to someone physically far away from you. And then, transparently, the extra-dimensional words pop out. Again, you're an innocent in the proceeding.

Just because the knowledge comes easily, don't dismiss it, however. Your inner sound byte or sight byte could be important.

For instance, one morning, my telephone rang. My long lost friend, Linda, was calling from Colorado.

"Okay, Rose, what is it?" she asked. "You've been on my mind all morning."

I had been planning a family vacation. Neither my husband nor I were terribly excited about these plans, which were to be finalized that day. Linda wound up inviting us to stay with her in Colorado. Our shared vacation was a blessing for host and guests alike.

We owed it all to Linda's Psychic Knowing. As someone who honors her inner languages, Linda recognized that I was reappearing in her life as suddenly as if we'd had an obvious synchronicity flash in the outer world. Had one of the books I've written tumbled off her bookshelf and hit Linda on the head, prompting her to telephone me, yes, that too would have been synchronicity—a meaningful coincidence.

With Linda's high consciousness, though, she didn't require an outer nudge. Spiritual life is economical. If the job can be done with a flash of Psychic Knowing instead of a hit on the head, so much the better. All Linda needed was persistent thoughts of someone far away. Because we hadn't spoken or written each other in a year, and Linda trusted her Psychic Knowing, she could take action based on what was "just" imagination.

Give yourself permission to do the same. Imagination can bring you fun and profit.

Imagination Alert—Q&A

Q: What if imagination also brings you shame and humiliation? Some of us have worked hard to establish our dignity.

A: Be careful whom you tell, that's all. Common sense is right when it warns you that many of the people in your life don't want to hear about imagination or Truth Knowledge and would think less of you if you forced them to listen. Choose like-minded friends to be your support group.

Q: Look, matter how many friends you have, imagination is scary. Very scary. A lot of wackos out there imagine things too, don't they?

A: Yes. That's their business. Your imagination is your business.

Q: What if I lose the ability to tell the difference between fantasy and reality?

A: Please, I'm not inviting you to throw common sense to the winds. Schedule just half an hour a day, in private, to be imaginative. That shouldn't destroy either you or your life.

Helping Imagination Along

Okay, you're convinced and ready to welcome imagination into our daily life. How can you, as an adult, develop more imagination? Have you no recourse but to watch reruns of "Barney"? Or must you hire a preschooler as tutor?

As a parent, I know how psychically expensive it can be to keep up with a kid's imagination. For an empath-in-training, only a relatively puny amount of imagination is needed. And, while teaching classes over the past decade, I've discovered a technique that will get you there relatively painlessly:

1. Starting now, eliminate these words from your vocabulary: "I don't know."

2. Whenever doing techniques for spiritual development, such as those in this book, give yourself permission to say whatever you know or imagine, even if you aren't sure it's true, *especially if you aren't sure it's true.* Yes, for the sake of propriety you can restrict the situations where you allow yourself to do this, but give yourself some time every day to verbally indulge your inner knowing.

3. Pay attention, from this time forward, to how other people use the expression "I don't know." Don't they use it to squelch imagination?

4. If the spiritually destructive words should pop out of your own mouth, here's what to do: Edit the ongoing tape that goes into your memory and subconscious mind. Say: "Correction, I really do have the ability to know."

5   Continue with your line of thought. Take a deep breath to muster up the courage to finish what you started to say.

6   Marvel at what you wind up saying, because right underneath each unnecessary "I don't know" lies forbidden fruit. Being so good, so sinfully delicious, this fabulous fruit intimidated your well-brought-up, prim, conscious mind. Well, let the rebel in you enjoy this juicy nectar.

After you've been free of "I don't know" for a while, you'll find that your imagination flows more freely than it has in years. Incidentally, this technique isn't bad for one's sense of humor, either.

Helping Imagination Along—Q&A

Q: WHAT AN ANTI-INTELLECTUAL IDEA! WITH ALL RESPECT, YOU MUST NOT WORK WITH MANY HIGHLY EDUCATED PEOPLE. ANY SCIENTIST, FOR EXAMPLE, IS TRAINED TO ADMIT LACK OF KNOWLEDGE. ARE YOU PROPOSING THAT WE THROW ALL JUDGMENT TO THE WINDS SO WE CAN WALLOW IN OUR PRETENDED OMNISCIENCE?

A: Oh, did I mention that one of the side benefits of this technique is to help a person to lighten up? Imagination doesn't co-exist with taking one-self so seriously.

Q: COME ON, HOW ABOUT THE LARGER ISSUE OF CREDIBILITY?

A: You're right. There is a larger issue: Who is testing you?

Q: EXCUSE ME?

A: When you volunteer the words, "I don't know," what's the context? Probably your critical faculties are at work, performing their usual task as gatekeepers to your imagination. But you're not in an oral exam right now. You're studying empathy. Whenever you're in that role, give yourself permission to be a free spirit. Say whatever pops into your head. Nobody has to grade you.

Q: WHAT'S THE HARM IN MAKING A SIMPLE STATEMENT LIKE "I DON'T KNOW"?

A: Have you ever studied affirmations?

Q: SURE. THEY'RE SENTENCES YOU REPEAT, OVER AND OVER, TO MAKE IDEAS FIRM. REPEATING AFFIRMATIONS LODGES THEM IN YOUR SUBCONSCIOUS MIND. BUT "I DON'T KNOW" ISN'T ANYTHING A PERSON WOULD PURPOSELY SAY AS AN AFFIRMATION, IS IT?

A: Still counts. What is being made firm, in this case, is self-doubt. Whenever people repeat this statement, they hammer home subconsciously that they don't believe they have knowledge.

Expressing yourself freely, you may not always be right. But if you give yourself permission to know what you know, you'll be right often enough—whereas putting down your imagination is always wrong.

Q: HEY, WHAT ARE YOU SUPPOSED TO SAY WHEN SOMEONE ASKS YOU A SPECIFIC QUESTION YOU DON'T KNOW THE ANSWER TO, LIKE HOW MUCH IS 24 TIMES 387?

A: Try "I don't have the answer *to that question*." This little escape clause protects your subconscious self-image because you're affirming lack of knowledge about one narrowly defined subject—no big deal. By contrast, it is a big deal (as well as unnecessary) to describe oneself as a not-knower. For most situations, an even more useful phrase to substitute for "I don't know" is "I wonder."

Q: Truthfulness is an important part of my belief system. What if imagination feels like lying?

A: Some of us hold so tightly to our integrity. That's wonderful. But what would be the harm if you were to say, "It seems to me that" or "I feel"?

Truth is relative, maybe even situational. Were you Moses, carrying down the stone tablets from Mt. Sinai, you would be held to one standard for certainty. Were you a parent, asked to lie to bring hope to your child before a serious operation, you might hold to a different standard. And if you were counting the bubbles in your bathtub, your standard for truth could be different still.

Here you are, training to become a skilled empath. Give yourself the benefit of classroom standards for truth, okay? You'll need this because, starting now, we're moving full speed ahead with your training.

In fact, we're about to smash a major boundary about your reality. Prepare to recognize something vital about your languages for empathic knowing... something universally available... something you've done since childhood... something so widely ignored that you probably don't even have a word for it.

Synesthesia

"Mom, when you put food coloring into my yogurt, you make it taste better." Perhaps it was inevitable that my son would notice this. I used to feed him health food in disguise, like "golden vanilla yogurt." A dot of vanilla, a dab of honey, plus the all-important dab of food coloring, added up to one of his favorite snacks.

America's food industry is onto this trick. How much appeal would canned gravy have if it remained its natural non-color? Of course it's tinted a suitable brown.

Occasionally food is colored in a strange way that doesn't jibe with your taste buds. Then you keep doing double takes. Ever try to eat a plain donut colored St. Patrick's Day green? Man, that stuff is hard to eat.

Why would it be important to us that color match taste? "Just imagination," some people would say. (And far be it from me to dismiss such an explanation.) Nevertheless, there is a technical term to explain it: SYNESTHESIA.

This little-known word (pronounced sin-ess-THEE-zha) means experiencing one sense in terms of another, even *many* senses combined together. Millions of moviegoers have been able to relate to the opening sequence in "The Sound of Music" as Julie Andrews' character celebrated the sight, fragrance, and feeling of being in the mountains. She sang, "The hills are alive with the sound of music." Think for a moment about all the senses packed into that "sound."

Moments of mystical, or celestial, joy always reach out to us through Synesthesia.

Synesthesia matters particularly to an empath because you Fly in Spirit at the celestial level, where all perception is concentrated in seed form. Naturally your experience of core reality will reverberate with this subtle, multi-sensory richness.

I believe that Synesthesia occurs when insights come from *beyond* regular sensory experience—where our physical senses just scratch the surface of life. When your consciousness shifts to life's deep spiritual core, you "make sense" out of this by expressing with your inner languages (the ones we'll go on to describe later in this chapter, plus aforementioned Truth Knowledge and Psychic Knowing).

Why use Synesthesia at these mystical moments? What you're reaching to describe is extra-sensory, meta-physical. You have transcended *through* your senses, rather than experiencing *with* them. Flying in Spirit, you have experienced deeply—not with a same-old, same-old isolated physical sense that fits neatly into some well worn conceptual box. Language that combines more than one sense is a very human way to express perceptions that don't come from the surface level of ordinary physical life.

By encouraging Synesthesia, you make Celestial Perception clearer and more conscious. Language with Synesthesia smashes boundaries. Notice what happens when you deliberately allow yourself to talk about *feeling* colors or *tasting* pictures. Crash! Down goes another wall of training to live in the boring mindset of a "responsible adult."

Kids don't edit Synesthesia out of their speech. They revel in it. "Those clouds look squishy." "That shirt is so red, it hurts my ears." "Your perfume puts sparkles into my nose."

Oh, yes, Synesthesia is also fun. See/hear/smell for yourself with these ideas for exploration:

1. Play that you're a wine expert. Next time you sip a drink (of any kind), close your eyes and describe what you're tasting in terms of color. And if words from other senses come up, too, don't censor them. My local newspaper carries a weekly wine column that is an unintentional tribute to Synesthesia. Today's column, for instance, includes these descriptions of wine flavors in terms of taste + more:

   □ silky
   □ primary
   □ vivid
   □ fine-grained
   □ taut
   □ earthy
   □ light
   □ soft
   □ nicely rounded

2. Next time you listen to music (and you're *not* driving a car), close your eyes for a while. Pretend you're a latter day Walt Disney cartooning your own version of "Fantasia. " Give yourself permission to choreograph the music with dancing lights in different colors. Sure you can do it! Wow!

3. Go to the nearest perfume counter. Take a whiff of one fragrance after another and find language to describe it. Maybe you'll find yourself talking about "high notes" and "low notes." Or your sensory languages may describe colors, textures, shapes, rhythms, more. And why not? Provided that you let yourself fall in love with a fragrance, you may tumble as Alice did upon entering Wonderland. (Chocolate isn't the only way to shift your consciousness to the celestial level!)

4. Wherever you are right now, look at a painting. What, no official "painting" is available? Make one. Use your hands to frame something nearby as if it were a painting—be it a tree, a lamp, bathroom tiles, or peeling paint. While you look at this "painting," touch it with your eyes. Feel the textures. Hmm, how did you do that?

5. Start noticing when people around you speak with Synesthesia. See? (Hear? Get it?) You're not the only one. Everyone shifts into *blending the senses* when having deeper perception of life.

Synesthesia—Q&A

Q: WHY SYNESTHESIA? HOW CAN COLORS AS DIFFERENT AS RED VERSUS BLUE COMPARE WITH MUSICAL NOTES LIKE MIDDLE C VERSUS F SHARP?

A: Our physical world is made of vibrations. They range from low to high. They make patterns. They move or grow still. Colors and music are two systems set up within physical reality that do this. Everything in nature can be experienced this way, provided your consciousness is awake enough to notice. When your consciousness flies to the level of Celestial Perception (deepest silence, speed closest to eternity, etc.), you find particles and patterns of God-stuff. Because you happen to be in a human body, it's only natural to express your experience in terms of any or all of your senses.

Q: AW, COME ON, ADMIT IT. AREN'T YOU JUST GIVING YOURSELF PERMISSION TO MAKE UP METAPHORS?

A: God, I suspect, is the one who is making up metaphors.

Q: I READ A BOOK ABOUT SYNESTHESIA, *THE MAN WHO TASTED SHAPES.* YOU MAY NOT BE AWARE OF THIS BUT NEUROLOGISTS CONSIDER TRUE SYNESTHESIA TO BE AN EXTREME, AND EXTREMELY RARE, CLINICAL SYNDROME—IN SHORT, A DISEASE. COULDN'T YOU FIND A BETTER WORD FOR WHAT YOU'RE TALKING ABOUT?

A: So far, no... and in fact I don't think I want to find a different word. The medical establishment is wrong not to recognize everyday Synesthesia. A whole continuum of experience can be present before there's a full-blown "disease."

Here's an example. Osteopaths, chiropractors, and naturopaths all understand what it means to have a yeast imbalance. But telling a regular M.D., as I did once, that you think you may have one. He snorted, "That's ridiculous. If you had a Candida imbalance, you'd be practically dead."

Really? Couldn't less extreme problems with yeast exist? Couldn't they, perhaps, be cured before the point of becoming life threatening? Holistic medicine depends on recognizing the sub-clinical varieties of human experience. This includes the health problems we can attend to before they become full-blown medical crises. Why define human experience only at the level of clinical emergency?

Here's another example, this time from the field of psychology. Abraham Maslow turned psychology on its head, as it were, when he had the idea of studying healthy people for a change. Just because founding father Freud developed his theories from working with people who were mentally ill, why must other psychologists structure their theories of human potential in terms of disease?

And speaking of research, I call on psychologists and holistic healers, linguistic experts and teachers, researchers from all disciplines, to pay more attention to Synesthesia. Study children. Study artists. Most of all, study empaths, because our use of Synesthesia can be incredibly accurate. We use it to translate from one inner language to another. Now, here comes an introduction to other intuitive languages, the most common ones I've found when training empaths.

Clairvoyance

"May we look at and into this world" sings an ancient prayer from the *Rig Veda*. While everyday sight enables us to "look at," **Clairvoyance** means to "look into" life at the level of Celestial Perception.

Perhaps it is the best known of our deep sensory languages. More important to know, it's the most widely misunderstood. For instance, perceiving the human energy field, or aura, often is mistakenly defined as "seeing colors." Yet auras, being energy bodies, can be defined in all the languages discussed in this chapter. Any language or perception can take you to Celestial Perception, not just Clairvoyance. Therefore, "Looking into this world" is a metaphor, rather than a demand for subtle sight. Clairvoyance probably is NOT your exclusive (or even strongest) means of spiritual knowledge.

After teaching aura reading for more than a decade, I'm convinced that, for the majority of people, the quantity of information available through pure Clairvoyance amounts to five percent *at most* of the total information you are set up to receive. What about the remaining information? It's processed in terms of your other languages, so that metaphysically speaking, each of us is built differently, with different combinations of language coming to us naturally.

Ironically, even when you *do* receive information through subtle sight, or Clairvoyance, it isn't necessarily colors. Have you ever had one of these experiences?

□ A teacher has explained an important new idea. A student goes Aha! You see the student's face light up. This light is not physical, nor is what you see necessarily a matter of expression. I call this glow an AURIC FLARE. When you *see* it (more than feel it/ hear it/smell it etc.—which are also possible), yes, that counts as Clairvoyance.

□ When you first meet a new friend, you see his face one way. But after your first in-depth conversation, his face softens somehow. You see him differently. Congratulations, you've moved past his personality's usual facade to make deeper contact with who he really is. Clairvoyance strikes again.*

□ At church, while you sit in a relaxed inward state, you notice a rim of light around the celebrants at the altar. Yes, you have just seen their auras. Two factors made Clairvoyance easier than most everyday situations: First, the people stood against a still background. Second, your awareness was relaxed and inward. It's important to understand that subtle sight, though apparently outward, really comes from inside. The deeper your consciousness, the more you'll see.

---

* Facade isn't merely a matter of personality or makeup. As your Clairvoyance develops, you will become aware of FACADE BODIES, that work like a suit of armor but exist on a psychic level. Each of us carries a mask, or facade, in every social situation. Sometimes it's transparent; sometimes it's thick. Sometimes it's a disguise, sometimes an exaggeration, occasionally even an obsession. The first time I became aware of facade bodies, I was reading photos for an interview with a Louisiana newspaper. As I started to read one face from a photo, a message hit me like a ton of bricks: "I'm so white." This surprised me, to say the least, but I kept on reading his face. Afterwards I found out that this was a photo of David Duke, notorious as a white supremacist.

- Clairvoyance can also show you special colors, like a black-and -white movie with just one detail colorized. For instance, when I read the aura of someone with Celestial Perception, I visually recognize/feel/know a bunch of golden glittery sparkles, like carbonated soda but made of energy. Do you have a color with special significance for you?
- Many of my students have noticed symbols or geometric patterns when they look at an aura. The meaning of this sacred geometry is revealed when using the technique for Questioning. Everyone's symbols are different. Perhaps you are set up to see stars, twinkles, or marks that look like an ongoing game of tic-tac-toe. Edgar Cayce, the famous psychic, channeled that charismatic people had hooks in their auras. They did, for him. But to another sensitive, the clairvoyant symbol could look like plus signs... or question marks.

Whatever form Clairvoyance takes for you, it's usually linked to your other languages—and those languages are the parts of experience that will wind up being more vivid for you. Think about your own experiences of looking deeper into reality. Didn't they involve sight triggering something else? Most of us need to activate Synesthesia plus more than one language, not sight alone, for a rich experience at the level of Celestial Perception.

This holds true not only of empathic travel but other soul-level or spirit-level experiences. For example, my friend Darshan Kaur Khalsa is a past life regression therapist with a growing client base on the East coast. In her words, "No matter what I tell clients, they start off expecting their experience to involve seeing things from the past. Most of them are more likely to hear or touch or experience in other ways. Their experience doesn't become vivid until they let go the expectation that they must see."

What matters is that your Clairvoyance enables you to see extra clearly. Just remember this. Despite a bias built into our image-bombarded American culture, seeing spirit clearly (Clairvoyance) is no more valuable than hearing extra clearly, touching extra clearly, or the other languages that follow. Several times, when reading auras, clients have come to me clutching their Kirlian photographs, saying, "Look at my aura in this picture. This should help you to read me."

Really? That reminds me of a story in Marshall McLuhan's book, *Understanding Media*, about two elderly women out walking together. One was pushing her granddaughter in a stroller. "She's lovely," cooed the other woman. "Oh, that's nothing," said the first. "Let me show you her picture."

Q: I WORRY ABOUT WHETHER THE SUBTLE STUFF I SEE IS CORRECT. WHAT DO YOU RECOMMEND TO KEEP US FROM MAKING SOME HORRIBLE KIND OF MISTAKE?

A: The most horrible mistake would be to worry about accuracy. How insulting! Your spiritual gifts don't deserve to be treated like the gangster in some movie who is being slapped around by the police. You set a pure intention, didn't you? Then assume your Clairvoyance is correct. As you nurture your knowledge, it will grow clearer.

Be kind for the sake of others, if not for yourself. Confident, clear perception will be a means for you to bless the world.

Q: WHAT ABOUT WANTING TO BE AS GOOD AS THE EXPERTS?

A: Unfortunately some clairvoyants assume that every other clairvoyant must see the same thing or see in the same way. We're so used to physical reality being one-size-fits-all. But it's ignorant, even arrogant, to assume that one's personal perceptions are so much holier than thou's, they must form the ultimate model for human Clairvoyance.

On several occasions, I've studied with spiritual teachers who made just this mistake. They even teamed up with artists to make colored drawings of "exactly" how auras were supposed to look. The funny thing about such drawings it that they contradict each other. Prove this to yourself by going to your favorite metaphysical bookstore. Check out the many books about auras that come with full-color illustrations, pictures that don't match up.

Q: My Clairvoyance isn't very good. All I see is the first layer of auras. When will that improve?

A: Don't keep score. You have many other languages to use in combination with clairvoyance. Currently I can accurately read eight layers of aura, but none of them primarily through vision. Carolyn Myss isn't clairvoyant either. Yet Dr. C. Norman Shealy has called her the most accurate medical intuitive he has encountered in 25 years of work with intuitives throughout the world. Myss's students wouldn't dream of faulting her for lacking clarity, yet in their personal lives, how many have felt their own abilities were lacking because their Celestial Perception didn't come with major visual flash?

Myss has joked publicly that she's a very "boring" psychic because her readings do *not* involve Clairvoyance. Rather than a personal fluke, this represents a universal lesson for everyone who has hungered after perception at the level of the angels.

Empaths, in particular, have too much valuable work ahead of them to bog themselves down by believing in our society's Myth about Auras.* We need to stop confusing the goal (information) with the means (the languages in which information flows to you). Speak your language without trying to fulfill anyone else's fantasies about how your spiritual life is supposed to show up! Later parts of this book will give you plenty of techniques to combine Clairvoyance with other languages. When you explore them, you'll amaze yourself with all that you know.

Q: Are you saying there's no hope for Clairvoyance if we're not visual, so we have to settle for the lesser abilities?

A: Clairvoyance is *not* better than the other abilities, just more famous. If you're not very visual, Clairvoyance can develop more but probably it will never be as strong as your other languages. Luckily you can use languages in any combination.

---

* See *Aura Reading Through ALL Your Senses*, pp. 22-27.

It may help to remember, what we're discussing are spiritual abilities. Beware of ingratitude or trying to copy someone else. A wise woman once said, "When God makes a toaster, He doesn't use it for air conditioning." Be what you can be best and make it glorious.

Q: I SUPPOSE I GET A LOT OF CLAIRVOYANT INFORMATION, BUT IT'S SO DARNED VAGUE. WHEN, IF EVER, WILL I BECOME REALLY CLEAR WITH MY CLAIRVOYANCE?

A: What needs clarity is the value you bring to your experience, rather than the experience itself. Clairvoyance often feels like sight without seeing. Don't let this paradox drive you crazy. And definitely don't try to push your subtle sight into sharp focus. When information comes to you in soft focus, let it be. Clairvoyance doesn't necessarily look like the pictures on your TV set, where you fiddle with the antenna to sharpen the image. Yet this isn't a matter of settling for vague experience. To sharpen your picture, bring in more of your *other* inner languages, plus Synesthesia.

Clairsentience

In the movie classic "It's a Wonderful Life," there's a scene where the hero, George Bailey, is tempted to work for the villain, Mr. Potter. To seal the deal, George starts to shake hands. Soon as he touches Potter, George realizes that he has made contact with something wicked and disgusting. So he pulls back his hand and cancels the deal.

Many of us can relate to that scene because, like the character of George, we are strongly clairsentient. CLAIRSENTIENCE means subtle touch. To give you an idea of how much you can learn from touch, think about handshakes you have known:

◻ The temperature of a handshake can tell a great deal. But when you probe with your consciousness, what you perceive transcends physical temperature. Coldness, for instance, could feel clammy in a way that communicates emotional distance. Or coldness could tell you that a person is frail or vulnerable. Other nuances include secretiveness, dishonesty, self-protectiveness, and an ingrained sense of social superiority. Which kinds of coldness have you met in a handshake?

□ Firmness in a handshake is considered desirable; advice for people who aspire to greater business success often includes a pep talk about making sure your handshake is good and firm. Well, firmness alone won't impress an empath with Clairsentience. You'll discover that the vigorous gripper could be wildly athletic or out of touch with his body; sexually interested in you or oblivious to your existence; pushy or timidly exuding a false confidence; enthusiastic or mechanical; coercive or shadowed with a victim energy. Which kinds of firmness have you shaken hands with?

□ Palm contact in handshakes translates into Clairsentience, too. No doubt you've received some handshakes where the other person's palm never touches yours at all, leaving a hollow space. Is this the sign of a habitual over-giver, someone who has forgotten to pause and receive from others? Or does this person prefer to make contact on a superficial level, not showing her deeper self until she knows you better?*

□ Grip position also conveys information to the Clairsentient. Have you ever received a shake that doesn't reach your entire hand? (The fingers-only version is the most extreme.) You may recognize a fearsome degree of daintiness, sexual awkwardness, pretense, disinterest, physical frailty, or fear. Ding! an alarm may sound when Clairsentience tells you this person is an emotional taker or a social snob. Or maybe the shake merely reveals a social butterfly whose attention, mid-shake, has flown to somebody else.

---

* Consider, too, the energetic meaning of the palm. It's a sub-chakra related to emotions. Therefore, those nuances of touching or withholding palms that you feel in a handshake relate directly to a person's willingness to be touched at the "heart."

Q: Could I have an empathic gift for Physical Oneness yet not be into Clairsentience?

A: Sure, and the reason becomes clear when you make a distinction between empathic gifts and empathic language. Empathic *gifts* mean that you fly in spirit to one or another level of subtle body. You could be drawn to body, mind, intellect, emotions, spirit—every empath's soul specializes, with some levels being more charming than others. Empathic *language* means the way you talk to yourself deep inside. So you could pick up information about Physical Oneness and express it in terms of Clairsentience, Clairaudience... you name it.

Q: Having been abused as a child, I suffer from a deep distrust of physical contact. Could I be clairsentient even if I hate touching people physically?

A: Certainly. Some of us have had experiences that make touching problematic—not only major traumas like abuse and rape but chronic illness, loneliness, or just having parents who were physically undemonstrative.

The good news is that enjoying Clairsentience in its non-physical forms—exploring auras rather than touching physical bodies—may help you to overcome the pain you have around the issue of touching. It may turn out that even though you have reservations about physical touch, you'll find that empathic experience registers in your mind mostly through the language of Clairsentience. Great! But even if you're forever turned off to the Clairsentience, the other languages within you are alive and well. Great again!

Recently I took a poll in a class of 20. "How many of you feel frustrated when you *can't* touch a person you feel close to: a little handshake, a hug, some kind of physical contact?" Most of my students waved their hands like crazy. But two students looked blankly at the hands raised around them as if to say, "Where are you from, Venus?" Clairsentience just wasn't high on their list of inner languages.

Q: Isn't Clairsentience awkward, though? You can use Clairvoyance whenever you like, but isn't it a little weird to wave your arms in front of a person's energy field? I always figured Clairvoyance was superior for this reason.

A: Some of my most revolutionary plug-in techniques will move you right past this seeming difficulty. Most important, though, remember that Clairsentience is a language. Superiority doesn't enter into it. You've been wired to speak some languages more easily than others. Everyone has. That setup of your body-mind-spirit was in place long before you picked up this book, and every set of gifts can lead you to mastery as an empath. Why worry about awkwardness? Learn how to use the gifts you've got.

Clairaudience

Listening to a talk radio show, you become impressed with the man being interviewed. His voice reveals a rare depth of heart. Then the interviewer ends the segment by saying, "Thank you, John Smith," and suddenly you realize that this interviewee is a newspaper columnist whose opinions you have known (and disagreed with) for years. Could happen! In fact, it did—to me.

Clairaudience has a way of opening up reality. It enables us to hear a deeper sound within ordinary sounds. When used in combination with empathy, this language resonates with fascinating knowledge. Here are some ways you may already be speaking Clairaudience:

- "Stop it," you say while talking to your teenage son, Michael. "You're not listening to me and I know it." When pressed to explain how you know Michael's not listening, you tell him you hear your words echoing back to you, as if bouncing against a wall. Michael scoffs: "A soundless sound—are you kidding?" But of course you can hear that kind of thing, loud and clear, if you have Clairaudience.

- When Michael was a baby, mouthing his first words, you heard him repeat a blurry-sounding syllable like "ookee opa." Other family members scratched their heads, but you instantly knew what it meant, "Cookie Monster." What were you hearing that other family members didn't hear? You heard Michael's intent.

□ As the weeks of his babyhood went by, you learned a whole range of meaning for "ookee opa. " It could mean "I'm tired and need a nap." or "My experience of life is exquisite in its immediacy." or "I'm bored. I need someone to play with me, *now*." How did you translate? Clairaudience.

□ Silence is one of the most fascinating ways that Clairaudience speaks to us. Imagine that you're alone in an elevator with a stranger. She says nothing, staring at the wall about a foot above your head. But the air is charged with electricity, and you hear its meaning in the silence around you. The stranger is cold and angry. Or she's drawn to you with a passionate, sexy intensity. Or she's bored, so bored you could cut the dead silence around her with a knife. Or, best case of all, she's endowed with such amazing spiritual development that you get a contact high. Right there in the elevator you might be able to hear angels sing.

Q: Could Clairaudience explain why sounds bother me that don't bother people around me?

A: Ever hear the expression, "Painfully aware"? It's common with Clairaudients. You may flinch from noises that others miss entirely. For instance, Milton isn't especially strict as a parent, but a major exception is how he handles noises. "Don't do that!" he yells when his son drags his feet, clad in socks, across the wall by his bed. Milton hates to sound like a wimp, but the noise sets his teeth on edge. Why? He hears the subtle breaking-down-under-pressure of the cotton fibers in the socks.

Inconvenient though it may be for Milton to have hearing that acute, Clairaudience goes with his magnificent gift as an Intellectual Shape Shifter. Even if Milton could stop that super-sensitive hearing at will, because it isn't always convenient, this would be a bad idea: It could blast a hole in his soul. Luckily, he can't, so he's stuck with sock noises.

Q: IF YOU CAN'T CARRY A TUNE, IS IT BECAUSE YOU DON'T HAVE CLAIRAUDIENCE?

A: Surprisingly, tunefulness has nothing to do with Clairaudience. William Butler Yeats, one of the greatest modern poets, couldn't carry a tune. Yet he had an uncanny ability to find words that would sing in the spirit.

One of my hobbies over the years has been to teach an adult education course in "How to Carry a Tune." When I give this two-hour class, students will enter timidly, barely able to warble "Happy Birthday." By the end they're belting out melodies like "Summertime" and not doing a bad job of it. Tunefulness can be learned by almost everyone, when a teacher can nurture abilities that have been squelched.

By contrast, Clairaudience can't necessarily be developed, not if you don't have it in the first place. Nor would you need to. In the words of Rabbi Elie Weisel, "There are a thousand and one gates to the garden of mystical experience. Each man has his own gate. Let us never make the mistake of desiring to enter the garden through any gate other than our own." Similarly, there are many gates for Celestial Perception. You'll know which ones belong to you by your relative ease at entering through them.

Q: WHAT'S THE DIFFERENCE BETWEEN HOW EMPATHS AND NON-EMPATHS USE THEIR CLAIRAUDIENCE?

A. All Clairaudients receive meaningful information through their subtle hearing. Clairaudients who fly empathically will be apt to pick up information in terms of sound and silence, to describe it in terms of sound, to remember it in terms of sound. Their experience of *otherness* may include an auditory component.

Q: AND IF YOU CAN'T DO THAT WITHOUT A BIG STRUGGLE?

A: Not to worry. Other languages may be on the tip of your tongue.

Gustatory Giftedness

Naomi's mother was very direct about it. "Come home from college for the holidays. I need to smell you."

The scent of someone we love is a tonic that reaches all the way to the soul. And those with GUSTATORY GIFTEDNESS drink this sort of tonic on a regular basis. They experience how taste and smell can bring you to the celestial level. Scientific research reveals that all human beings unconsciously *react* to fragrance. Gustatory language, by contrast, is conscious. It holds your insights as an empath in ways that are very individual and precise. Count yourself gifted in the gustatory tongue if you can relate to one of the following examples:

- When someone feels happy or sad, tired or relaxed, confident or fearful, you can smell it.
- One of your favorite aspects of sex is the progression of fragrances around your lover.
- Stepping into a crowd of people, the stench of alcohol sometimes hits you like a physical blow, while others seem oblivious.
- You taste flavors in food that other people don't seem to notice. Many commercially popular processed foods, in particular, taste absolutely fake... as if garish shades of marigold, crimson, and light green were supposed to blend into a pleasing shade of orange.
- Smell or taste become active for you as Synesthesia. A kiss will smell blue or purple or pink. With gustatory language, sense-blended experiences like this aren't just flights of poetry. They are prose—how everyday life shows up for you.

Q: WHAT IF YOU ARE ONLY SUPER SENSITIVE TO SMELL ON CERTAIN OCCASIONS? DOES THAT STILL MEAN YOU HAVE GUSTATORY LANGUAGE?

A: Absolutely, and the frequency of these occasions will increase when you use techniques to exercise your empathy on a regular basis.

Q: DOES IT COUNT AS GUSTATORY GIFTEDNESS IF YOU SMELL SOMETHING IMAGINARY?

A: Always trust your imagination, once you have set an intention. Many of my students have noticed fragrances that seem to arrive out of nowhere. For instance, Jonathan is a Healing Touch practitioner. When he works on a client's energy field, sometimes he has perceptions that seem wacky, like a hospital-antiseptic kind of smell or flowers that are not in the physical room and have nothing to do with the client's physical body.

Jonathan has learned to use these perceptions as one of his languages for experiences of Physical Oneness. This empowers him.

Q: MAYBE I SHOULDN'T ADMIT THIS, BUT I KEEP COOKBOOKS ON MY NIGHT TABLE. IT'S MY FAVORITE BEDTIME READING. I CAN TASTE THE RECIPES JUST BY READING THEM.

A: Tasting food when you read about it shows Gustatory Giftedness, so congratulations. If you examine your abilities more closely, you may discover additional dimensions of Synesthesia. For instance, I once published a cookbook where Gustatory Giftedness worked in a way that involved Clairaudience, Synesthesia, and the next gift we'll discuss, Holistic Knowing.

To create a new recipe, most cooks begin by designing it on paper. I'd start by picking a couple of interesting ingredients, like eggplant and tomato sauce. My senses are wired so that I can switch on a way to translate taste into sound, like notes with overtones. So when designing recipes I would play around, filling out the chords by adding ingredients until the sound was full. The recipes tasted good in real life, too.

Holistic Knowing

Speaking of music, ever notice that some people are naturals with chord instruments while others prefer one voice at a time? If you like to play flute or violin, that's a different sensibility from the keyboard enthusiast. One man's musical meat is another man's poison.

HOLISTIC KNOWING is like being the kind of musician who favors playing a chord instrument. It makes you come alive to Hold a Space for many people at once, rather than empathically sharing with just one person at a time. Connecting with the wholeness of a situation, Holistic Knowers relish the experience of a big "us" that enfolds many people, rather than the smaller "us" that contains just "you" and "me."

Here's a way to decide if you're strong in Holistic Knowing. Can you relate to the pesky side, such as what I call Volunteer Party Host Syndrome? Here's how it works. Say that you have gone to a party at Walter's house. His job description for Party Host is radically different from yours. To him, the job is over once guests cross his threshold. To you, that's when a host's work really begins. Immediately after arrival you sense that Walter isn't hosting, he's guesting.

How does this affect you, the guest with Holistic Knowing? Not only do you notice guests who are standing alone and appear visibly pathetic, you find the less obvious casualties of host neglect—guests who put up a brave front but nonetheless are having a terrible time, like that poor soul in the red dress who flits a bit too vivaciously from one conversation to another.

One look at her aura across the room, one sound bite from the hollow-voiced conversation around you, the smell in the room—whatever empathic gifts of yours combine with the language of Holistic Knowing, and OUCH, you can feel it. Nobody here has set up a lost-and-found for partygoers. You wind up talking to the suffering guest, then seek out other neglected guests and pull them into your conversation.

After the party, you might slap your forehead and ask, "Why did I spend the whole party acting like a host when I was a guest? What's wrong with me? Am I... co-dependent?"

Probably you're not, just empathic. Some would argue that behavior like this shows poor personal boundaries, maybe even an acute need for therapy. However, that interpretation misses the point about empathy. Volunteer Party Host Syndrome shows a gift for empathy in general and Holistic Knowing in particular. Recognize this language, use it on purpose, and you'll be able to do the following:

□ Spellbind an audience. Hold the group in the palm of your hand when you speak, teach, act, sing, or dance. (Assuming that you also have some skill in those areas!)

□ Preside over a large family gathering without leaving anyone out—meanwhile suffering a minimum of personal exhaustion.

□ Lead any group of people, be it a workplace situation, a club meeting, or class, so that everyone feels included.

□ Build a team, helping people to support each other with their varied strengths.

□ Keep many people in your mind, or heart, at once.

Q: How is Holistic Knowing different from being a leader? Or is it the same thing?

A: Holistic Knowing is one of many ways to be a leader. Surprisingly, this language does not necessarily go with having a winning personality. People may not even notice you. Indeed, the act of Holding a Space is most powerful through silence.

Q: Whenever I take a class, I prefer to sit in the back. I guess it's because I like to connect with the whole group. Could that be Holistic Knowing?

A: Exactly—and probably nobody will notice what you're doing except other empaths in the room who speak the language of Holistic Knowing.

Q: Could you give an example of Holistic Knowing not involving a social situation?

A: When you build a sand castle, write a story, put on sunscreen before going outside—whenever you take an action that involves completion, people with Holistic Knowing take pleasure in perfect economy. Holistic Knowing can involve knowing exactly when something is done. You stop precisely there and feel a delicious sense of rightness.

What has made this experience qualify as Holistic Knowing? You were aware of the many parts making a whole. That whole satisfied you more than any one part could.

Q: How can Holistic Knowing help you as an empath?

A: Empathic skill makes you a juggler. Not only can you merge and flow on purpose with any one person at any one time, but you are in a privileged position where you can purposely merge with more than one person, appreciate the energetic interplay, maybe even facilitate it. Holistic Knowing is a most valuable language for empathy.

Q: Heaven help me, I have no clue what you're talking about. What if all this discussion of Holistic Knowing makes no sense to me whatsoever?

A: Then you're in the majority. Most people don't speak this language. Remember, empaths are set up to speak different languages. All that matters is identifying which ones you *do* speak.

Analytical Awareness

Whenever my mother used to practice the piano, my sister and I would run for cover. As if caught in a recurring nightmare, we would hear the same Chopin etude again and again. Mom would start at the beginning. Then clunk, she'd stop halfway at the very same chord. Back to the beginning, she would go, over and over and over.

As an adult I realize that I, of all people, am in no position to laugh at my mother's technique for wrecking perfectly good music. Feebly attempting to practice the violin, I inflicted the same kind of torture with Bach's double violin concerto. Of course, people who actually learn to play an instrument practice differently. They work at the hard parts until they figure them out. Alas, neither my mother nor I has much of a flair for the language it takes to do this, Analytical Awareness.

Musicians who practice properly have a peculiar kind of curiosity. They unravel knots. Analytical Awareness, with music or anything else, involves jumping from level to level until a puzzle is utterly solved.

Sometimes it's called having a restless mind, so let's immediately distinguish Analytical Awareness from being scatterbrained. Analytical Awareness means that you understand what's happening at the surface level, then jump to other levels, one by one. The challenge is learning to take enough time when processing this language, so it doesn't babble at an unintelligible fast-forward speed.

Artist Georgia O'Keefe spoke for many who have learned the secret of slowing down with Analytical Awareness (and a right brain sensibility) when she described her art:

> A flower is relatively small. Everyone has many associations with a flower.... Still—in a way—nobody sees a flower—really—it is so small—we haven't the time—and to see takes time like to have a friend takes time. If I could paint the flower exactly as I see it no one would see what I see because I would paint it small like a flower is small. So I said to myself—I'll paint what I see—what the flower is to me but I will paint it big and they will be surprized [sic.] into taking time to look at it.

When you can take the time to look at her paintings, you'll see the work of an artist with tremendous Analytical Awareness. If you speak this language comfortably, it's likely that you use it most easily for Intellectual Shape Shifting. But it also facilitates other empathic gifts. For instance, I've read the auras of doctors who have magnificent Physical Oneness, and it's made all the stronger by their Analytical Awareness.

To summarize, let's use an example from the world of toys. Empaths who can speak Analytical Awareness move like a Slinky®. Other empaths move more like Play Doh ®.

Q: Wow! Did you say that nobody can be a good musician without Analytical Awareness?

A: Yes, that probably is a requirement to perform music as complicated as a Beatles song—more so for more sophisticated music. Of course, it wouldn't hurt if you also had a good ear and were physically coordinated....

Q: What a relief! Ever since childhood, I've felt guilty about being lazy at practicing the piano. It seemed I had everything: a good ear, a good teacher, and I could really feel the music. But I couldn't push myself hard enough to practice properly. You're saying that my lack of Analytical Awareness was the real culprit, not my lack of push?

A: All the motivation in the world won't give you a spiritual language that's not part of your inner programming.

Q: But isn't it important to push yourself to do the difficult things? Couldn't you call that the key to success in life?

A: Depends on how you *define* life. In the material world, sometimes there's no substitute for hard work. Spiritually (including exploration of your empathic self), it never helps to struggle. Joseph Campbell, author of *The Hero with a Thousand Faces*, had the right idea when he advised people to follow their bliss.

Q: What always works for me is to analyze my strengths and limitations. Then I overcome them. For instance, if I could speak all the languages you've described except for Analytical Awareness, that's the one I would focus on.

A: When you develop *any* one of your spiritual languages, you develop them all. It's like growing up physically. As a child, did you say, "Arms, it's your turn to grow; come on toes, stretch"? Or did the sequence of growth arrange itself? So will your language for empathy, assuming that you follow your bliss. Incidentally, from your question it's obvious that you're strong in Analytical Awareness. Just play it back.

Q: How can you say Analytical Awareness is helpful for empathy? When I tried to Hold a Space before, my mind jumped around like a puppy. What can I do about it?

A: Adjust your timing. Analyze *after* you travel, not during the journey. Otherwise you're putting on the brakes when you drive. So relax into your experience, rather than analyzing it; encourage yourself to bring in other languages, such as Clairsentience.

Q: Won't shutting up my mind make me even more frustrated?

A: Forget shutting. Keep your attention open with some extra big Vibe-raising Breaths. Also, realize once and for all that you can afford to relax. Unlikely though it is that someone like you would turn intellectually lazy, even for a short time, it wouldn't last. Analytical Awareness would reassert itself at the soonest opportunity.

Q: Could you give an example of how an empath could slow down Analytical Awareness?

A: Say you're Holding a Space with Dolores, exploring her thought process. In seconds, you move through the way she does what she does. Although it's tempting to dart back to your usual way of thinking and actively figure out what has happened, you can make a choice to let yourself linger.

Q: Why? I don't get it.

A: By allowing your mind to ease up, you open deeper into experience. Focusing your Analytical Awareness will block deep empathy. Save it until after you've traveled empathically. Otherwise, one starts thinking, "I know it all." Actually, knowing all *about* IT is different from knowing IT *directly* through personal experience.

Language It

Consider the languages described in this chapter in terms of a SPIRITUAL INVITATION. That's the green light to go full speed ahead on your journey toward higher states of consciousness. You'll recognize a spiritual invitation when you feel an increase in interest, charm, enthusiasm, or curiosity... plus a sense of delightful familiarity.

Part of your invitation to empathy is your languages of the spirit. Now you've had the chance to consciously recognize the ones that are important to you. To hasten your progress, set the intention right now that for the rest of today you will gently pay attention to your own use of language for spiritual experience.

Do this for a few days and, effortlessly, you'll gain a healthy self-consciousness about these deep structures for spiritual experience.

Analytical Awareness gives you layers; Holistic Knowing puts them together. Gustatory Giftedness adds fragrance and taste. Clairsentience brings meaning to any touch, whether to the physical body or an energy body. Clairaudience awakens truth through sound while Clairvoyance awakens truth through sight. Truth Knowledge is the language moves you into oneness with seamless spontaneity whereas Psychic Knowing is an even wilder kind of language—not quite as strange as the proverbial speaking in tongues but at least as spiritual and far more useful.

Whenever you give yourself permission to relax and move into an empathic voyage, Synesthesia will stimulate all your precious gifts for language. Over time, you will slip into a higher state of consciousness, fully in touch with reality but with the added dimension provided by very human ways that you, personally, language the finest spiritual nuances.

So-called ordinary life mixes touch and sight, smell and taste, hearing, knowing, breaking apart and putting together. Although theoretically we can separate these modalities, in practice they mix and mingle. Your favorite old winter coat has its touch, its colors, its musty closet smell; maybe you take for granted its multi-part structure, its body-covering completeness, even the familiar sounds as you put it on, all this making one garment. Therein lies life's richness of experience and hidden potential for language.

Now your Synesthesia experiences can—make that *should*—gain the same comfortable richness. Sometimes the feast will appear as if by magic, a complete banquet richly laid. Other times, you'll receive just one magic bean, a tablecloth, or the flower that eventually will form a centerpiece. In such cases, what will help? Language. Imaginatively used, it can turn line drawings into 3-D.

As you open yourself up to uninhibited language, you open up your flights of spirit. After you've traveled, what then? How will you be able to use your experiences? Will they fade like a dream, real only in that self-same dream world? Language gives staying power.

Therefore I urge you to make the effort to language your experience. Wait until you come back, of course, rather than being self-consciously wordy during empathic experience. Immediately after you come back from journeying, you're in a special transition zone—not unlike the gabby stage some of us fall into right after making love, which some have dubbed *birdsong*. After empathy, go ahead and talk about your experience.

As you'll discover, finding language is fun. Quicker than certain alleged cereal guys say "Snap," "Crackle," and "Pop," you'll find distinctive ways to language your empathic experience.

Here is some of the language my students have used: spongy, bouncy, metallic; heavier than me, lighter than me, more serious; slower moving, vibrationally lighter, fairylike; resistant, fluffy, magnetic; warm, cool, hot; happier to be in her body, more sensuous than me; more analytical, bigger mind, fascinating, always so complicated.

Do these particular bits of language impress you? Maybe not. One person's epiphany is someone else's cliché. So what? For that matter, who cares whether your words will impress anyone else? Languaging has value for *you*. It makes your experience clearer, more real, and longer remembered. In addition, the very process of languaging strengthens coordination between your subtle faculties and your everyday personality.

Finally, today's language serves as a basis for tomorrow's language. Over time, so much speech accumulates that you learn what you mean by it, not unlike the mysterious way your onetime babblings of English eventually turned fluent.

8. *P*lug in, *S*witch on

Fly in Spirit big time with this chapter's collection of techniques for exploring all six types of empathy. At first it may surprise you that they begin with some kind of aura reading—at least this will surprise you if, deep down, you were expecting advanced empathy to be no more than a slight variation on your everyday perception.

However, aura reading means waking up Celestial Perception, lifting you to higher consciousness as a basis for knowing. Why settle for vaguely picking up signals when, consciously, the rest of you hardly knows what you're doing? When you bring your conscious mind to the level of auras, and afterwards travel empathically, wow! Not only do you Fly in Spirit. You know you are making the trip.

The major discovery in this chapter... perhaps, too, the major discovery in this book... is the concept of PLUGGING IN. Remember how auras are made of electro-magnetic energy? You can use your consciousness as if it were a lamp.

When you plug a lamp into a light socket, then switch it on, you can light up an entire room. Similarly, you can use intention and one of your languages for aura reading (like Clairsentience, Clairvoyance, or Clairaudience) to form an energetic connection with someone. Once this is done, the whole person will be illuminated for you, as if in the glow of a subtle spiritual light. Then you can travel at will throughout that person's energy field. Your empathic experience will be both conscious and, over time, increasingly vivid.

You'll understand this travel experience in terms of your strongest personal languages, as described in the previous chapter. Even unskilled empaths vaguely sense that they have used one of their inner languages to set off a shift in consciousness. For example, ever see Shirley Temple's amazing performance in "The Little Colonel"? The tiny tot danced with legendary tapper Bojangles Robinson, matching him tap for tap, beat for beat. Amazingly she did this with almost no rehearsal. As an adult, Temple was asked how she managed to do this. She told the reporter, "I would learn by listening to the taps. I would primarily listen to what he was doing and I would do it. I can't explain that too well, except that I could hear it."

Explaining this in *our* terms, what Shirley did was to plug into Bojangles' aura by means of Clairaudience. Then she was free to use her gift of Physical Oneness. In that flow of energy, empathically connected with his body, of course she could match him tap for tap. His body had become her body, for all practical purposes.

All empaths, natural or skilled, slip into travel experiences—even if we never manage to tap dance as well as Shirley Temple could by age six. You have *your* ways, the areas of purity in life where you travel without needing any technique at all. But the disadvantage with such experiences is that, usually, you can't cause them to happen on demand. They happen when they happen. Techniques make the difference. Master this chapter's techniques to plug in. Then you'll have practical ways to switch on profound empathic travel.

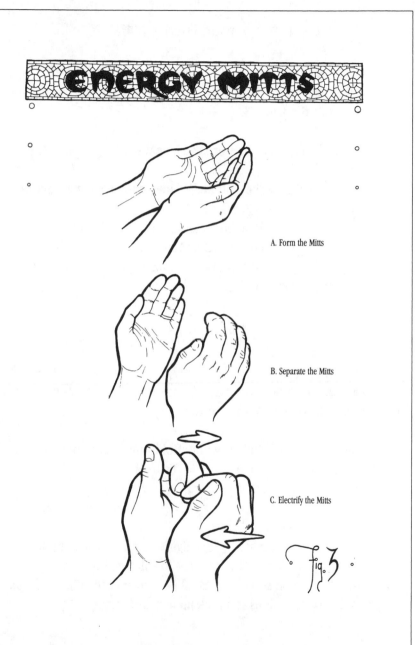

ENERGY MITTS

A. Form the Mitts

B. Separate the Mitts

C. Electrify the Mitts

Fig. 3

Put on Your Energy Mitts

Turn your hands into tools for Clairsentience. I call them ENERGY MITTS because they help you to catch energy the way baseball mitts help you to catch a baseball. See figure 3.

1. *Cup your hands*, as if you were catching water from a pool. (See figure 3A.)
2. *Separate your hands* but still keep thumb and fingers together on each individual hand. (See figure 3B.)
3. *Electrify Your Mitts.* Rub the fingernails of each Mitt back and forth across the fingernails on the other Mitt. This charges up the auric energy coming out of this part of your hands, like turning up the volume on a radio. [See figure 3C.]

Aura Bounce

Now put those Mitts to work to catch energy... and knowledge. (You'll be able to see the hand positions used by previewing the illustration for a later technique, "Bouncy Affirmations.")

1. Spread your hands shoulder width. Hold your Energy Mitts so they face each other, palm to palm. (See figure 4a.)
2. *Slowly bring your Mitts together until you bump up against a something made of energy—a subtle something*, not a solid something. (See figure 4b.)
3. Bounce your Mitts out again. (See figure 4c.) That back-and-forth movement is the basic Aura Bounce. To enhance it:
4. *Repeat* this motion several times. Close your eyes to help you focus more on the sensations you pick up in your Mitts.

A. Positive   B. Negative   C. Positively Renewed!

Fig. 4.

5. *Vary the speed of the Bounces.* (By the way, while doing this you are allowed to breathe! Some newbies tense up as if they've been asked to do brain surgery. Take it easy.)
6. Take a deep breath and *language your experience.* Whatever words come up, they're fine, even if they don't sound especially fancy or lofty. It was a breakthrough for my students when they found words like "sticky goop" and "wet purple fuzz."

Energy Mitts & Aura Bounce—Q&A

Q: Different people in the class held their hands at different distances—why?

A: Several reasons: First, remember the layered energy bodies that make up the human aura? With Aura Bounce, each hand bumps against one or more layers. Stereo information comes to you, where each hand separately bumps into the edge of an energy body that sticks out of the other hand; then your brain puts the input together.

Does this seem hopelessly confusing? Don't worry. Becoming skilled as an empath doesn't depend on visualizing this stereo stuff while you Aura Bounce any more than an artist must constantly remember that every image he draws on a page must be processed by his optic nerves and be introduced to his brain *upside down*. Good old science....

Intellectually reassuring though it may be to explain how things work, trying to remember the mechanics while you actually do something can make you crazy! For most of us, it's enough to know the practical part. To turn on the light, use a switch. To feel your aura between your hands, bounce your Energy Mitts together until you get there, wherever *there* is.

A second reason why people feel auras between their hands at different distances is that people are spiritually set up to pay attention to different layers of spiritual life. Therefore, some of you will feel aura borders when your hands are two inches apart, others will be more attracted to subtle body borders six inches apart, and so forth. And that will be because the close-in layer carries information about physical survival, the six-inch layer stores information about life from the perspective of the intellect, etc. Each layer corresponds to a kind of data. In this book, however, I've purposely avoided discussing what the different auric layers are about. It adds theory that you won't need for your direct experience as an empath, and I've had to include plenty of abstractions already, about language and consciousness—things that *are* directly relevant.

A third reason why people feel auras at different distances is that their energy bodies come in different sizes. A bigger aura sticks out more. So a roomful of people doing the Aura Bounce correctly will show plenty of variation in the distance between hands.

Q: If I noticed a couple of different stopping places on my own aura, were those different energy bodies?

A: Exactly right! When you peel an onion, can't you stop at different layers? Well, an advanced version of Aura Bounce lets you do something similar.

Advanced Aura Bounce

Auras have layers. Don't just take my word for it. Bounce into this next exercise.

1. *Place your Energy Mitts far apart,* as far as you can comfortably hold them.
2. Slowly *bring them together.*
3. *Bump into one layer*, or boundary, or texture. Pat the edges gently to acknowledge what you have there.
4. *Rest* your Mitts right where they are. Take a Vibe-raising Breath to clear your mind.
5. *Slowly bring your Mitts closer together until you bump* into the

next layer. Again pat the edges gently in acknowledgment.

6. *Repeat Steps 4 and 5* until you've come through the last energy layer (your Mitts will practically touch each other).

7. Now for the finale: Drop your hands to your sides. Take a few Vibe-raising Breaths. Form your Energy Mitts. Innocent as a kid making snowmen, scooping up snow with no defined limits whatsoever— just going by what feels good— *do one free-form, simple Aura Bounce.* Stop at the layer that feels most comfortable. That layer is your specialty at this time in your life.

Advanced Aura Bounce—Q&A

Q: Wow! What have I done to deserve being so good at this?

A: Amazing, isn't it? Just by virtue of your being *human*, your aura has all those layers. By virtue of your *choice* to explore spiritual life, you're able to appreciate those layers with your consciousness. And by virtue of being an *empath*, you're going to learn to Fly in Spirit from one layer to another, at will. Awe-inspiring as this is, guess what? It's positively mechanical compared to the inner richness of experience you'll have later. But let's keep developing your spiritual abilities one step at a time or, in this case, one hand at a time.

Find Your Primary Sensor Hand

You can go on to use the Aura Bounce on other people, plants, or pets. Discover a hidden world of information, utterly fascinating. But you won't need to use both Mitts to explore this, any more than a ball player needs a matched set of baseball gloves. Choose just one hand, and for best results don't base your choice on whether you're right handed or left handed.

Did you know that you have a built-in version of handedness that relates to subtle energy sensing? Everyone has one hand that works especially well at receiving information. (The other hand is your POWER HAND, for sending energy. Use that hand if you do healing work.)

In your role of empath, however, what matters most is receiving. The hand that does this better is your PRIMARY SENSOR HAND. To sort out which hand is which:

1. *Interlace your fingers* as though preparing to twiddle your thumbs.
2. *Wiggle the thumb that is on top.* That belongs to your Power Hand. Is it left or right?
3. *Wiggle the thumb that is underneath.* That belongs to your Primary Sensor Hand. Use it for all one-handed techniques (such as all the rest of the aura-touching techniques in this book).

Have fun now exploring a few different people's auras with your Primary Sensor Hand. Bounce against one, then another and another. After each exploration, be sure to language your perceptions. Not that you need feel obligated to share that language out loud. Go somewhere private and say the words or write them down.

Even better, show a friend how to feel auras and take turns exploring, then languaging your experience. Children under 10 make especially interesting exploration buddies.

Find Your Primary Sensor Hand—Q&A

Q: WHEN I AURA BOUNCED DIFFERENT PEOPLE WITH MY PRIMARY SENSOR HAND, I DISCOVERED SOMETHING WEIRD. YOU WERE RIGHT——DIFFERENT PEOPLE DO HAVE DIFFERENT AMOUNTS OF ENERGY IN THEIR SUBTLE BODIES. WHY?

A: Lo and behold, you've bumped into one of the mysteries of spiritual life. Aura size relates to amount of life energy, spiritual energy. It has nothing to do with the person's height or physical beauty or other ways we're used to distinguishing people.

What's going on? Subtle energy is relative. You can't necessarily predict who's going to have more or less. Aura size for each individual changes too, by the way.

Q: WHAT DOES IT MEAN WHEN PEOPLE HAVE BIGGER AURAS?

A: There are plenty of possible meanings:

- One reason for a big aura is that you're healthy, happy, and awake.
- Higher consciousness—such as you're developing right now—can expand your aura.
- Soul-level talents can show in a bigger aura, especially around a particular chakra. For example, singers and other musicians with major sex appeal have enormous second chakras.
- People who are, physically, on the heavy side often have bigger auras—more about that in the chapter on "Grounding."
- If you enjoy speaking in public, you have learned to hold an energy space for your audience. And the better you do this, the more your own aura grows to meet the crowd. Having done many live media interviews, I've found it fascinating how topnotch broadcasters unconsciously expand their auras when they go on the air.
- For more nuances about auras, see my earlier book, *Aura Reading Through ALL Your Senses.*

Bouncy Affirmations

One of the most fascinating influences on a person's aura size is thought. That's right, the thoughts you have from moment to moment directly affect the size and quality of your aura, as the following technique will demonstrate. (See figure 4.)

1. Form your Energy Mitts, polish them up, then *do the Aura Bounce* until you make contact with a blob of energy between your hands. Freeze. *See the distance* between your Energy Mitts?
2. *Drop your hands to your sides* and, for now, forget about them. *Say the following affirmation* out loud three times with your eyes closed: "I love myself."
3. Open your eyes. Form your Energy Mitts, polish them up, then *do the Aura Bounce* a second time. Freeze. *See the distance* between your Energy Mitts now? (See "Positive" on figure 4)
4. *Drop your hands to your sides* and, for now, forget about them. *Say the following affirmation* out loud three times with your eyes closed: "I am about as important as a little ant running around on the sidewalk." (Please, please don't let this be the key sentence you take from this book. This is an experiment. Book reviewers, have mercy!) *Repeat Step #3.* (See "Negative" on figure 4.)
5. Go back to the truer affirmation of Step #2. *Say it three times* and repeat Steps #2 and 3. (See "Positively Renewed" on Figure 4.)

Bouncy Affirmations—Q&A

Q: Now I'm really upset. My aura size is whooshing in and out because of what I say?

A: You're not the first one to be shocked at how much auras can change, based on what you say about yourself. Negative self-talk smooshes down auras, just as positive speech expands them.

No need to obsess about censoring every little sentence—just avoid badmouthing yourself, such as repeated use of those dirty little words "I don't know." Chronic self-put-downs = low-self esteem = low amounts of energy in your subtle bodies = low reserves of physical vitality and immunity.

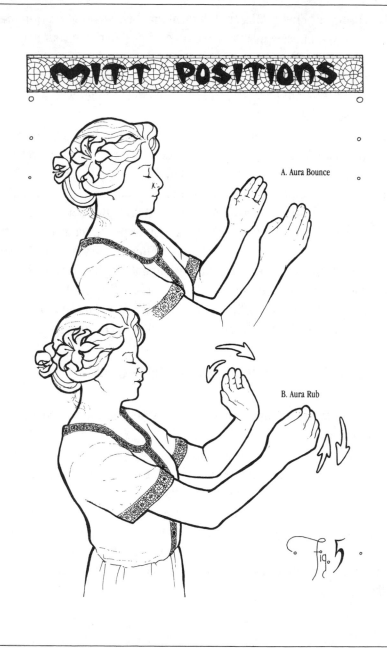

MITT POSITIONS

A. Aura Bounce

B. Aura Rub

Fig. 5

Aura Rub

Now that you've experienced how your aura can expand or shrink, you're ready to explore an even more interesting aspect: quality. What is this energy like? And how much can it tell you?

1. Form your Energy Mitts. Polish them. *Do the Aura Bounce*. Freeze at any position where you feel yourself making contact with energy. (See "Mitt Positions," figure 5a.)
2. Move each Mitt inward about one inch. *Gently rub* your Mitts sideways, palm opposite palm.
3. Close your eyes and *savor the texture*. (See figure 5b.)
4. *Language* your experience. How about some weird words with plenty of Synesthesia? Free yourself up to imagine and associate. (All words are good except those that put yourself down as a knower.) Some words my students have used are soft, silky, hot (as in sexy), vibrant, thick, and indigo.

Aura Rub—Q&A

Q: What's the point in moving your hands back and forth? Didn't you think we looked crazy enough before?

A: There is a method to the hand waving. It's contrast. Ever take a long, slow bath and wonder if it's safe to add more hot water? Stewing in your own juice, you get so used to the temperature that you have no clue what it is any more... until you swish the water around enough to feel it . Well, that's the basis for the Aura Rub. Like bathtub water, the quality of your aura can become numbingly familiar. Moving your Mitts stirs things up.

Q: Can you do Aura Rub on other people? If so, do you still rub your hands back and forth?

A: Yes and yes.

Q: WHEN I DID THE RUB, I FOUND I WAS PLAYING WITH AN ARMOR-LIKE COATING ALL OVER MY BODY.

I guess you'd say I language it with Clairvoyance. Somebody told me that this layer of the aura is called the web. It's so neat, I could play with it for hours. Do you think I'm becoming obsessed?

A: *Fascinated* is a fairer way to put it. Of course you're interested. Do parents call babies obsessed when they play with their toes? With auras, different people are attracted to different layers at different times. Perhaps you'll go on to study healing techniques where you can use your skill with this web to help people all over the planet. Brainwave: How about you call it the worldwide web?

Q: COULD YOU HURT YOURSELF BY DOING THE AURA RUB?

A: Highly unlikely—but if you feel uncomfortable, stop.

Q: HOW ABOUT HURTING OTHER PEOPLE?

A: Healing Touch practitioners, who work specifically on their clients' auras, have certain guidelines which are useful for doing Aura Rub or other techniques where you're touching another person's energy field:

- Do only brief sessions for elderly people or children. (That means no more than 10 minutes.)
- Before starting your session, inquire if your client takes blood thinners. Avoid prolonged sessions of aura moving (again, more than 10 minutes)with clients on this type of medication.
- People with migraines may react to even a light auric touch in a way that is ultra-sensitive. If your client complains, back off. (And if you have someone in your life, including yourself, who regularly gets migraines, I'd strongly recommend that you learn Janet Mentgen's amazing Healing Touch technique for re-moving the "pain spike." It really works.)

Of course, the techniques we use here to receive information from auras do not involve prolonged rearrangement of anyone's energy field. If that's your interest, study with a qualified teacher. I'd especially recommend Healing Touch, a multi-level training for moving the human energy field. Instruction includes Therapeutic Touch, Pain Drain, and other practical techniques. For information about classes near you, contact the Colorado Center for Healing Touch, Inc., 198 Union Blvd., Suite 204, Lakewood, CO 80228, 303-989-0581; E-mail address is www.ccheal@aol.com.

Aura Security Blanket

Plain good manners require that you close off someone else's aura after you've been poking it. They feel more secure—as if neatly tucked in under a security blanket. And the technique is so simple, you'll want to do it routinely whenever you've dipped your hand into someone else's aura.

1. Start with good manners. *Tell your client* what you're about to do before you do it, e.g., "I'm going to close off your aura now, since I've been touching it. This will take just a minute."
2. Stand in back of your client. *Grasp your client's shoulders*, one hand on either side of her neck.
3. Close your eyes. Breathe slowly and deeply. *Hold a Space* for your client. Feel how you're connected energetically.
4. *Set the intention for your energy to disconnect.* Feel the energy within your client shift, sealing itself back up like a self-motorized, zip-lock bag.
5. When you feel that your client is complete energetically, or after one full minute (whichever comes first) open your eyes. *Return to awareness of yourself as a skilled empath, an individual.* Inwardly affirm, "I have strong, clear personal boundaries."
6. *Let go* of your client's shoulders. Say something like, "All done."

Aura Security Blanket—Q&A

Q: WHAT HAPPENS IF YOU FORGET TO CLOSE UP AN AURA AFTER YOU WORK ON IT?

A: Both your subject and you will be left with a lingering feeling of incompleteness. You know how funny it feels if someone gives you half a massage or half a kiss. So take responsibility for giving proper closure to anyone whose aura you physically probe for more than a few seconds.

Plug in with Clairsentience

Of all the Energy Mitt techniques, this is my favorite discovery for connecting with someone or something empathically.

1. *Request permission* of your research subject.
   - For a human subject, ask in words, e.g., "May I connect to you with a special empathy technique? I'll hold my hand away from your body, in your energy field."
   - For an animal, ask in thoughts.
   - Living plants are such perpetual energy givers with people, you need not ask a thing. Still, it would be a courtesy to say or think, "I'm about to connect with you empathically. Thank you for letting me do this."
2. Take out and polish your Energy Mitts. Rest your Power Hand at your side. *Prepare to use only your Primary Sensor Hand.*
3. Approach your research subject. Do an *Aura Bounce* with your Primary Sensor Hand. Stop at the boundary you just felt. Now *move your hand inside* just a tad and leave it there. You're plugged in.

4. Mentally *ask any empathic question* that is ethical.* You will receive an answer. For example, ask how your research subject experiences emotions or mental activity or spiritual knowing.
5. When you are done, *remove your hand.* Share any information you feel would be appropriate. People usually love to hear about the special things you've noticed about them.
6. *Close off your subject's aura.* Thank your subject.
7. *Return to awareness of yourself as a skilled empath, an individual.* Inwardly affirm, "I have strong, clear personal boundaries."

Plug in with Clairsentience—Q&A

Q: WOW, HOW DID THAT WORK?

A: Being plugged in means that you are connected empathically and energetically, much like a lamp plugged into a wall socket.

Using your Primary Sensor Hand plugs you in with Clairsentience. Some empaths prefer plugging in with Clairvoyance, by looking in the direction of a person's aura. These are the two main ways to connect, even if other inner languages, like Gustatory Giftedness, speak to you more. Plugging in will make the empathic signal stronger, intensifying all your inner languages.

Q: WHAT IF YOU DON'T NOTICE ANYTHING IN PARTICULAR, EITHER BY LOOKING OR TOUCHING?

A: No problem—just keep yourself open to receiving information. A lamp doesn't automatically light up just because it has been plugged in. You must switch it on. As you'll discover, plugging in happens automatically with empathic techniques but usually you must do something extra to turn on specific information.

---

* What wouldn't be ethical? Don't pry into specific thoughts, attempting to read the person's mind. Thoughts are private, whereas thinking patterns are not. So it's okay to research, "How does he process emotions?" but not "What does he feel about me?"

And this information will come to you *empathically*, not as a slice of knowledge so much as a piece of your heart (or intellect or spirit or body). It is YOU learning about the part of yourself that is the other person.

Q. THE SKEPTIC IN ME HAS TO ASK, HOW CAN I KNOW FOR SURE THAT I'M REALLY PLUGGED IN?

A. Along with the skeptic grumbling inside you, every empath has a trusting voice. That part of you has the best answer to this question. All I can add is a reminder that once you set up the conditions for doing the technique, you're connected. You really can trust that.

If you dip your hand in water, it will get wet. You don't have to keep examining your hand to reassure yourself. "Ooh, is it really wet?"

Similarly, once you plug into a person's aura with your Primary Sensor Hand (or Clairvoyance or Clairaudience), it's done. You're plugged in. Knowledge can begin to flow.

What will happen if you make an extra effort to push away doubts about whether yes, indeed, you are really plugged in? You'll push yourself right out of the experience.

Q. STILL, HOW CAN I TURN UP THE VOLUME FOR THAT TRUSTING VOICE?

A. Put a *little* more attention on the beginning of the process, rather than the end. Rather than focusing in a critical way on whether you're getting good enough results once plugged in, take some extra time to prepare yourself. Use some of the methods you learned earlier: Do a few extra minutes of Vibe-Raising Breaths. When making your request to Get Big, take an extra minute to breathe in the presence of your inner teacher. Setting your intention, ask for something new or ask in a new way, inspiring your spirit.

We Fly in Spirit under grace. In the life of every empath, there come repeated realizations of this, at increasingly deep levels. Each deepening brings greater trust.

Q: BUT HOW DOES PLUGGING IN WORK?

A: Plugging in works like making a phone call on the level of Celestial Perception. To get a dial tone on the cosmic telephone, you Get Big and set an intention. The "number" you dial is a chakra. Techniques, like those in this chapter and the next are like dialing someone's phone number. Automatically the information will flow.

In this chapter, we've emphasized plugging in through clairsentience. However, as long as you connect consciously with another person's aura, it can be done through any of your in-built languages for Celestial Perception. I've emphasized clairsentience here because most of my students find it the easiest way. Techniques in our next chapter will give you a chance to explore even more outrageously.

*P*ersonal *N*otes

When I did the Aura Bounce and Aura Rub, here's where I'd rate my confidence on a scale from 1-10, with 10 being the top floor and 1 being the basement:

Note from Rose to newbies: If you're new to exploring auras, it's common to begin at around 3. Keep at it until you reach a 5 or higher. The techniques in this chapter, more than anything else in this book, are easier to do if you can have support from other people physically in the room with you, people who are at least a 7. I wish I could be in the room with you right now, so we could share the fun of doing these techniques. If you feel stuck, find someone—could be a friend or a local teacher of aura reading. Failing that, consider a one-hour session with me, over the phone or in person. For details, see my website, www.rose-rosetree.com.

My biggest Aha!s from doing Bouncy Affirmations:

One affirmation that makes my aura really big:

Amazing experiences when Plugging in with Clairsentience:

9. Travel Techniques

In preparation to travel bigger and deeper than ever before, let's summarize what has been covered so far. A natural empath, you've learned, routinely Flies in Spirit without effort, lifting burdens for others. Skilled travel starts by choosing to become conscious about your own consciousness. You've come to recognize your built-in specialties as an empath, such as Emotional Oneness and Intellectual Shape Shifting. And you have become receptive to receiving information about your travel through highly personal languages for Celestial Perception, such as Clairaudience, Gustatory Giftedness, and Clairsentience.

Techniques have empowered you to put self-knowledge and gifts into action. You've learned to turn empathy OFF by Coming Home several times throughout the day, which develops a natural self-awareness at many levels: emotional, physical, intellectual, and spiritual. Remember, all that's needed for this is a *simple* awareness—as effortless as tracking other things that people in our society observe constantly, like facial expression and designer labels.

Along the way you learned how to put on an Energy Shield. Then you activated your aura sensing abilities, beginning to plug in and question.

Altogether, you have turned over the pieces of the jigsaw puzzle. Now comes the fun of putting them together. It's spiritual self-awareness. And it's fun—more fun the better you get at it. Travel techniques, like this chapter's ways to Fly in Spirit, are designed to make you more adept at using your God-given gifts. These techniques are awareness accelerators, not necessarily for use on a daily basis. Rather, you can use them on special occasions when you are ready to blast forward. Afterwards, even without employing specific techniques, empathic travel will become more vivid in your everyday life.

Over time, you will discover a growing sense of oneness when you're with others, as if you're present together on the level of consciousness. When something happens to another person on that field of consciousness, you (as a skilled empath) can choose to say YES. Then (and only then), will you share in the experience full force—whether to be of service or for the deep learning that is your birthright.

The Heart Journey

The Heart Journey can take you deeper than ever before into the experience of otherness. The secret is to plug into your client's heart chakra, which is located in the center of the body, around the location of the physical heart. This chakra stores information about how a person gives and receives love, plus other higher emotions like compassion, nostalgia, and spiritual yearning. Problems can show up here (such as patterns of victimization and anger), but so do inspiring gifts of the soul.

1. *Find a willing subject.* Ideally this is a partner who would like to travel as well. Then you can take turns doing the technique. However, any consenting partner will do. We'll refer to that person as your client.
2. Sit or stand facing your client.
3. Establish a point of reference—yourself. Close your eyes and take seven Vibe-raising Breaths. *Do the technique for Coming Home.*

THE HEART JOURNEY

Fig. 6

4. *Get Big* by connecting with a source of spiritual inspiration.
5. *Set an intention*, such as: "I choose to learn what is going on with this person, emotionally, physically, and mentally." or "My purpose is to go outside my personal frame of reference and gain wisdom."
6. Form your Energy Mitts. Polish them. *Do the Aura Bounce in front of your client's heart chakra*, using only your Primary Sensor Hand. Soon as you reach an aura boundary, hold your hand still. (See figure 6.)
7. Now *move it forward one inch*, palm still facing your client, so that you are plugged in.
8. Close your eyes. *Allow yourself to travel inside your client's energy field.* Rather than focusing awareness to figure things out, let go and fly.
9. When you're ready to end the journey (anywhere from 30 seconds to 5 minutes), bring your hand back to your side. Plant your awareness firmly inside your own physical self with a few Grounding Breaths and *do the technique for Coming Home.* Open your eyes.
10. *Share what you noticed* with your client. Please don't worry about being precise. Just language it.
11. *Ask your client for feedback.* Enjoy it as an enrichment of your experience, rather than a test to see if you were "right." If you are taking turns with your client, repeat Steps #2-10, trading places.
12. *Return to awareness of yourself as a skilled empath, an individual.* Affirm, "I have strong, clear personal boundaries."

The Heart Journey—Q&A

Q: I FELT A LOT OF SADNESS. SHOULD I HAVE TOLD MY PARTNER, AND RISKED DEPRESSING HER EVEN MORE?

A: Sharing can actually uplift your partner. Haven't you noticed that when another person validates your pain, it can bring healing? Just give it a light touch. And, if you can, finish by describing something else you noticed. So many exquisite things about a person reveal themselves when you take The Heart Journey.

Q: WHAT DO YOU MEAN BY "GIVE IT A LIGHT TOUCH"?

A: Describe in terms of what *you* felt. You just did this when you said, "I felt a lot of sadness." That's far gentler than saying "Hey, you have a lot of sadness." Either way, your partner will get the point.

Q: MY PARTNER COULDN'T RELATE TO MY COMMENTS. DOES THAT MEAN I WAS WRONG?

A: People are like accordions. Our minds are collapsible. Depending on how we fold up within ourselves, different aspects of how we're doing will become either conscious or unconscious.

So what you experienced may well be true but hidden from your partner's conscious mind.

Q: WHAT IF EVERY TIME I TRY THIS TECHNIQUE, MY PARTNER SAYS I'M WRONG?

A: Pay attention to repeated feedback from partners. If it indicates that you keep traveling to sadness, anger, or other negative emotions, most likely you have some unfinished business. Usually you can take care of this on your own, once you give yourself the assignment of clearing it up. If not, reach out for professional help, whether from the counseling community or with an alternative health practitioner.

Q: I'M AMAZED AT THE DEPTH OF MY EXPERIENCE ON THE HEART JOURNEY. FOR YEARS I'VE BEEN DOING MEDITATION ON MY OWN, BUT IT WAS ALWAYS AN ABSTRACT FEELING. THIS EXPERIENCE WAS SO MUCH MORE COLORFUL. HAS ALL MY MEDITATION HAS BEEN A WASTE OF TIME?

A: Meditation is the best investment of time you can make in your spiritual life. The same goes for contemplation and prayer. All of them expand your awareness; simultaneously they reduce the effects of stress and aging on your physical body. Another plus is how they can set the stage for higher states of consciousness.

Q: WHAT EXACTLY ARE HIGHER STATES OF CONSCIOUSNESS?

A: Higher states of consciousness change your relationship to God. Mind-body-spirit make the journey together—none of these states is merely a notion. So a mere idea or a mood about closeness to God won't get you to a state of consciousness where you can *live* that closeness.

Regular spiritual exercise can get you there, though. While you're doing your technique of contemplation or prayer, mind-body-spirit are purified. Results are cumulative, over the years.

Here is an overview of the stages in developing higher states of consciousness:

□ Everyday human consciousness is the most common state on the planet. Here you identify with your experience at the level of environment, body, mind, intellect, or emotions—one, then another, then another.

□ Consciousness of consciousness is the next step. Intellectually you understand what consciousness is. At will, you pay attention to your own awareness—take one step back and witness it.

□ Or you can take one giant step forward, through a spiritual exercise or as a gift of grace. Awareness of the Self means that you experience yourself as being a spiritual presence. It seems different from your usual form of human presence... whether lighter, more pulsating, tinier, vaster than usual....language may vary but what stays constant is the deep joy you feel after making contact with the Self. With repeated experience—and, of course, techniques come in handy to make this kind of experience repeat more often—you can travel at will to this level of who you are.

□ Celestial Perception comes next. Somehow you have earned access to the realm of auras and angels, permission to learn deep human secrets. Gerard Manley Hopkins is one poet who specialized in languaging what it is to have Celestial Perception. In "The Windhover," a masterpiece of Synesthesia that Hopkins, himself, considered his finest poem, there's a reference to "the dearest freshness deep down things." Celestial Perception is that singing joy. It isn't God-talk or wishing, rather it's an experience that comes and goes. I developed the techniques in *Aura Reading Through ALL Your Senses* to help people who are ready to open up this level of consciousness. Techniques in this book, by contrast, are especially for empaths.

▫ All-time Inner Silence is a state of ENLIGHTENMENT. Whenever you ask within who you are, even if you're standing in the midst of a three ring circus, the answer is Silence. Physiologically, your mind-body-spirit system has the habit of functioning with a minimum of internal stress. From this point on, your life belongs entirely to God. As discussed previously, your consciousness may tend to glorify others or to unify with them. In either case, you can give service that is supremely helpful, balanced—and so effortless, it's funny.

Q: I AGREE THAT MEDITATION HAS GIVEN ME A BASIS FOR DOING THE HEART JOURNEY, BUT YOUR TECHNIQUE GAVE ME SUCH A DIFFERENT KIND OF EXPERIENCE. WOULD YOU COMMENT ON THIS EXTRA DIMENSION?

A: Empathy techniques are, to put it mildly, a supplement to meditation practice. You see, there are millions of empaths like you with huge consciousness who hardly know what they've got. Some of you have been doing meditation techniques for years, waiting for some cosmic declaration of "enlightenment" before you purposely *move* your consciousness. Other empaths haven't done spiritual exercises but, but by virtue of living fully at a time of rapid spiritual evolution, their third eyes have come along for the ride. By the time they become interested in exploring consciousness, they find themselves right on God's doorstep.

Either way, you fortunate empaths are ready for travel techniques. Depending on your soul's deep choice, you'll move to experience that glorifies or unifies. It's not enough, you see, to realize yourself as a huge, abstract field that throbs with energy. Wonderful though that is, your life will improve enormously when you awaken perception at the celestial level.

Contrary to the prevailing wisdom today, celestial life isn't just for dead people and spirit guides. Nor has someone like you fathomed that hidden level of life by virtue of decorating your home with angel pictures. Why settle for gossip, however lofty the conversation? And why settle for a mundane perception of life when hidden deep within everyday reality is this celestial level? To get there consciously, stretch all your empathic gifts, speak all your inner languages... like Clairaudience, which is particularly helpful for the next technique.

Deep Listening

This technique is *not* for those who believe children (or anyone else) should be seen and not heard. Instead, this technique helps you to connect by hearing at the celestial level. Once you plug in this way, whether you're strongly Clairaudient or not, the empathic gifts that are strongest for you will move your consciousness into another person's way of being.

1. *Find a client.* Ideally, your client will be a fellow explorer who would like to travel as well. Then you can take turns at Deep Listening. However, any consenting partner will do. Explain that after you take a minute of silence, you will need him to extend one arm so that you can listen to the palm of his hand. Explain that you will not otherwise touch him or converse until you have finished listening. In this position, your client will need to wait patiently until you are done. Afterwards, he'll be rewarded by receiving a brief empathic reading.
2. Sit or stand to face your client.
3. Remember who you are. Do the technique for *Coming Home*.

DEEP LISTENING

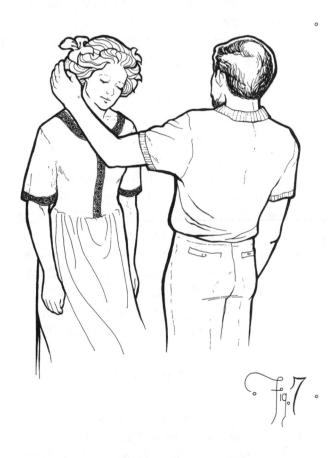

Fig. 7.

4. *Expand your awareness:* close your eyes and take seven Vibe-raising Breaths.
5. *Get Big* by connecting with a source of spiritual inspiration.
6. *Set an intention*: "I choose to experience what it is like to be this person. My purpose is to gain wisdom."
7. Ask your client to extend his arm. *Position yourself to listen.* Then close your eyes and allow yourself to travel into your client's subtle bodies. (See figure 8.)
8. *Pay attention* to your experiences. They're all meaningful in the context of learning about your partner.
9. When you're ready, *mentally ask questions* like "How does this person experience feelings?" and "What is it like to live in this person's body?"
10. Again, pay attention to your experience. *Answers will come* in terms of your strongest languages.
11. When you feel you have learned all that you are going to learn this time, *separate* from your client, including physically moving your ear away from his hand. Time for *Coming Home*: Bring attention back to your own body and feelings.
12. *Open your eyes.* Thank your client. Describe what you noticed.
13. *Ask for feedback* from your client, if desired. And if you are taking turns as partners, repeat Steps #2-13, trading places.
14. *Return to an awareness of yourself as a skilled empath, an individual.* Affirm, "I have strong, clear personal boundaries."

Deep Listening—Q&A

Q. Does it matter which ear you use for listening?

A. Many of us do have a preference. When you have an important conversation on the telephone, which ear do you use? That's the one for Deep Listening.

Q: WHEN I CONNECTED, I HEARD A BABY CRYING. SHOULD I TELL MY PARTNER WHAT THAT MEANT TO ME? OR IS IT BETTER JUST TO SAY WHAT I HEARD?

A: When you're new to sharing your comments with a partner, you might prefer to offer the raw material, e.g., "I heard a baby crying. Does this mean anything to you?" As you grow more comfortable with Flying in Spirit and languaging your experience, you'll find an interpretation that feels right intuitively. There's no problem with offering this so long as you phrase it with humility.

Q: WHAT DO YOU MEAN BY "PHRASE IT WITH HUMILITY"?

A: Suppose that, when you heard the sound of the crying baby, the underlying feeling reminded you of your frustration as a new mother. You might say, "I experienced frustration, like when I was a new mother and I didn't know how to cope. Does this have anything to do with your feelings right now?"

Q: AS OPPOSED TO SAYING WHAT?

A: "You have an Inner Child who is crying his heart out. You should heal your Inner Child."

Q: IS EMPATHY ABOUT GIVING PEOPLE ADVICE LIKE THAT?

A: No! To consciously help someone by means of your empathy, 98 percent of the help comes through your depth of Holding a Space. As appropriate, you can supply an extra two percent in the form of words. Words coming from empathy will not be coercive, judgmental, or deterministic—i.e., "You should." "You're bad." "You are supposed to."

Q: I FEEL REALLY TERRIBLE NOW. GUESS I CHOSE THE WRONG PERSON TO TRY THIS TECHNIQUE WITH. HOW COULD I HAVE KNOWN IN ADVANCE?

A: There is a certain art to choosing a partner for empathy techniques. Pay as much attention as you would before crossing a street. Rather than blindly rushing in, take a minute to ask inside, "Is it wise for me to join empathically with this person?"

Intuitively, we always know the truth about partnering choices. Carl Rogers, the great psychologist, found that people who meet with a new therapist can tell within minutes whether or not that particular therapist will be able to help them. When people disregard their inner turnoff, they can spend years in therapy with very limited success.

Q: THEN WHAT DO YOU TELL A PERSON WHO TURNS YOU OFF, "NO WAY"?

A: Bring back your best manners from high school dances. When an unwanted partner asks you to dance, you don't have to sock him in the jaw. Just say, "Not now, thanks."

Q: WHAT IF YOU FORGET TO ASK FOR GUIDANCE BEFORE YOU FLY?

A: Finish up the technique and don't worry. If you team up with someone you don't especially enjoy, what's the worst that can happen?

At a dance, what you stand to gain or lose is fun, so an undesirable partner may steal a few minutes of fun. But with Listening Deep, your goal is wisdom. No matter how dismal your companion, after you've finished (and affirmed your strong, clear personal boundaries), all that will remain is wisdom. On to the next person or the next technique....

I Want to Hold Your Hand

At last, we come to the technique pictured on the cover of this book. It shows one way that an empath plugs in to facilitate travel. She starts in handshake position. After Getting Big and Setting an Intention, she can effortlessly plunge into any consenting person's energy field.

On the cover, the empath's travel in spirit is pictured symbolically. You can see one of her subtle bodies moving downward into the body/energy field of her partner. For the cover photo, the empath is shown moving through his crown chakra, into his body. And you can see her growing delight as she comes closer to merging with his consciousness. Actually, the travel could come from any angle; it's easier to *do it* than to find a visual way to symbolize it in a picture.

The bottom line: Don't expect an out-of-body experience when you do this technique, but do expect a mind-boggling experience of Physical Oneness. Ever wonder how it feels to be in a body other than your own? Here's your chance to find out. I named this technique in honor of a song by the Beatles. Ideally, you'll do it with a partner who would like to travel as well. Together, read the complete instructions. Refer to them as you go through the steps one by one.

1. *Stand facing your client* as though both of you were preparing to shake hands (which you are, in a way).
2. Remember who you are, using the technique for *Coming Home.*
3. *Expand your awareness.* Close your eyes and take seven Vibe-raising Breaths.
4. *Get Big* by connecting with a source of spiritual inspiration.
5. *Set an intention,* such as "I ask to experience how it feels to be in my partner's body. The purpose of this empathy experience is to develop physical forms of empathy."
6. *Start to shake hands* with your partner but don't pump. Once you have grasped each other's right hand, hold still. Close your eyes and stand in that position.
7. *Allow yourself to be in your partner's space.* Gently pay attention to whatever comes to you now, through imagination and Synesthesia, in any of your intuitive languages. But don't talk. Remain in the silence.
8. After you've had your fill, *disengage your hand.*
9. *Give thanks* inwardly to whomever you connected with in Step #4.
10. Bring yourself back to outer reality. Take several Grounding Breaths. Feel self-awareness fill up your physical body. Do the technique for *Coming Home.*
11. When you're ready, *open your eyes.*
12. Tell your client what you noticed. *Language it.*
13. *Share feedback.*

14. *Return to an awareness of yourself as a skilled empath, an individual..* Affirm, "I have strong, clear personal boundaries."

I Want to Hold Your Hand—Q&A

Q: HEY, THAT'S AS CLOSE AS I'VE EVER COME TO MY CHILDHOOD DREAM OF BEING AN ASTRONAUT. HOW DID I DO THAT?

A: Thank your empathic gift for Physical Oneness. Your light body just merged with that of your partner. Because you stayed conscious, you could enjoy the otherness of this experience.

Q: I FELT SCARED AND WANTED TO COME BACK TO MY BODY RIGHT AWAY. SO I DROPPED MY PARTNER'S HAND AND OPENED MY EYES. NOW I FEEL ANXIOUS. WHAT DID I DO WRONG?

A: You always have the right to come out of an empathic experience. But it's important to come out properly. Otherwise you could feel rough for a while. I'll talk you through a better re-entry:

Okay, close your eyes. Choose inwardly to bring full awareness back inside your body. Feel your body fill up with pure YOU-ness. Take a moment to give thanks inwardly for what you experienced with the technique. (Sure, you received more than you bargained for, but that's no reason *not* to give thanks.)

Now take 11 Grounding Breaths. Open your eyes, taking plenty of time. Say out loud, "I choose to psychically disconnect from my partner. I have strong, clear personal boundaries."

Q: UNLIKE HER, I DIDN'T GET MORE THAN I BOTHERED FOR. I GOT A BIG FAT NOTHING. WITHOUT BEING RUDE, ARE YOU AND THE OTHER PEOPLE HERE KIDDING? THIS ISN'T A TECHNIQUE FOR TRAVEL.

A: What did happen? Did you ask to be in your partner's space?

Q: WHEN I ASKED, I'M TELLING YOU I GOT A BIG FAT NOTHING. I FELT REALLY STUPID, PRETENDING TO BE GOING ANYWHERE. THE ONLY THING I NOTICED WAS THAT, FOR A MINUTE,

I FELT HEAVY AND KIND OF CONSTIPATED AND DIFFERENT FROM NORMAL, WHICH MADE ME EXTREMELY UNCOMFORTABLE. THAT'S NOT THE GLORIOUS KIND OF THING YOU CALL OTHER-NESS, WAS IT? YUCK.

A: You've raised an important point. Otherness doesn't necessarily make you feel glorious, not unless you're swapping bodies with someone who feels like a king or queen. Other people's strengths and problems are not necessarily the same as yours. Still, it's magnificent that you can experience them at will, even if that means "heavy and constipated." Eventually you'll enjoy how the otherness of another person's experience can be totally different from your expectations.What an adventure!

Q: LIKE HER, I COULD TELL YOU 100 THINGS THAT DIDN'T HAPPEN FOR EVERY ONE THAT DID. HOW CAN WE CULL THE WHEAT FROM THE CHAFF WHEN WE DO YOUR TECHNIQUES?

A: Aha! Language comes to the rescue again. When describing your experience, talk *only* about what happened right. Ignore the rest. Think of what happens when a baby learns to walk. Parents coo over the time the kid lands upright, not the hundred times he falls. That's smart. If all his parents did was criticize, it could take little Jimmy 10 years to start walking.

Reinforce your empathy as if you were being your own good parent. Don't make a big deal about anything but your deeper glimpses of empathy. Gradually they'll happen more often and become increasingly vivid.

Q: TALK ABOUT EXPERIENCES THAT ARE KIND OF EMBARRASSING, I'M A WOMAN, RIGHT, AND I DID THE EMPATHY TECHNIQUE WITH A MAN. I ABSOLUTELY LOVED BEING IN A MALE BODY. BUT NOW I'M STARTING TO WORRY. COULD IT MEAN THAT I'M GAY?

A: Don't worry. Physical Oneness won't change your sexual orientation, whatever it is. Meanwhile, isn't it interesting how men and women have such different ways of being in their bodies? Vive la difference! Techniques in the next chapter will help you to explore it more fully.

*P*ersonal *N*otes

Was The Heart Journey amazing or what? Highlights so far:

Deep Listening experiences the first time I did the technique:

Aha!s and experiences when I did more Deep Listening:

Who was my first client for I Want to Hold Your Hand? Highlights?

What was it like for me the first time doing I Want to Hold Your Hand with a person of the opposite sex?

Which gifts and languages for empathy are my favorites these days? Examples of personal experience with them:

10. And There's More

Here's a chapter to empower you even more as an empath. We'll start with a mind-boggling technique, go on to a spiritual exercise that expands you even bigger, and conclude with something very practical. All the while you'll be refining your skill with language, too. Empowered, you'll Fly in Spirit with increasing clarity.

Taste Someone Else's Reality

Admittedly this next technique for Physical Oneness requires that you take a leap of faith. Imagine, you're about to taste another person's reality in a very personal, physical way.

Does your partner trust life on earth? Strangers? Friends?

Psychologist Erik Erikson has discovered that, in the first year of life, every human being goes through a major life lesson involving Trust versus Mistrust.* Consequences can last for a lifetime; they show in the root chakra. Primal trust also involves what Caroline Myss, in *Anatomy of the Spirit*,

---

* Erik Erikson, *Childhood and Society*, (New York: W.W. Norton, 1963), pp. 247-251.

calls "the tribe"—people in society whom you unconsciously consider to be your extended family.*

What Myss and Erikson haven't explored, to my knowledge, is how each of us carries our experience of being physical, and belonging to our tribe, in terms of the usual taste in our mouth. "Usual" means at least half an hour after eating or drinking.

For instance, notice the taste in *your* mouth right now? Question what it shows about your trust of reality and your tribe.

Like that taste in your mouth, you've held your own view of being physical for a long time. Though it feels like second nature, your familiar taste will shift to reveal your partner's experience. Here goes another fascinating exploration of otherness!

1. *Find a client.* Either plan to take turns or find a client willing to receive your empathic reading.
2. You may sit or stand. *Position your client to stand with her back to you.* Both of you, take a vacation from talking until Step #9.
3. Honor who you are with the technique for *Coming Home.*
4. *Expand your awareness.* Close your eyes and take seven Vibe-raising Breaths.
5. *Get Big* by connecting with a source of spiritual inspiration.
6. *Set a very specific intention:* "I choose to connect with the way this person experiences physical reality and belonging in society. I choose to experience this in terms of the taste in my mouth. The purpose of this empathy experience is to gain wisdom."
7. *Plug into your client's aura through vision*: Aim your eyes at the base of your client's spine. This corresponds to the root chakra of the aura, the part about Trust versus Mistrust of physical reality and belonging. Although you may be used to exploring the base of the

---

* Trust problems show in root chakra damage. Like other difficulties that show up in the aura, this can be healed through appropriate use of alternative medicine. Caroline Myss' *Anatomy of the Spirit* (New York: Harmony Books, 1996) is full of healing stories.

spine from the front, the chakra energy radiates at the back as well. Be confident that, simply by looking, you have plugged in, regardless of whether you're convinced that you have seen anything clairvoyantly. (If you strongly prefer plugging in by touch to seeing, feel free to do that instead. Do the Aura Bounce and the plug in.)

8. *Travel:* Close your eyes. Take a few Vibe-raising Breaths. Notice the taste in your mouth. Know that this is your partner's taste, and that it has meaning.

9. Open your eyes, looking again at your client's root chakra. Ask your client to listen without making comments while you *describe what you experienced.* Language your experience of the taste and what it means to you as a way to hold reality.

10. Close your eyes again. Give thanks inwardly to whomever you connected with in Step #5. *Do the technique for Coming Home.*

11. Bring yourself back to outer reality. Take 11 Grounding Breaths. Feel the inner part of you fill up your physical body. Now your body contains only your energy. When you're ready, *open your eyes.*

12. Turn to face your client. *Receive your client's feedback on what you described.*

13. *Return to awareness of yourself as a skilled empath, an individual*, mouth taste and all. Affirm, "I have strong, clear personal boundaries."

Taste Someone Else's Reality—Q&A

Q: Here I had this completely different taste in my mouth. I interpreted this to mean that my partner doesn't entirely trust physical life. It was amazing. What did I do to deserve this kind of knowledge?

A: The obvious answer is that you dared to do the technique. Looking deeper, you deserve the knowledge because as an empath you've been doing spiritual service all your life—even if you weren't conscious of it.

Now that you're becoming aware, you'll attract chances to learn at a faster rate. Every new bit of learning expands your consciousness and, consequently, your skill for doing service the next time.

Q. HOW DO YOU INTERPRET A TASTE, ANYWAY?

A. Sometimes an interpretation will come so easily, you can't miss it. A fresh taste will remind you of joy at being alive while a stale taste will make you feel bored and boring. If the meaning of a taste doesn't come easily, use the technique for Questioning later in this chapter.

Q: WHAT IF YOU DO THIS TASTING TECHNIQUE ON SOMEBODY REALLY MESSED UP? COULDN'T AN UNPLEASANT TASTE STAY IN YOUR MOUTH FOR A LONG TIME AFTERWARD?

A: Yes, which is why you need to use common sense when choosing your partner. This goes for any empathic technique. If you get majorly messed-up vibes from a person, avoid joining with him.

Q: WHAT IF YOU HAVE TO DEAL WITH HIM ANYWAY, LIKE HE'S YOUR BOSS?

A: Deal with him on the level of objective, everyday reality. Open up your empathic boundaries only with people who interest you, or who can downright inspire you.

Darshan

So long as you're going to be a conscious empath, why not use it to bask in the light of the glowiest people you can find?—the best, the brightest, the holiest. With Spiritual Oneness, anyone's way of holding reality can become an open book to your unfolding perception. You won't *own* the other person's experience, which is as it should be. Considering how hard each of us must work to develop our consciousness, would it be fair if you could peek into someone else's spiritual life and instantly trade up? However—and it's a glorious however—you definitely can visit another person's spiritual space whenever you like.

Sanskrit has the perfect language for this. DARSHAN (pronounced DAHR-shahn) means the glow one feels in the presence of a saint. India is famous for its multitudes of saints, sometimes set off from the crowd by their monkish robes. But no country has a monopoly on people with glorious auras.

Empaths discover that costume is ludicrously irrelevant. You'll find high consciousness walking around in pricey business suits or wearing a cheap uniform at your supermarket's checkout counter or in the guise of a harried librarian at your nearest under-budgeted public library. New mothers often have a temporary dispensation of huge spiritual glow, so don't let their rumpled wardrobes and exhausted faces fool you. Saints of every description make excellent darshan material.

To some, darshan means physically sharing a space with someone whose vibes you would like to have rub off on you. In India, people travel for days to sit at the feet of a saint. In America, one of our greatest contributions to spiritual life is our entertainment industry, because most of our "stars" really do shine, having unusually bright or transformative auras. Instead of spiritual pilgrimage India-style, we Americans spend hours daily, in the comfort of our homes, worshipping at the altar of television. And to some degree, it works. Regardless of what a show's about, our spirits get a lift when stars do their exquisite auric modeling.

Stars also provide gossip material, of course. Wherever people seek inspiration, it's human to notice the outward things: how the saint or celebrity looks; the layers of dress and mannerisms; the outer likes and dislikes. Yet the part that truly brings joy is darshan.

Spiritual wisdom shows all over a person's aura and is especially concentrated at the third eye. As an empath, you can easily plug in to this sacredness. And then the best darshan the world has to offer can come as close to you as a kiss. So pucker up:

1. *Find a subject* to join with by means of Spiritual Oneness. This can be a co-explorer of empathy, like a buddy who is going through this book with you. But it can also be anyone who happens to be in the

room with you.

- □ You need not be concerned with consent for this particular exercise.
- □ Houses of worship are excellent places to try this technique, partly because ordained clergy (of any religion) often carry a special grace while they give a service.
- □ Also, your subject for this technique will be easier to read if she isn't moving a lot, and people in houses of worship keep relatively still.
- □ Wherever you do this technique, you'll want the person you're studying to be positioned at an angle from the front where the forehead shows clearly.

2. *Prepare your perspective.* Do the technique for Coming Home.
3. *Expand your awareness.* Close your eyes and take seven Vibe-raising Breaths.
4. *Get Big* by connecting with a source of spiritual inspiration.
5. *Set a specific intention:* "My purpose is to experience God as known by this person."
6. Choose either Clairvoyance or Clairsentience to plug into your subject's third eye. (Remember, that's the part of the forehead between and above the physical eyes.)
   - □ For Clairvoyance, open your eyes. Aim them at your partner's third eye. Gaze in an easy, unfocused manner. As usual, don't try to see. Just be.
   - □ For Clairsentience, form your Energy Mitts. Polish them. Hold up your Primary Sensor Hand. Bounce against your partner's aura. Move your hand inward slightly, about an inch. As usual, know you're plugged in. Allow information flow to you. With Clairsentience, you may prefer to close your eyes. With Clairvoyance, leave them open.
7. Take a few Vibe-raising Breaths. *Hold a Space with your subject's spirituality.* Accept the experiences that come to you.
8. If you like, *ask questions* inwardly while you are empathically

joined. As usual, right after you ask each question, let go and pay attention to Vibe-raising Breaths. Your answer will come without effort.

9. *Decide when to separate.* Bring your attention back to your own body and mind. Close your eyes. Thank whomever you connected with in Step #4. Do the technique for Coming Home.

10. *Open your eyes.* Language what you noticed. With a partner, talk directly. Otherwise, keep your observations to yourself or write them down, if practical. Thank your subject, verbally or silently.

11. *Ask for feedback*, if appropriate. When you are taking turns with a partner, repeat Steps #2-11, trading places.

12. *Return to awareness of yourself as a skilled empath, an individual.* Affirm, "I have strong, clear personal boundaries."

Darshan—Q&A

Q: How important is accuracy in doing this technique? I had an amazing experience, but I don't know if it was more about me or my rabbi, the person I joined with.

A: Isn't it enough to expand spiritually? We're used to our limits of consciousness. This technique enables you to expand beyond your limits, as far as your spirit will take you.

Q: If three different people all focused at the same time on my rabbi (who is extraordinary), would they all have the same experience?

A: Probably not. One of the signs of a great spiritual teacher is the ability to send a meaningful message to every person in the group, regardless of level of consciousness, uplifting each person.

Q: What's a level of consciousness?

A: Level of consciousness means degree of spiritual awakening. It's like those Russian dolls that come hidden within each other. You've seen them.

The big doll, made of wood, shows a smiling woman. Unlike a real-life woman, however, she unscrews at the neck. After you remove her head and body, you'll find a smaller but otherwise identical version of that same doll. You can twist her head off, too, and proceed in like manner to find smaller and smaller dolls until you arrive at the tiny little Russian woman deep inside.

What profound spiritual symbolism! That big, clunky doll corresponds to human perception at the outermost level life—ordinary reality. Going within, we find hidden levels that are progressively more intelligent, aware, and joyful. Finally, at the level of the innermost doll, comes awareness of celestial life, complete with clear perception of God and angels.

Q. So what does this have to do with my rabbi's ability to uplift everyone in the congregation?

A. Picture the worship service with people who look like those nesting dolls. Those with surface-level consciousness look like the big dolls. Others may look like the next size smaller dolls, and so forth. And there you are, with tiny doll consciousness. The rabbi's darshan can speak to you, along with every other size doll in the room.

Invariably, no matter what size of doll you're living at any given time, you experience everything from your level of consciousness. Also true: consciousness evolves over your lifetime, gradually shifting into progressively more celestial experience. The beauty of religious ceremonies and hymns is that they can shift along with you. For instance, think of Passover songs or Christmas carols. Each year those sacred melodies bring fresh tears to your eyes because you're listening with higher consciousness.

The Darshan technique enables you to sample the beauty of every religion... and every doll size. This doesn't break the spiritual law about experiencing life at our level of consciousness, just bends the law a bit.

Q: For as long as I can remember, I've seen colors around people. Sometimes these auras look plastic, which to me has always meant that people are phony or unevolved. Should I make use of this to screen out whom I'm going to choose for the Darshan technique?

A: Each of us knows which people attract us spiritually, and it's smart to choose them for doing the Darshan technique. Definitely avoid merging with anyone whom you dislike. Especially steer clear of anyone who seems disturbed or downright evil.

All this notwithstanding, the Darshan technique has a special benefit for you, considering your habit of judging people as phony.

Q: WHAT DO YOU MEAN? AURAS ARE MY SPIRITUAL PERCEPTION, AND IF THEY'RE TELLING ME PLASTIC, THAT MEANS PLASTIC.

A: It's wonderful that your perception of auras has been a lifelong gift and that it's so vivid. Still it could be time to reconsider some of your earlier interpretations. Because we evolve spiritually over the years, sometimes we can outgrow habits of judging—why not choose, instead, to practice discernment?

The quality you call "plastic" is a result of your wonderful ability to discriminate different textures of auras. Instead of standing outside or putting down, jump in deeper. What is it like to Join in Spirit with these differently-textured auras?

You may find that some relatively unglowey auras belong to people who carry fear of their own spirituality. (In general, the larger the cross a man wears, the smaller his third eye and the greater his fear.) Fundamentalists (in any religion) may equate any changed perception with craziness or "the Devil." Other relatively static auras show resentment due to disappointment from religious authorities in the past. Merging temporarily with people through the Darshan technique will teach you compassion, rather than superiority. It's a much more interesting lesson.

Q: THIS DARSHAN TECHNIQUE BLEW ME AWAY. HOW DID YOU DEVELOP IT?

A: By degrees—Spiritual Oneness has been a long-time gift but, as you know, having gifts don't necessarily mean that you use them with skill. Originally I stumbled onto Spiritual Oneness in a way that couldn't have been more clueless. Here's the story.

Until 1971, I lived exclusively on the East Coast. Never had I traveled farther west than Illinois. Then a business trip took me to California, including a five-hour stopover at the San Francisco airport. While I waited in the lobby, anyone who happened to see me probably figured I was on drugs, since I was staring at strangers with such extreme rapture—falling in love because the people at this airport had "the biggest foreheads I'd ever seen."

That's right: These Californians had gigantic "foreheads." So open, so free, it was as though these people came from a different planet. I was thrilled to the core.

Actually I was seeing auras without realizing it. Like most people, I believed in a myth about auras that included the notion that auras must be perceived as colors around people's bodies. Frankly, I expected auras to look like the neon lights around a cheap motel—you know, the kind that blink off and on, "Vacancy! Vacancy!" (For more information about this silly myth, in its various parts, see my book *Aura Reading Through ALL Your Senses*.)

It took many years before I began to appreciate that what had fascinated me so about my first sighting of a large group of Californians was their wide-open third eyes, not their physical foreheads. It took many more years to move to progressively deeper empathic perception, helped by the techniques in this book.

Along the way it was a major breakthrough to understand that empaths can connect with anyone, directly at the level of auras. Third eyes can be the most fun of all to explore. The Darshan technique is one of my very favorites.

All the techniques you've used from this chapter will expand your knowledge until you can travel at will without using formal techniques. Nevertheless, techniques remain a delightful playground for all empaths, no matter how sophisticated. And language continues to be a requirement for any skilled empath.

Your Inner Dictionary

Languaging your experience *is* getting easier by now, right? Not that the words are necessarily perfect nor your descriptions complete—because there's always going to be a tantalizing gap between the rich experience of otherness and that relatively meager part of it you can record verbally (and, thus, take home afterward). As you've discovered by now, every technique to Fly in Spirit gives you the opportunity to question, to go deeper into your experience and find language. This process strengthens a form of coordination between your spiritual self and your everyday personality. Words become the ultimate souvenir.

To language your experience so far, you've developed the habit of probing—even pushing yourself—to find words. Now you're ready to make use of a simple technique that will help you to systematically find even more depth of language (and with it, depth of conscious experience).

Each of us, I believe, is writing a book of life. In a way it's the ultimate scripture. Unlike The Bible of your religion, universal and read by millions, you are writing a personal story—breath by breath and day by day. And since you happen to be writing your life *as an empath*, your INNER DICTIONARY is the one-of-a-kind reference book about your scripture.

Linguistic experts will tell you that standard reference books for language are an illusion. Sure, a group of scholars can spend $5 million to update the *Oxford English Dictionary*. Yet nobody actually talks like that. A printed dictionary is a compromise for the sake of convenience, a social agreement that decrees words shall carry specific universal meanings. In reality, even on the simplest level of conversation you can imagine, different people use different words to mean different things.

When it comes to the deep levels of your travel as an empath, with your very individual gifts and your built-in spiritual languages for expression, how much more complicated language becomes. Newcomers to my classes used to frustrate me (and themselves) by expecting that I would simply "give them the dictionary" about celestial perception. Gradually, I started helping each person to develop a personal Inner Dictionary.

Don't let the prospect intimidate you. It's easy. You start with a notebook. Draw a line down the middle of each page to form two columns. Head the first column, PERCEPTIONS. Head the second column, INTERPRETATIONS.

Now that you're becoming more skilled as an empath, you can start to record language from your travels in this special journal. After each technique, write your words in the first column. Later, when you have a quiet moment, use the following version of the Questioning technique to write interpretations for each item into the second column. Here's a step-by-step description of the process.

Questioning, in Depth and Detail

1. *Prepare* a list of questions for your session of dictionary writing: items you have written in the Perceptions column of your Inner Dictionary. Also prepare a quiet space where you won't be interrupted. Include some recording equipment, either a tape recorder or some scrap paper and a pen. In addition you'll need a notebook or computer to compile your various sessions of research for your Inner Dictionary.
2. Close your eyes and *take a few Vibe-raising Breaths*. This will prepare your body-mind-spirit to settle down for the deepest possible experience.
3. *Set an intention* and Get Big in preparation to add to your Inner Dictionary.
4. Choose one item to research, e.g., When doing a previous technique, you saw an image of umbrellas unfolding. *Question one item at a time.* e.g., "What do *umbrellas* mean?"
5. Immediately let go. *Take a few Vibe-raising Breaths.*
6. Whatever pops into your head, *record it* immediately. Open your

eyes just enough to accomplish this. Close your eyes again as soon as you can, to remain in an inward state.

7. *Repeat Steps 4-6* until you come to the end of your list of questions, or you feel tired, whichever comes first.
8. *Give thanks* for your session of Questioning.
9. *Ground yourself* with some Grounding Breaths.
10. Open your eyes. Review and evaluate what you have recorded. Transfer these notes to your official Inner Dictionary on computer or in a notebook.

Questioning, in Depth and Detail—Q&A

Q: What if the first thing that pops into my head is how stupid I feel doing this?

A: Keep going. What's the second thing? Write it down. Don't slow yourself down by debating your doubts. Questioning is like learning to ride a bicycle. Although you'll find bumps along the way, the thrill of the ride is to keep going and feel the flow. A new cyclist wastes a lot of motion at first, but with practice that stops—and not by criticizing the awkward moves but by disregarding them. Use your courage to keep going until the process becomes easy.

Q: Rose, do you mean to tell me that every time you take an empathic journey you still stop to write all this stuff down in a notebook?

A: Of course not. After a year of doing this technique, you'll find the process of dictionary-making becomes second nature. By then you'll have accumulated a basic vocabulary of your empathic language.

Q: Will my dictionary ever be finished?

Maybe not, but you'll become fluent at understanding most of the subtle sense language that comes to you. As for new words, you'll become

Page from Rose's Inner Dictionary

The purpose of writing an Inner Dictionary is to keep track of personal language for empathic experience. This sample reconstructs my process of reading celebrities for one of my media interviews.

PERCEPTION	INTERPRETATION
Face seems to peel off in a layer at the top of her photograph, as though she is purposely leaving out a lot of who she is.	Here is someone who knows how to project thought forms—give a desired impression that may bear little relation to who she really is inside. This woman would be good at TV, probably a TV broadcaster[turns out, she was]; she comes across as cute and perky. But she's carrying uncommon seriousness underneath. Wish she'd trust people enough to let more of it show. Bet she'd be even more powerful that way.
Akasha—space energy—is in this man's third chakra. Wow! Rare to see that much in someone who isn't an astronaut. And it isn't everywhere in his aura the way it would be for an astronaut, just in his third chakra plus some in his crown chakra and above.	Incredible, huge intellect that contains the deepest spiritual energy. I love the way he can use it to balance all that comes before him. And not like a judge, even a great one. It's bigger. He's an old soul with tremendous wisdom and compassion. What a huge energy presence, too, with no need to dominate others. He's here making himself available as a resource.

confident when questioning about additions to your dictionary. The opposite page shows a sample from my own Inner Dictionary .

Q. How do you come up with a good question in the first place?

A. You're right to be concerned about getting the question right. Questions reveal your underlying assumptions about power, reality, spirituality. And some assumptions won't produce good answers. Let's say you're connecting empathically with a woman I read for one newspaper and you discovered that her face seemed to be covered with some unusual layers. Of course you'd want to question, further. Here are some examples of questions *not* to ask, and why.

- "Does that make her evil?" Questions involving judgment only bring up more judgments, not more truth. Ask questions that can help you gain wisdom rather than opinions.

- "Will she get married soon"? Don't try to mix psychic reading and empathy. If your goal is to do a psychic reading, use techniques expressly for that.

- "When did she get these layers? Where was she and what happened?" Questions like these, again, suggest the intent to do a psychic reading—this time of a very literal kind. Detective work about specifics is not the purpose of Flying in Spirit. Better to ask what the layers mean now, because that relates to being of service and gaining wisdom. (Psychic Knowing may pop up, unasked, when you question, but then it will be related to helpful information. Otherwise, don't bother with it.)

- "Oh brother, layers. Nobody else talks about layers. Have I messed up again?" Testing or criticizing yourself does not count as a legitimate question. Take a few Vibe-raising Breaths and start over.

- "But I didn't want layers, I wanted colors. How come I didn't see colors?" It bears repeating: Each of us has certain languages and perceptions that are woven into the spiritual fabric of who we are. Instead of expecting yourself to "perform" a certain way, it's better to let yourself explore the way you already do.

Joining in Spirit

Synchronicity is afoot. As I begin to write about this technique, my empathic child comes and stands by the side of my chair. For three minutes, in utter silence, he watches me tap the computer keyboard. Normally this kid us is not voluntarily quiet. Amazed, I say, "You really want to stand here and be that quiet?"

Matt shrugs, then fidgets. He dances out of the room.

Suddenly I realize that Matt has physically come to Join in Spirit with me. Moreover, his graceful exit exemplifies Step #2 of the technique that follows. But first things first. Let's go for a basic definition.

JOINING IN SPIRIT means that you help another person by empathically linking your energy field with hers. She is someone who has *asked* for your help. Perhaps she has asked long term, by signing up as a close friend. At the other extreme, the request could come from someone who is practically a stranger.

In either case, it's your choice, whether or not to link your consciousness. To appreciate the importance of choice, let's compare Joining a Spirit with Holding a Space. With the latter, you *initiate* merging your consciousness with that of another person. With the former, you *respond* to someone else's invitation. Either way, making the choice to go ahead means that you will merge your consciousness. But when you initiate the connection by Holding a Space, your motivation could be curiosity or fun, as well as service. When someone else asks to Join in Spirit with you, the invitation is usually based on that person's need. Make a point of becoming consciously clear about what is involved:

- To Join in Spirit *not* on purpose is draining and shows weak personal boundaries, a desire for martyrdom, co-dependence, or unskilled empathy.
- To Join in Spirit when you are conscious but *reluctant* is also draining... and something you're unlikely to do after you've read the next few pages.

□ As for consciously Joining in Spirit on purpose, when you do want to, that is a blessing for everyone involved. Not only are you helping someone, you're refining your skills as an empath.

How great a blessing can it be to Join in Spirit with someone? Permit me to brag—at least about what it's like to be on the receiving end. Dr. Bill Bauman, my mentor for the past seven years, has sometimes offered to Join in Spirit with me when I was in great need. When he did this, I would feel his comforting presence energetically, a cross between a long-distance hug and a silent telephone call lasting for hours.

Sometimes heavy emotions, like fear and self-blaming, would lift. Sometimes it would simply be easier for me to know my own mind. Several times, the results were so dramatic, I counted Bill's presence as a miracle.

Bill never told me directly how to give this kind of blessing. But when I was spiritually ready, I figured out how to follow his example, and others have felt the benefit. I feel deeply honored to pass this technique along, now, to you.

The unique thing about learning to Join in Spirit is that you can read about how to do it whenever you like, but as for practicing it—you'll have to wait for a chance.

Here's what I recommend. Read the following section now, then bookmark it in your awareness as though it were a useful address on the Internet. You'll know when to return to these instructions.

I. Recognize when someone is calling to Join in Spirit with you

Perhaps earlier that day you have had a conversation where a good friend tells you he is going through a rough time emotionally. Someone you care about could be in the hospital. Or a family member could be taking a highly rigorous test. Circumstantial clues like these can help you to recognize what is happening when that person tugs on your energetically. (From now on, let's refer to "that person" as your client for Joining in Spirit.)

How will you recognize when your client calls to Join you in Spirit? That varies according to your inner language. Perhaps the person's face will flash before you. You may hear the sound of his voice in your ear, smell a fragrance that reminds you of him. Or perhaps you'll catch yourself thinking of him in a daydreamy sort of way.

Whatever subtle clue comes to your awareness, make a conscious mental note. That client is calling you to Join in Spirit.

2. Decide whether to engage

Just because you're called doesn't mean you must come. We're talking about giving a blessing, not responding to an obligation. Question whether you would like to do this. Maybe your answer isn't yes or no but "Maybe another time." Honor whatever answer you receive.

When your inner answer is "No" or "Maybe another time," tell the person. To do that, hold the person in your mind and think your response. Consider it done. Now go about your business, whatever it is, and don't respond to further calls from that person. (Probably there won't be any because that person will call on someone else in spirit.)

If your inner answer is "Yes," allow yourself to be with that person mentally. What happens next is much like answering someone's physical telephone call. You stay on the receiver, listening, making the occasional comment, as needed. This conversation isn't about you or your needs. It's a form of service.

3. Get Big

Because the service you are doing is spiritual, you need not to do it alone. After you choose to connect, inwardly call on the Ascended Master or Archangel of your choice.

4. Decide when enough is enough

Who decides when you have Joined in Spirit long enough? You do.

Sometimes you'll feel that your client is doing better now and doesn't require your help.

Sometimes you'll feel tired or start to worry about fulfilling your responsibilities. Enough is enough. Without further ado, tell your client good-bye.

Often your client will be done in minutes, and will release you even before you get around to thinking about good-byes. Otherwise, the choice to hang up the spiritual telephone is yours, so remember to make it.

5. Stop when you feel like it

Have no pangs of conscience about deciding that this session of Joining in Spirit has gone on long enough. Once you have joined, even for a second, your recipient has received worthwhile help, even if this hasn't registered fully yet. Besides, any spiritual helper you have invited into the conference call will stay with your client as long as needed, regardless of whether you hang up. It's easier for beings of light to give long-term blessings without burning themselves out. Respect your human limits and give only what you have to give.

- □ Do the technique for *Coming Home*.
- □ Thank any being of light you have called on to help you.

6. Be yourself

Return to awareness of yourself as a skilled empath, an individual. Affirm, "I have strong, clear personal boundaries." What can you take from the experience of Joining in Spirit? Remember anything you have learned about how to give this kind of service. Otherwise, forget the details of your client's problems and get on with your life.

Joining in Spirit—Q&A

Q: Isn't it selfish to say no when somebody needs you?

A: Staying in balance about your empathy is never selfish. As an empath, it's your first responsibility. Joining in Spirit takes energy. In fact, we can be very specific about the kind of energy taken:

- Emotional forms of empathy take emotional energy.
- Intellectual Shape Shifting takes guess what? Intellectual energy.
- Physical forms of empathy take subtle energy related to your physical body plus energy related to the coordination between your body and the rest of your body-mind-spirit system.
- Spiritual Oneness takes less energy than other forms of empathy. Nevertheless, all forms of conscious empathy take energy. It's important not to overextend. Sometimes an empath needs to stay home, and that's that.

Q: But what if you feel guilty about saying no?

A: What's the worst thing that would happen if you said no?

Q: The person might die. The person might flunk out of school. The person might go stark raving mad. Hmm, maybe all this does sound a bit extreme. That's what my fears say, anyway. Okay, get this. What if the person you refused to Join in Spirit was your mother?

A: Spiritual crisis at the level of life-and-death intensity, even when concerning your mother, is the responsibility of that person and God. And God has messengers, you know: angels. No empath, however skillful or kind, is going to put an angel out of a job.

Q: But if the client, as you call it, has asked you to help. If you say no, haven't you done something wrong?

A: Look, the client has sent you an *invitation*. Responding does not brand you as right or wrong, good or bad. You've been invited to give, to learn, to make that other person's business your business. Sometimes your spirit will tell you this simply is not appropriate.

Q: But what if you were this person's LAST HOPE?

A: Please, let's remember context here. Were you physically swimming next to a drowning man, yes, you might be a last hope. But being called to Join in Spirit is not of that order. After you say no, your would-be client is free to telephone around.

On the inner planes, most of us carry a little black book with many juicy entries, and they're not restricted to names we have written down consciously with a full address and phone number.

Your spirit has taken note of all the promising names. There's a saint who sat with you on a bus this morning, who'll most likely be available even though she's a near stranger. There's an incredible spiritual being, disguised as a normal person, who saw you today at your neighborhood post office. Friends and lovers are connected with you since childhood, maybe even lifetimes before that. Thus, in spirit, you are linked to a world-wide web of resources. So is any would-be client.

Q: Still, isn't it possible that somebody considers you her only resource, even if others could be available?

A: Yes, unfortunately. That somebody has made a mistake for which you are not responsible.

Q: When I joined in spirit with my friend Margaret, I felt an outpouring of deep sadness. She had told me earlier that day about something bothering her. Could I have been imagining the whole thing about Joining in Spirit?

A: What if you were? Imaginary Joining in Spirit still counts. Imagination is how it is done!

Seriously, chances are you weren't making up what happened. As you gain experience with Joining in Spirit, you'll recognize the truth of it more clearly.

Depending on your empathic gifts and your preferred inner languages, experience will fall into certain patterns. For instance, you may notice physical sensations in your body (from Physical Oneness) and language them to yourself in terms of textures and images (from Clairsentience and Psychic Knowing). Let Joining in Spirit become an experience of learning for you about your ways to know truth, as well as a form of service to your friend.

Q: Hold on. I've got a major ethical question here. Can't things get a little weird if you call in a spiritual helper your client doesn't believe in?

A: Good point. Let's say your Uncle Walter, who is old and ailing, calls on you. When you Join in Spirit, you call on Jesus because he's the one you depend on to lift your spiritual burdens. And you happen to know that Uncle Walter can't stand Jesus.

Here's where the simplicity and innocence of Joining in Spirit keeps you from having problems. Because Walter has called on you, and your way is to call on Jesus, you have every right to do so. If he doesn't like the energy, he'll hang up very quickly.

However, let's be very clear about which do's and don'ts are involved in making a conference call when you Join in Spirit.

- □ DO feel free to support your client by listening.
- □ DON'T give advice. Don't send out a single thought that includes the word "should," such as "You should divorce that bum." or "Here's what you should tell your kid...." (This would constitute psychic coercion.)
- □ DO feel free to call on your favorite spiritual helper to join with you both and lift your client's burden.
- □ DON'T coach that spiritual helper about what to do. For instance, don't say, "Buddha, convert her to follow your path of detachment." Let the Buddha work in His own way. (Don't give him one more reason to be a laughing Buddha!)
- □ DO take the mission of Joining in Spirit as lightly as you can. Let the client's experience flow through you. Feel it. Know it. Then let go of it.
- □ DON'T resist changing your mind. If you feel frightened about what you're starting to experience when you Join in Spirit, act calmly and wisely. It's fine to say, "Okay, that's all for now. Good

luck." and hang up. It's fine to say, "Take that burden, Goddess Athena," then marvel at how your own sense of burden eases up. But it's definitely NOT fine to stay Joined in Spirit when it drains you, in which case you won't help either your client or yourself.

- DO thank your spiritual helper afterward. Bask in how your relationship becomes even more glorious because of this new dimension of service.
- DON'T think for a minute that you have the right to push your personal spiritual helper on anyone else. Especially when a person has come to you for help, don't take advantage of that vulnerable state to pray in the manner of revival meetings, "Jesus, come into this person's life." Never presume that you have the right to improve upon another person's religion.

Q: WHAT IF YOU DON'T FEEL COMFORTABLE BRINGING IN ANY SPIRITUAL HELPER AT ALL? IS IT STILL SAFE TO JOIN IN SPIRIT WITH PEOPLE?

A: Sure, but over time you will find that your ability to Join in Spirit grows enormously when you are willing to call on a specific being in a light body.

Angels can fly because they take themselves lightly. We empaths fly faster when we let angels help us take ourselves lightly. When we accept the company of angels, saints, and spiritual masters, they create a kind of flight momentum, just as birds who fly in formation generate an updraft.

*A*ffirmations

1. It is safe for me to open up more as an empath. My ability to serve others, with balance, grows every day.
2. I accept people as they are. Phooey on the habit of judging!
3. No psychic coercion for me—I don't give it, nor do I take it. I am the only authority in my life.
4. As an empath, I am always free to move in spirit. In my freedom is my power. In my freedom is my safety. My empathy thrills the heart of God because it awakens freedom for all on earth.
5. When empathy overwhelms me, I return to awareness of myself. I am a skilled empath, a master of my gifts.
6. I break the pattern of carrying around other people's stuff. I am an empath, not a garbage collector. What doesn't belong to me, leave immediately!
7. I banish guilt. Whether or not I use my empathy in this particular situation, I give enough in life. I refuse to join empathically with others because *they* demand it.
8. I stop believing there is virtue in pain. I explore pain just long enough to learn there *is* a lesson. I reach clear through to the joy of God; I learn my lessons and move on.
9. First I take care of myself. Each day I do work that thrills my soul.
10. Either I Join in Spirit with others or I don't. I am very clear about when I choose to do service. Since God has made enough empaths to go around, I can afford to take it easy.

Part III

Lifestyle Matters

"When we die, we're not going to be asked why we didn't become a Messiah or didn't find a cure for cancer. Instead, we will be asked, 'Why didn't you become you?'"

—*Souls on Fire*
Elie Wiesel

II. The Lifestyle You Deserve

This chapter explores many facets of the lifestyle you deserve as an empath. Let's start by making room for you to even *have* a life as an empath. Contrary to the popular expression, nobody needs to "get" a life. Society more or less dictates that you excel at each of the following types of life, at a minimum:

- A Thrilling Sex Life
- A Prosperous Wage-earner Life
- A Glamorous Dress-up Life
- A Dutiful Child Life
- A Bountiful Parent Life
- A Conscientious Car Owner Life
- An Immaculate Housekeeper Life
- A Healthy Food Provider/Nutritionist Life
- A Medically Impeccable, Well Exercised Life
- A Community-oriented Good Citizen Life
- A Responsible Budgeter Life
- A Wild (though Disciplined) Vacationer Life
- A Saintly Spiritual/Religious Life

You get the idea. Empaths don't need to get a life. We need to *claim* a life. What do you want to be as you grow up? For that matter, who have you been all along?

Name Yourself Right

"Call me Ishmael" wrote the narrator of *Moby Dick*. If he'd lightened up with his name, perhaps the novel would have been a bit shorter. Confess, did you wander all the way through to the end of Herman Melville's classic? Would it have made a difference if the book had started, "Call me Snapple"?

Seriously, our names (official and otherwise) always have consequences, which makes it scary that you may have been named wrong, officially or unofficially.

Has one of your unofficial middle names been "too-sensitive"?

Chances are excellent that your parents called you that, due to their own lack of knowledge about how to raise you as an empath. Envy the well-adjusted child whose reaction to being called "too sensitive" is a look of disbelief and the breezy reply, "Too sensitive for what?"

Every toddler needs to learn potty training. Just as surely, every young empath needs to learn how to come back home and give empathy a rest. As you grew up, your soul also cried out for knowledge about grounding, how to bring yourself down to earth. Empaths need more of that than other people, so many suggestions on how to do this will follow in a later chapter. Safe to assume, as a rising empath, you haven't been given so much as a clue about grounding.

Before you prepare to ground anything, though, let's complete the task of naming, especially removing any habits of mis-naming.

What names for yourself have you written in your ongoing autobiography? (Everybody writes one, even if it stays unpublished and subconscious.) Have you been using any put-downs over the years? Gadzooks, what tone of voice hath thou been using?

American society, in general, mocks sensitivity and ignores true empathy. Sometimes people are praised (on TV or off) for emotional displays that supposedly show empathy. These performances, however, are more likely to be histrionic displays about victimhood. If *that* is supposed to be empathy, and if you've been given no name for what you do, it's all too easy to pick up the latest trendy label about some psychological problem, like "co-dependent."

What are the true names for yourself?

It should help that you now have six shiny new monikers for different types of empathy: Physical Oneness, Physical Intuition, Emotional Oneness, Emotional Intuition, Intellectual Shape Shifting, and Spiritual Oneness. How about holding a garage sale for the old names? If nobody else wants to buy them, trash 'em.

Empaths in Society

So many empaths criticize themselves unnecessarily for being different. Even when they accept themselves as sensitive, they don't accept their empathy.

"All my life, I've had to work on my weak boundaries," Mary told me. She's a social worker with exceptionally good Emotional Oneness and Spiritual Oneness. Until we talked, she didn't appreciate how directly her struggles with "boundaries" were related to the talents she uses as a therapist.

What's the equation each of us should have learned in school?

Empathy = flexible boundaries

For Mary to worry about so-called "weak boundaries" would be ridiculous. What she has is strong empathy, a God-given gift for spiritual exploration. Assuming that Mary learns to value her strength and use it on purpose, she has no good reason to criticize her flexible boundaries.

If only the average empath knew as much as the average weight lifter. Here's what I mean. First thing you learn, when you start weight lifting, is the drill for building muscle. *Body building requires that you alternate workout days with rest days.*

So when Bruce lifts weights on Monday, he knows he will have to take Tuesday off. Hardworking muscles need a day to heal. Bruce can afford to rest because it will enable magic to happen. His muscles will grow back stronger than ever.

Likewise, we empaths strengthen our boundaries when we alternate Flying in Spirit with giving it a rest.

Maybe weight lifters have an advantage because they need to use special equipment. Serious himbos don't make do by hefting a couple of soup cans from the kitchen. Either they join a gym or they pay big bucks for home equipment. And since they receive basic training about how weight lifting works, they know better than to judge themselves for needing time off. Bruce isn't likely to fret: "I've had a lifelong problem with lazy muscles that won't let me work out every day."

Physical muscles have their way of working. So do your empathy muscles (which make you a *light* lifter, instead of a weight lifter). Your consciousness is so flexible, it can do the equivalent of perfect splits and effortless backbends. Enjoy this. Don't blame yourself for it.

And if your current lifestyle includes "working on yourself" for being "too" empathic, phooey!

Objective-Subjective Balance

To be a tightrope walker, you don't have to work for the circus. Every day you balance on a skinny little rope that separates objective life from subjective life.

Objective reality means the things that happen in the physical world, like receiving a telephone call. Subjective reality means inner experience of those things, like how you *feel* about receiving a particular telephone call.

Both realities matter. Balancing matters too, because otherwise people tend to become either excessively objective or excessively subjective.

OVER-OBJECTIVE people are insensitive. "You've got to prove it to me," they insist, fussing over even the smallest departures from scientific fact. Furthermore, over-objective people will accuse you of "making it up" whenever you can't defend what you've said in literal terms.

Nobody enjoys being willfully misunderstood. What's worst about dealing with over-objective people? Could be the terrible tone of voice with which the accusation "making it up" is typically spoken, implying that you're a crazy good-for-nothing. Should you try to call your accuser's attention to this terrible tone of voice, he—being over-objective—will most likely denounce you for making up the implied insult, too.

Hurtful though it can be to deal with over-objectivity, let's be fair and look at the other side of the coin, being OVER-SUBJECTIVE. One person's fascinating marathon narrative of psychological conflicts and issues can be somebody else's yawner.

How can we empaths avoid becoming ludicrously over-subjective? Grounding activities help people like you and me to find OBJECTIVE-SUBJECTIVE BALANCE, with a happy medium between paying attention to what is outside and our rich inner lives. Eventually someone's sense of humor (hopefully yours) will remind you there's more to life than empathy.

Humor

Even when you've been conscientiously using empathy techniques, Coming Home more often than you Fly in Spirit, sometimes you'll slip into old habits and slave away with your gifts. Don't feel discouraged. Balance will come to be a habit. It's the inevitable result of your continuing education as an empath.

Humor helps to bring balance. Collect stories like this one, related to me by a student:

Ellen talked on the phone with her twenty-something daughter, Connie, who spent the time complaining about a terrible stiff neck. For half an hour, Connie related her troubles while mother Ellen patiently listened.

Next morning, Ellen woke up with an unbelievably stiff neck, beyond any stiffness she known before. Acute pain lasted for days. The poor dear gobbled up aspirin, hobbled around, felt mentally baffled as well as physically uncomfortable. What was it with this pain in the neck?

Next week she happened to call her daughter again.

"How are you doing, Connie?"

"Fine, Mom."

"Want to hear an amazing coincidence? I started having neck problems, too."

"Gee, Mom, that's a shame. Mine stopped. Right after we talked, all my pain was gone."

Education in Moderation

The Berenstain Bears never prepared you for this one. As a parent, you may have read countless problem- solving tales like *The Berenstain Bears and the Messy Room* and *The Berenstain Bears and Too Much Birthday*. But what is to become of Brother Bear, or you, after too many seminars? Do you know your own mind? If you were alone with it a dark room, would you even recognize it?

Especially because you're an empath, you're probably very good at any technique you try. Growth seminars, evening workshops, weekend intensives—all of these can be very appealing. Although as a teacher and author, I might seem to have a vested interest in not saying this, the fact remains that *most empaths need more time at home, doing nothing*.

One seminar or retreat per season is plenty, unless you're an enthralled beginner. Between times, on your own or with friends, explore what interests you at your own pace. Make your own informal support group of like-minded buddies. At a more advanced level, apprentice yourself to the best teacher you can find. (Rare is the teacher who'll turn away a truly motivated student.)

When I give classes, I invite each participant to "pick up" at least two other students. Unless your teacher does this for you, take the initiative.

Share your name and phone number with people who seem to be on your wavelength. Fellow students at your adult ed. center—or your favorite bookstore or health food store—can make wonderful companions on your journey; there's nothing terrible about making the first move toward friendliness. Lose those hang-ups society has taught you about seeming too forward or needy.

Students perpetually tell me they wish they had more like-minded friends. Many of my workshops have resulted in follow-up groups, where students meet at each other's homes to continue their learning. How smart!

Regardless of how often you wind up attending classes, as a rising empath you'll need to alternate serious study with casual meetings with friends and un-pressured closeness with family. Add plenty of unstructured time to be alone. And be guided by your inner sense of timing.

Respect Your Inner Timing

Timothy has single-handedly declared war against wearing a watch. He seems to be winning, too. Not that he expects his "war" to change other people, just that he has decided, personally, to stop following other people's timetables instead of his own. During the day, Timothy will do an occasional reality check, consulting his internal watch before asking someone, "What time is it?" His inner clock is getting pretty darned accurate.

Whether or not you wish to follow Timothy's example with physical clocks, it behooves every empath to pay attention to inner timing.

Stephan Rechtschaffen, the physician who founded the Omega Institute for Holistic Studies, has developed a fascinating concept about the creative use of time. *Timeshifting,* the subject of his book, means learning how to transition smoothly from a fast pace to medium to slow... and back again. Too often, he says, Americans live only at one pace: fast forward.

Aside from "little" inconveniences caused by living at breakneck speed, such as exhaustion, rushing is no good for empathy. Empathy, as you may have noticed, happens in a timeless kind of time. Each day brings us countless opportunities to linger in the presence of others, empathically using our most developed gifts or quietly exploring the underused ones. Habits like rushing and multi-tasking block an empath's development.

C. Leslie Charles offers the best assortment of strategies I've seen yet to counteract perpetual rushing in her how-to, *Why Is Everyone So Cranky?* This gem of advice is typical:

"Your level of resistance [to slowing down] is in direct proportion to the extent of your need."*

Empathy techniques can help, because they don't just require that a person slows down. They offer an immediate reward for doing so. Techniques to turn empathy off, like Going Home, bring physiological balance that can last for hours. Techniques to turn empathy on, like Darshan, can give you the high of Celestial Perception.

So even if you have only ten minutes a day to explore empathy, set your watch (inner or outer). Let this be a respite for you, in the here and now. Let digital or analog ticking become irrelevant.

Taking a Sabbath helps, too. A glorious day to rest and relax can be yours, if you make the choice.

No Numbing Allowed

Tempting though it is to medicate away your empathy with alcohol, prescription drugs, non-prescription drugs, or massive doses of your favorite comfort food, you know the truth. Numbing yourself is a poor substitute for developing skill as an empath.

Even psychoactive medication may not be needed as often as it's commonly prescribed. Although some individuals need it to function, many do not. As noted by Dr. Elaine Aron in *The Highly Sensitive Person*, HSPs easily become over-aroused yet that doesn't necessarily mean they need medicine. She tells the personal story of a routine checkup. When she told

---

*C. Leslie Charles, *Why is Everyone so Cranky?* (New York: Hyperion, 1999), p. 72

her family doctor about her work on sensitivity, he became visibly upset. Calling it shameful that "This problem is undertreated by medicine," he pulled out his prescription pad to put Aron out of her misery, saying, "Thank God it's easily cured, just like diabetes."

Wryly she told him she thought she could survive without his pills.*

Could there be ways in *your* life that you try to numb your sensitivity? Now that you've been a practicing empath for a while, maybe it's time to re-evaluate that aspect of your lifestyle. Of course, it would be a mistake to discontinue medication without consulting your doctor. Periodically, though, it can't hurt to ask your doctor to re-evaluate your meds. If you're subjectively changing and growing at a fast rate, maybe there's some corresponding physical readjustment, one that warrants lightening up on the pharmaceuticals.

Anyway, most of our numbing "drugs" are self-prescribed: excessive shopping, too much TV, recreational eating. If you can identify something like that in your lifestyle, see if you eliminate it. And guess what? To break the cycle of any numbing (or addictive) behavior, one of your best helpers could be your old friend, the technique for Breaking out of the Amusement Park. As cravings arise, right then, allow yourself to be with yourself. What's going on? Be with it. This takes great courage, of course, but you'll find the rewards are even greater.

In *Nourishing Wisdom: A New Understanding of Eating*, nutritionist Marc David gives an inspiring account of his struggle to break the habit of food cravings. He used what he calls The Holding Technique: "Breathe through a craving, fully experience all the sensations that arise, allow emotions to be fully expressed, and arrive at the place where you no longer need yield to the desire."** Like Breaking out of the Amusement Park, this technique uses your consciousness to nurture your own body-mind-spirit.

---

* Elaine Aron, Ph.D., *The Highly Sensitive Person* (Secaucus, NJ: Birch Lane Press, 1996), p. 196
** Marc David, *Nourishing Wisdom* (New York: Harmony Books, 1991), p. 127

Breaking bad habits is hard. Make it easier by including brief periods of Darshan technique with someone who inspires you. Then come back to your dear old self. As an empath, you're practiced at Flying in Spirit to help others. How about some service to you!

Another option with numbing behavior is to consider it a wake-up call. When you realize you've been numbing yourself, ask, "Could something else in my life be out of whack?" Use the Questioning technique.

Everyone has points of vulnerability, and it may be unrealistic to hope that they will ever go away completely. A loving self-awareness can help you remember to notice signs of strain early on, then follow up with a gentle intent to rebalance your lifestyle. Catching yourself mid-act in numbing behavior could remind you, for instance, that you're chronically over-tired, over-committed, overworked or overachieving. And let's not forget an especially common problem for empaths: Over-giving.

Appropriate Give and Take

Take care of yourself. Just about everyone needs a gentle reminder from time to time. Take care of yourself, in body-mind-spirit.

How easy it is to give to others when you unconsciously wish they would give to *you*. Alas, giving empathy to others will not force them to bestow it on you... or even to notice you, necessarily. Understandably, you may sometimes be tempted to use empathy to push yourself into someone else's space, when you've been feeling excluded.

For instance, let's say you're having dinner with your spouse. He's elsewhere, except for the portions directly involved in self-feeding. Over-subjective or over-objective, preoccupied with work, wishing he could be watching TV—whatever is going on, he's distant. You can feel it from the first moment he puts butt to chair and fork to mouth.

As he sits before you in all his uncommunicative glory, appropriate behavior would be to deal with his distance in practical ways. You could question him, try to involve him in conversation, or excuse yourself and dine alone with your copy of John Gray's *Men Are from Mars, Women Are from Venus*.

Anything practical would be preferable to what you, an empath, may be tempted to do instead. For crying out loud, when the guy needs space, don't barge in by joining with him empathically. Nobody can beat you at hide and seek, if you're the one who's seeking. As an empath, you can torture your spouse by joining him anywhere, at any time.

But don't do it just because you wish he would want to join you. Remember, skilled empaths set an intention before they travel. Be honest with yourself about yours and you won't come to someone else when what you really want, in your heart of hearts, is for that person to come to you.

Showing Off? Why?

When was the last time someone insisted on telling you how he was feeling and you didn't want to know? Well, it's even worse if he insists on telling you how YOU were feeling.

Not everyone wants feedback from empaths, even if it's like refusing a six-inch slice of lusciously gooey chocolate ganache layer cake.

Huh? What kind of a weirdo would refuse a free piece of cake like that?

Under certain circumstances, that kind of weirdo could be YOU. For instance, you might turn down the cake offer first thing in the morning for breakfast on the day before entering national finals as Miss America. Even the most confirmed chocoholic must admit, there's a time and a cake for everything. Sometimes that cake is best made out of fresh whole air. Smart bakers know better than to thrust their goodies on people who can't eat them.

Similarly, we empaths must resist the temptation to offer insights that weren't asked for, a.k.a. giving gratuitous advice or, to put it even more bluntly, just plain showing off.

Congratulations if you're conscious enough about empathy to struggle with this form of temptation. When you start using your gifts on purpose, every day feels like Christmas. There you go unwrapping packages (which actually are people's outer facades). Of course you want to cheer—or at least wave the wrapping paper around to show everybody else how many presents you found under the tree.

Beside this wholesome sense of excitement, there's a more iffy matter, the very understandable desire to win status points. When you can know things that others don't, the urge to flap your tongue may be stronger than a dog's need to pant on a hot day.

Of course you may yearn to tell, if only to make up for the status points you've lost over the years by revealing that you couldn't handle watching a thriller with the rest of the gang; or by feeling your head would burst if you didn't request that your date would turn down the music; or by the other countless, chronic ways that empathy + sensitivity = vulnerability.

You couldn't hide it then so, by gum! Why hide it now?

Actually, many of us who are seriously empathic are carrying serious pain. The desire to show off can mask a wish to get even.

Empaths are intense. We gravitate away from small talk and towards big talk about feelings, ideas, or spiritual truth. When non-empaths sense how deeply we know, often they don't like it.

From childhood on, can't you remember times of being made fun of because you "knew too much?" Even if you recognized that your critics were mostly responding to this relentless knowing of yours, what could you do about it, other than making yourself feel dead inside?

Get-even-pain caused by being an empath is a trap, no better or worse than any other kind of emotional pain. How can you untrap yourself? Take a lesson from a classic toy you probably played with in childhood, the Oriental thumb puzzle. It's a colorful tube-shaped puzzle, made of interwoven straw. To start, you place one thumb in each side. Then you try to pull your thumbs out. The harder you pull, the tighter you're stuck.

Eventually you learn to let go, letting your thumbs to move toward each other in a conciliatory gesture. By the time you escape, you've learned a lesson from one of the most spiritually potent toys ever devised. It teaches the wisdom of reconciliation.

Especially with empathy, it's wise to forgive the pain you may have suffered because of it. Using your empathy to get even wouldn't really help, even if it were possible. You and the people you've pulled against have been linked by your empathy, just like two thumbs caught up in the same straw tube. Resistance only makes the tension worse. To solve the problem, let go.

In most cases, adults can completely release being bound up in relationship with people who don't like us or our empathy. Granted, as children we had little choice about our significant others. Growing up, we have gained freedom of choice. Now we can not only choose our roommates, we can surround ourselves with surrogate brothers, sisters, parents, and as many friends as we have room to hold in our hearts. Birds of a feather flock together, even if they didn't hatch in the same nest.

So it's wise to seek out peers for sharing your empathic insights. Make friends who respect that you travel in spirit. Choose significant others who love you for celebrating empath's Christmas every day.

Replace Judgment with Discernment

"Judge, lest you not be judged." Jesus offered pretty scary advice here, didn't he, when you think about it? Yet the words are comforting, too, because they imply that if we judge less often, we'll be criticized less often.

Imagine what a relief it would be to face with less criticism from others. Imagine a complete absence of self-blame. Wow, would that still be human life? For me, handling judgment is an ongoing lesson. Fortunately, empathy empowers us to choose discernment rather than judgment. Let's define both terms:

DISCERNMENT means noticing differences, no value judgments required. People tend to be good at discernment for one of the following reasons:

- Analytical Awareness is one of your soul's strong talents.
- In school, you had at least one really good science teacher.
- You've slogged through school all the way to a Master's degree or a Ph.D.
- Religious training has emphasized your powers of discernment.
- A role model once showed you how to live with genuine discernment.

JUDGMENT, by contrast, means discernment with an attitude. Instead of stopping at the point of noticing differences, a judger goes on to decide whether each difference makes a person good or bad. People tend to be habitual judgers for one of the following reasons:

- Analytical Awareness is *not* an important language for your soul's expression.
- You grew up with at least one relative, friend, or teacher who was highly critical. (If that person was also sarcastic, you got a double dose of training.)
- Your education, socially or academically, has emphasized judging.
- Black-and-white thinking has been encouraged in matters like religion and politics. People are either right or wrong. Period.
- News media have taught you to be judgmental. (Controversy sells. Under the guise of objectivity, reporters fill their stories with judgments—one side pro, one side con, and the more outrageous, the better.)
- You watch TV on a daily basis. TV teaches smart-ass judging disguised as cleverness. Judgment underlies the most sophisticated commercials, echoes in the banter among news anchors, comes with a laugh track in sitcoms. Alarmingly, even shows for children teach, like, how to have attitude. Who isn't smart enough to consider himself smarter than somebody else? Duh!

For perspective on judgment vs. discernment, consider food. And start by watching a baby eat. You'll be reminded that babies approach food with no discernment whatsoever. Just when you think you have successfully fed Junior a mouthful of pureed carrots, out it goes... in installments.

Innocence about food reflects more than a baby's inherent talent as a performance artist. Babies haven't yet learned to discriminate between keeping food in versus drooling it out. To their innocent mouths, no food is good, no food is bad. Instead each bite is a new and strange adventure.

Next comes the antithesis. Once youngsters learn to discriminate, judgment becomes incredibly intense. Except for a few favored foods, most items achieve instant rejection. Spicy food, vegetables, even perfectly acceptable foods when mixed together, are judged "bad."

By adulthood, some people remain picky eaters. (Extreme example: I read an Ann Landers column where a woman boasted that she had never eaten a piece of fruit or a vegetable in her entire life. Talk about being a nay-sayer!) Most of us, however, develop a balance between innocence and judgment. We've learned enough discernment to leave food we don't like on the plate, so we don't have to shriek, like a Dr. Seuss character, "I do not like green eggs and ham."

Empaths need to understand that people, like food, can be tasted with either innocence, judgment, or discernment. As adults, we can't unlearn our hard-won categories of experience. Yet we always have a choice between simply noticing (discernment) versus sneering at what we notice (judgment).

Judgment closes off empathy while discernment keeps the door open. Especially in cases where we are troubled by anger or hatred, empathy helps us to break the judgment habit and find forgiveness.

A wise person has said, "Make your words soft and sweet because one day you may have to eat them." Words that express discernment rather than judgment also help us because they can remind us to switch on empathy which, in turn, can move us back to innocence.

CAVILING, complaining about people's little faults, diminishes the speaker. Habitually done, it may even grime up one's aura. Refusing to cavil is worthwhile, then, if for no other reason than to keep yourself clear as an empath.

Generosity and Forgiveness

As we survey the ideal, soul-nourishing lifestyle for an empath, let's not fail to include generosity. Educate other empaths who cross your path. Be generous in telling the truth about *their* empathy: what it is; why it need not be a weakness; how it can show up in ways that have nothing to do with society's gooey, maudlin understanding of "empathy"; how techniques can set you free to consciously Fly in Spirit.

Like attracts like. Therefore, many of your friends are probably empaths. Perhaps you'd like to invite them to join you in an Empath's Spirituality Group. Many women today are forming Spirituality Groups, as described in *Sacred Circles: A Guide to Creating Your Own Women's Spirituality Group* by Robin Deen Carnes and Sally Craig. Male empaths need friends, too. Why not bring together your own group to explore Flying in Spirit?

Empaths grow into their gifts at their own rate. Some may take years to show interest in developing the power of empathy. The biggest nay-sayers to inner life may surprise you some day when they reveal themselves to be empaths who, at last, are ready to recognize and use their gifts.

Other people I've known over the years, male and female, have amazed me by their spiritual awakening. Seemingly un-empathic when I knew them superficially, years later they reappeared with more vulnerable hearts or humbler minds.

At one of my seminars, I found myself repeatedly staring at a participant named Deborah. What made her so familiar? During our first break she told me. She had been in my local chapter of the La Leche League, a support group for mothers who breast-feed their babies. From the way I connected with the women in that group years ago, I never would have guessed that Deborah was an empath—and a very gifted one, it turned out.

Had I connected empathically with the La Leche ladies, I might have found many with strong empathic talents, not just Deborah. Several in the group, however, were zealots about causes with which I didn't agree, and they hurt me with derogatory comments about my lifestyle. Indirectly they helped me to develop generosity of heart—forgiveness—even if it took me years.

Yes, whenever we travel into another person's space, empathy offers us forgiveness. Thus, we empaths don't have to settle for pushing ourselves to forgive, then doing it superficially, grimly or piously, as a religious duty. Finding forgiveness can be fun.

How do you find it? To forgive a person from your present or past, Get Big. Say to a spiritual master or Archangel, "Take the burden of my feelings about this person and help me to forgive her completely." Stay connected in silence, and you'll move in your consciousness, with thoughts and images flickering by, until you reach a place of peace.

Forgiveness like this is available to anyone. You need not be an empath... except to enjoy the "dessert" part of the meal. As the forgiveness process unfolds, out of habit, you'll find yourself Holding a Space for the person in question, then traveling empathically. Gradually you'll understand from the inside out how she ticks. This is a far cry from more common practices where people "work at" forgiveness by forcing themselves to see another person's point of view. Why settle for a dry theoretical understanding? Empathy is an experience. Bite into it like a strawberry and you can taste the juice.

Another option for an empath is to do travel techniques for forgiveness in the same way you would approach any empathic journey. Bring the person to mind and plug in through sight, hearing, or touch. As usual, you will enter the mind, the heart, the body, or the spirit. It's that easy.

Afterwards you will breathe easier, too. In the palace of your nostrils, you'll find a fresher air.

Forgiveness, I hasten to add, is needed in relatively few cases. More often than we are actively hurt by relationships, we find ourselves feeling isolated. Perfectly good potential relationships don't seem to "click." To heal this, all we need is simple generosity. As empaths, we can afford to be generous at welcoming people back into our lives and giving them a second chance. Years after you have grown used to using the power of empathy, half-strangers may surprise you by doing a Deborah—revealing a curiosity you never knew existed. In fact, they may have noticed you were an empath even before you did.

The Play within the Play

"All the world's a stage," Shakespeare wrote. As an empath, you are privileged to peek behind the theater curtain. In life, as in a theatrical performance, people project their roles with varying degrees of effectiveness. Words, body language, and dress can make an impression. Or not.

When you Hold a Space for a person, however, you can appreciate any role being played. Then, just as actors are more than a role, your empathic search can be rewarded with visits to other layers, all the way down to patterns about the interpersonal movement of spiritual energy. It's like discovering a play within a play—worthy of the great Bard himself.

So, in your lifestyle as an empath, what are you to do with this richness of experience?

Sometimes you'll want to fit comfortably into the surface action. Other times, you'll choose to go back and forth: learning empathically what other performers do, then pulling awareness back to the surface level of the unfolding drama.

In the play within the play, on the level of auras, some performers function as ENERGY MOVERS. Their auras pulsate, scintillate even. You can observe how such actors awaken others energetically, even when nobody else consciously recognizes what is happening.

Other actors, you'll discover, are ENERGY HOLDERS. Some do it on an emotional level, holding onto feelings with the long memories attributed to elephants. Others hold energy on a physical level, keeping alive the memory of aches and pains or pleasures. What fun, to notice! You'll observe what happens when other performers make contact with these energy holders and, temporarily, take on their patterns.

Finally, you'll find fascinating ways in which some actors serve as ENERGY DISRUPTORS. They shake things up, in a way that may or may not seem destructive on the surface. Regardless, the job is necessary. Psychotherapist Virginia Satir has observed that an important role in family dynamics is played by certain people who act as The Distractor. Psychology has, in fact, given us many words for behaviors that go with energy disruption mode: confrontation, passive-aggressive behavior, and so forth.

Yet a psychological label doesn't necessarily open our awareness to the nuances, which are the best part. Disruption need not be pathological, either. You'll find that some disruptors are transformers or boundary smashers or destroyers of spiritual ignorance. Energetically, observe how people respond to them. It's fascinating.

Surface behavior can be the exact opposite of what's happening aurically. For example, disruption may seem to be going on whereas, deeper down, participants are both maintaining their energy patterns. An extreme, jarring portrayal of this kind occurs in Edward Albee's drama, "Who's Afraid of Virginia Woolf?" As an empath you'll find that, despite apparent arguments, a couple can maintain a loving connection. Although it may not be how *you* would wish to show love, it's their chosen dance, for now.

Yes, at the level of Celestial Perception, there are many surprising ways for our spirits to create the play within the play. Each person aurically models a way of being, and empathy reveals it, up close and personal. Another benefit of skilled empathy, at the level of life's inner play, is that it can address one of the deepest kinds of worry for highly spiritual people.

Have you ever had the fear that you won't manage to do what you came here to do? On the level of energy, you'll discover that you—and everyone else—has a role to play. Even in the midst of worrying, "Will I ever do something important?" you already are. You're doing it with your energy... sending out your vibration to others, with the potential to help them learn and grow and connect with others in a particular way. This opportunity is offered to everyone on earth, at a spiritual level, in every relationship.

Observing the play within the play, you'll appreciate how this applies to you. Then you can reassure others, based not on easy generalizations but clear experience. For instance, Elizabeth came to me to discuss a breakthrough she had received through her prayer group at church. A "Holy Fire" now burned in her heart, she said.

"How is it that I could have such a profound spiritual experience yet outwardly my life is unchanged?" she asked. "What am I going to do with this?"

In responding, it helped that I could join both her pain and her light. I told her, "Whether or not you do a thing with it outwardly, your life is changed. You're carrying that Holy Fire with you wherever you go. On the inner, it's available to everyone who chooses, and that's all you can be responsible for."

The same goes for you, too. Your empath's light does shine. Just by being in a room, your own way of being radiates. Energetically you demonstrate a way to be, and everyone in the room with you receives this message. Usually a person's spirit takes note while conscious levels of the personality do not. As a skilled empath, however, you'll stop being oblivious. Daily life offers us thousands of little choices. Once a day or more, you can choose to pay attention to this great play within the play.

Meaningful work, kind actions—there are innumerable ways for a spiritual person to fulfill the burning desire to make life better for others. In purely spiritual terms, viewing the play within the play will open awareness to your service, everyone's service, through the act of auric modeling.

Auric Modeling

What we are shows. It shows far more than you probably think.

Imagine that you are attending a big designer's fashion show, watching models parade down the runway. Will you notice how they are dressed?

"No brainer!" you say. "This is a fashion show, for crying out loud. Besides, how people are dressed shows *everywhere*, all the time, to anyone who bothers to notice it."

Of course... and you don't need to wait until you're seeing an official Fashion Show to notice. You wear clothes. That qualifies you to relate to anyone you choose at the level of being dressed.

Similarly, everyone's aura shows all the time, too. It shows fully to everyone in the room who cares to notice. At this Auric Fashion Show, your spirit recognizes the spirit of others. And, depending on your soul's choice, you may be changed by contact with some of these souls. Consider it, if you will, a form of out-of-body sex. Two or more participants meet together, merge, and walk away afterward.

Of course this does *not* involve physical jollies. For all the awareness most of us have about the proceedings, we might be making love in our sleep. And afterwards, if we remain unconscious about what happens energetically, that's like giving ourselves the full numbing equivalent of a knockout blow to the head.

When will the reality of auric sharing reach you on a conscious level? Depends on how much your consciousness has developed.

Even a man who's oblivious to the spiritual level of life will consciously notice the presence of someone who is either extremely wonderful, extremely awful, or extremely similar to himself.

Want to notice more? Start by becoming aware of AURIC MODELING. Whenever two people are together, each one models, or demonstrates, a way to move energy as a spiritual being. If you were in a room with a wall-size TV, you'd receive input, wouldn't you? Well, auras put on a big show, too, in their own dimension. And our spiritual selves get the message, regardless of how much we pick up consciously. The difference, when you engage consciously as an empath, is that you have the fun of exploring how people react to auric modeling from others. Here are examples drawn from some of the auras I encountered when writing this part of this book:

□ June carries most of the liveliness of her aura below the belt— a polite way to say she lives mostly for power and sex. Her heart chakra is heavily armored and, at the throat, she models tightness and stored up anger. Yet everyone's aura shows deep gifts of the soul, and June is no exception. Since June's not very awake spiritually, her gifts don't show very clearly. Yet deep down she models a sweet, direct appreciation of life. "What you see is what you get," her aura sings wherever she goes.

□ If June is a chickadee, Dave is more of a rare bird, feathered with exceptional Analytical Awareness. Dave's aura is somewhat developed at the third eye, huge at the third chakra, and he moves through life as an expert information sorter.

True, all is not yet perfection. For now, there's a numbness at Dave's heart chakra plus a chronic clog at his throat. Speaking up for himself is an ongoing struggle for Dave; he knows so much more than can express. Altogether, what Dave models most successfully is how to keep the mind active. Being with his spirit is like taking a laxative for sluggish thinking. Who will welcome his presence? People with intellectual daring will they'll love entraining with those jazzy mental rhythms.

Dave's just starting to awaken his gift for Intellectual Shape Shifting. When he's using it with power, he'll be able to tell which people are bright enough (in the way he is bright) to listen to what he has to say. Then, I predict, his clogged-up throat chakra will clear right up.

□ Daisy is a TV talk show host with a reputation for being caring. Seeing her photo in a magazine, I quickly notice that her aura shows some soft-heartedness. But, for now, her third eye is closed in a state of disinterest to genuine spiritual experience—and why not? Her surface life is working so well for her right now. (Many people don't start to awaken spiritually while they are rich or successful.)

Since Daisy's not spiritually seeking yet, she doesn't have the oomph that might transform her soft-heartedness into Emotional Empathy, and she's even farther from being an Intellectual Shape Shifter or Physical Empath. What the woman does have is sex appeal galore, bouncing right out of her second chakra! Daisy will have charisma for earthbound people like June, whose energy fields respond mostly to sexiness.

□ Julio is a transformer. He moves through life at hummingbird speed... even though most people fly more like pigeons. In addition, Julio's aura shows strong gifts of Spiritual Oneness and Emotional Intuition. What you're most likely to notice around him, however, isn't the empathy. It's the prod he gives your soul to release old habits and make way for the new.

Human nature being what it commonly is, making people uncomfortable is the story of Julio's life. Even when this transformer never opens his mouth, some people will form an intense dislike to him and show it. Therefore, a major part of Julio's learning as a human personality, as opposed to a spiritual presence, is not to take it *personally* when people react to his aura.

□ Gail is Julio's exact opposite. She's spiritually set up to move slowly and thoroughly through life. Currently her heart chakra reveals a pattern of holding onto pain from past relationships, but what's fascinating when you explore this more deeply is her rigorousness as spirit. She's a relationship scientist, dissecting every possible specimen. While relationships are going on, she pulls 'em apart. After they're dead, she keeps on probing.

How will Gail effect people who prefer the hit-and-run form of dating? She'll slow-em down and unnerve them—literally, give them "the creeps." Other people, spiritually set up for thorough learning and teaching, will find Gail's presence comforting.

□ Ray is an empath with major talent for at Physical Oneness. When he's not Flying in Spirit, most of Ray's awareness is bound to his physical body. Yet he's also awake at a very high level of oneness with all of creation. Trying to balance these two extremes is an ongoing struggle for him—picture two gears gnashing against each other. Not surprisingly, Ray's third chakra shows fatigue, and he's out of touch with his heart. When Ray is with people, they may react to his courage at holding himself together. Alternatively, they may identify with his struggle or feel the parts of him that are not functioning strongly yet.

You get the idea. As you attune to auric modeling, you'll discover one more reason why empaths need never be bored in life, not when other people share the planet.

Beyond the fun of observing it, auric modeling has a very personal meaning for you. Did you realize that your aura always has an impact on others? Sure does. Wherever you go, your energy presence demonstrates what it is to be an empath. Your whole life, whether aware of auric modeling or not, whether skilled as an empath or not, you always have modeled empathic sensitivity. Now, by becoming balanced and stable as a skilled empath, your auric modeling will help you to bring hope to other empaths whenever you meet them.

12. How to Parent an Empath

One of a parent's sacred responsibilities is to better the quality of life for each new generation.

This chapter will show you many practical ways to help your empathic child to grow up confident, balanced, and empowered. Nor need you be an empath yourself—or the same kind of empath as your child—in order to help. However, if you, yourself, *are* an empath, it may be healing for you to revisit childhood through this chapter and, this time, get it right. One word for this is REPARENTING. Each of us has the option of rewriting our history as though we had grown up with different parents, choosing the best role models imaginable.

Think about it. What if you had been raised by skilled empaths? Had they nurtured your gifts, what different habits might you have developed? Well, whatever habits you didn't learn then, you can set in motion now. And your Inner Child will thank you.

Unless your upbringing has been highly unusual, the people around you most likely taught distrust of genuine spiritual gifts. As an example, let's revisit a traditional tale told to children. It holds a lesson for us all, parents especially.

The Emperor's New Clothes

Long ago, a vain Emperor was approached by two swindlers who promised to make him a glorious suit of clothes. He fell for it like a ton of gold bricks.

Although the swindlers accepted lavish payment in return for the clothes, they only pretended to make them. Observers were shamed into pretending along with them, for the swindlers cleverly said that people who were unable to see the invisible clothes were unfit to hold their jobs.

Eventually the Emperor paraded down the street wearing only his invisible clothes, plus a thick gloss of denial about his nakedness. All his subjects joined in the pretense, except for one young boy.

"The Emperor is naked," shouted this boy. At once the elaborate deception collapsed. Everyone admitted the truth, the thieves were caught and punished, and the Emperor had to live forever with his public humiliation.

Thus goes the traditional tale, a story of deception and vanity. But what if, beneath the surface, there lies a parable about society's fears of spiritual growth? Let's try out this different version....

The Emperor's True Clothes

Long ago, a wise Emperor sought teachers who could bring him to a higher level of consciousness. Two worthy teachers arrived and began to instruct him.

Unfortunately, the common people weren't ready to understand the Emperor's spiritual pursuit. Gossip arose that he was wasting enormous sums of money on pure vanity—something as useless as nonexistent clothes. Meanwhile, the Emperor developed his spiritual gifts. He learned to Fly in Spirit.

Eventually there was a news leak about the nature of the Emperor's private activities. The people demanded that he display his so-called wisdom by giving a public demonstration. Since he thought he was such a great empath, they said, let him give detailed readings of several volunteers! Everyone could watch, then decide if the Emperor was crazy or what.

Parading his knowledge against his will, the Emperor was exposed to the ridicule of people who expected carnival entertainment, not the subtler delights of spiritual wisdom. Some observers, those with open minds, may have felt inner stirrings of truth. Crowds, however, are not geared to subtleties. Eventually the most childish person in the group burst out laughing:

"He's a fake. He's crazy. He's making this up."

Soon the mob joined in the general laughter. (Oops, bad karma! Anyone who mocks a genuine spiritual seeker will have a hard time later finding genuine teachers for himself.)

As for the Emperor, was he shamed forever? Hopefully not. I prefer to think that he just learned not to cast pearls before swine—exactly what parents need to teach their empathic children.

As a parent, you are charged with creating a safe, private place for your empathic child to become a skilled explorer. That place is home. Even if the home you remember didn't nurture the empathic side of your growth, you have help in creating a better environment for your child. Let's start with learning about the special kind of empathic grace that comes to all mothers.

Pregnancy—A State of Empathic Grace

Pregnant women glow. Where does this mysterious glow come from?

It comes from the level of auras. During pregnancy the spirit of the unborn child joins with the mother. Energetically they dance together. Using techniques for empathy, you'll have great fun exploring this. Just find a pregnant woman and Hold a Space with her. Emotionally, physically, and especially spiritually, what you perceive can be a revelation.

A pregnant mom carries two energy fields. It's as though she were a kangaroo with a little energy joey tucked into her pouch.

When a mother is very conscious about her own awareness, she'll notice that she becomes a conscious channel for her unborn child's spirit. She links up, as though the phone company has rewired her to make conference calls.

Even the mother's physical vision can change to reflect this unique spiritual partnership. Personal example: During pregnancy, my driver's license came up for renewal. Lo and behold, for the first time in 33 years, I passed a vision test without glasses. Stunned at the miraculous improvement, I learned that eyesight often changes during pregnancy. Ask your optometrist. She'll recommend that you not buy new glasses until after childbirth, because vision can change back afterwards.

Why does vision change? Spiritually the explanation is simple. When you're pregnant, an extra person is looking out through your eyes.

Even if you notice no physical change, what about the rest of your outlook? That can change, too. For instance, during pregnancy I slipped into a dramatically different mindset about driving. Customary timidity was replaced by feelings of adventurousness. After my child was born, alas, the fearless driver drove away and took the eyesight upgrade with him. As for the spirit I no longer physically house, ever since we drove Matt home from the hospital it has been clear that, unlike his Mom, he delights in car rides. And his eyesight tests 20-20.

Unlike vision changes during pregnancy, which happen only sometimes, each pregnant woman, without exception, gains temporary access to a new set of gifts. Empathic fathers sometimes feel them, too.

When you do travel techniques as an empath, look out for subtle changes to your perception during pregnancy. Even your gifts for empathy may change. Or you may find your perceptions slipping into a new language, like Analytical Awareness. Enjoy yourself(selves) while it lasts.

Child Care Means Spacing Out

From childbirth until your child is a Two or Three, you may have noticed something funny about your state of mind: You have no mind.

In your past life, pre-parenting, you may have been a top flight executive. Now you can't even organize a diaper bag.

The baby wants to feed on demand. You only wish you could *think* on demand.

Sure, you can find excuses. The need to sleep for more than a couple of hours at a time may have something to do with your mental fog. Besides, what is a toddler? It's a highly independent person who combines the highest level of physical energy she'll ever have in her life with the lowest level of fear, plus zero common sense. No wonder you have to work non-stop as a security guard.

Now let's look deeper. While your child is little, there's an entirely different reason for a mother's trademark spaciness. So-called bonding between mother and child has an esoteric meaning. BONDING is widely understood to mean a close emotional tie between mother and child. Spiritually it means more. Together you two have formed an empathic connection, as if you were hot-linked on the Internet. Effortlessly, at push-button speed, your consciousness shifts from child to mother and back. [Note: Of course a father, adoptive parent, or committed caregiver can bond just as closely as any biological mother or father. Only for simplicity do I refer to all these intimate ways of being a parent as "mother."]

Mothers, give yourself credit. Think you just space out meaninglessly into the ozone? Ha! Energetically, you shift your aura to cradle your baby. Research this any time you can find another mother who is feeding her child, especially a breast-feeding mother. Yes, it's worth a trip back to the mall, if you can't find this anywhere else. Hold a Space with a Madonna and child. You'll delight in the way the mother's aura wraps around her baby, often tinged with an exquisite celestial glow.

And whether they breast-feed or not, mothers nourish their babies with consciousness. No wonder Moms seem spacey. Or bonded. Or empathic. ATTUNEMENT is yet one more name for it. Researched with fascinating, even microscopic, precision by psychiatrist Daniel Stern,* attunement is a form of closeness that shows in a certain kind of play between parent and child. It reassures babies that Mom senses what they feel.

Stern has found that, approximately once every minute, parents skilled at attunement made gestures to show connection, such as a mother's matching her voice to the pitch of her baby's squeal. Unlike simple imitation, these gestures mirror back the child's inner feelings.

Lacking empathy, the attunement Stern measured would be a shallow mirror reflection. But when mothers attune, they serve as empaths, signaling an energetic connection.

Empathy also creates the profound parental sharing that Dr. Jean Shinoda Bolen calls "the diffuse, shared awareness" of motherhood. In *Goddesses in Every Woman*, this Jungian analyst remembers how, when her own children were young, they would mysteriously know whenever Mom shifted away from her usual unfocused, nurturing attention. Whenever she would shift to a more purposeful style of consciousness, immediately they'd start to cry. How could kids in another room, occupied in baby games of their own, tell that Mom had picked up a school book to study? "It seemed as if the kids had ESP when my attentive-to-them, scanning-for-details mental state was replaced by focused attention, which 'tuned them out.'"**

---

* Daniel Goleman, Ph.D., *Emotional Intelligence* (New York: Bantam, 1995), pp. 100-101 describes the research by Stern.

** Jean Shinoda Bolen, M.D., *Goddesses in Everywoman* (New York: Harper & Row, 1984) p. 133-134. Bolen also explains in detail how "Each of the three goddess categories has a characteristic quality of consciousness." Women who are strongest in the qualities of Hera, Demeter, or Persephone, have diffuse awareness—similar to what I call being an empath.

What does this behavior signify? I take it as confirmation that mothers nourish their children by Joining in Spirit with them. When the spiritual feeding stops, kids notice.

Which mothers have this kind of diffuse awareness or natural skill at attunement? Stern and Bolen find that some do it far better than others. I suspect that all mothers are initially offered this gift, much like the ability to breast-feed, but it lasts only so long as it's used. Like milk, empathy flows on demand. The mothers who hold this special awareness longest are what I call natural empaths.

With every passing year, from birth through the first years of elementary school, such a mother feels as though she is getting more of her own life back. And it isn't just that baby-sitting duties grow progressively easier. Toddlers, pre-schoolers, kindergarteners, and first graders demand progressively smaller shares of empathic linkage.

The Shadow Side of Empathy

Mothers worry, right?

Sometimes mother-guilt nags at you until you doubt every single choice you've made about raising your child. Irrational fears may plague you. You could go teary eyed with remorse over what you packed for the kid's school lunch. When the guilt list seems endless, consider this:

Mom worries can be empathy in disguise. Much of the time, empathic mothers experience worry as a reminder of *connection* to their children.

Remember, you always have the choice to switch empathy off. Or on, big and vivid. However, becoming clear about your choices can be extra confusing when you're prodded by maternal guilt. Society has taught you an enormous vocabulary for problems and pathology... but precious few words to acknowledge empathy. Under the circumstances, it's common to interpret the part of you that connects with your child by using the words you *have* been taught—like worry. "What's wrong with my kid? If I'm thinking about her when she's not here, something must be wrong."

So consider this counterculture idea. Just because your child pulls energy, that doesn't necessarily mean anything is wrong.

Take it from an experienced energy worker. Family members and friends are always bound by CORDS OF ATTACHMENT. Energetically we support each other through our give-and-takes, an energy exchange as natural as a heartbeat. Being an empath, your experiences of energy connection with loved ones will be more vivid than the experiences of non-empaths. Therefore, if worry has been taught to you as the most acceptable vocabulary for interpreting your magnificent energy flow, guess what? You'll think you worry a lot—at least until you're a skilled empath.

So the next time you catch your mind drifting into doom-and-gloom thoughts about your child, question whether you have received an invitation to Join in Spirit with her.

- When the answer is "No", try Coming Home. Remember that little word, *projection*. Find out what is really bothering you.
- When the answer is "Yes," send a hug. You may even feel one return to you, a hug with the different-from-you flavor of your loved one.

Another way to break the worry habit is to use the technique of Questioning. Find a few quiet minutes, close your eyes, and steady yourself with some long slow breaths. Then ask inside, "Why am I having these thoughts about Junior?" Remember to let go of your question, by shifting your awareness onto some Vibe-raising Breaths. In the silence, an answer will come. Guaranteed, it will be more productive than the habit of worry.

Here's the bottom line: You deserve to parent without habitual worry. If your habit is really misinterpreted or misdirected love, you can train your mind to stop grabbing attention in a negative way. When loved ones pop into your awareness, welcome it. Then choose to pay attention to your inner languages, rather than society's languages of worry and guilt. Inwardly are you set up to speak the language of sight or sound or fragrance? Recognize your personal signals as the empathic equivalent of a telephone call.

In the words of my own son at Six, "A telephone is a kind of transportation for your mind." When your empathic phone rings, answer it. Find out if it's really an invitation to Join in Spirit. A call to empathy, even if it first sounds like worry, can be a blessing.

Know Thyself

Whoever hacked those words onto the Temple of Apollo at Delphi had a point. Sure it's a good idea to "Know thyself." And one of the ways to best help our children is to guide them into a recognition of who they are.

Granted there's a certain stage of parenting when advice to help kids gain self-knowledge seems so unneeded, it's ludicrous. Survivors of the Two's know what I mean. Toddlers operate under fascinating rules about what constitutes "mine":

- □ If I want it, it's mine.
- □ If I look at it, it's mine.
- □ If I ever played with it, it's mine.
- □ Even if I have long since put it down, it's mine.
- □ Who cares if you happen to be holding that thing in your hands right now? It's mine, and don't you forget it.

What happens at this stage, of course, is that kids score an A+ on the subject of Recognizing Mine but utterly flunk the subject of Recognizing Yours. Both classes happen to be required subjects, not only during childhood but throughout every semester of life at our one-room schoolhouse, The Learning Planet.

In some ways, Recognizing Mine and Recognizing Yours may grow easier after Two, but ask any recovering co-dependent and you'll learn it ain't necessarily so. Empaths need to become honor students at self-knowledge because they travel so readily. At the drop of a hat, they enter into another's head or heart.

And, golly, "they" probably includes both you and your kid. Therefore, we parents of empaths need to help our children to become very clear about recognizing:

- □ My toys, your toys
- □ My ideas, your ideas
- □ My opinions, your opinions
- □ My needs, your needs
- □ My definition of reality, your definition of reality

Defining Friendship

Why is it so important for empaths to learn about different levels of friendship? In a heartbeat, they nestle into a friend's heart, mind, body, or spirit. Fortunate is the child who, early on, learns to set boundaries with friends, based on the fact that friends fall into different categories:

STRANGERS are people you don't know at all, even if you bump into them on a regular basis, like a certain kid you often pass when walking to school.

ACQUAINTANCES are people with whom you share a common interest. You may spend time together, like teammates at soccer. Different activities throw you together. You share small talk, sometimes "shop" talk, too, about the particular activity you have in common.

BUDDIES are people you actively like and who seem to like you, too. You learn each others' names. You seek out each other's company. With a buddy you start shifting from small talk to big talk, entrusting the matters that matter.

CLOSE FRIENDS trust each other enough to bring their relationship to a level of genuine intimacy. You have favorite topics of conversation. Joking around, you shift into big talk, may even share important secrets.

A BEST FRIEND is the closest type of friend. The name is misleading. Youngsters may have several "best" friends: one at school, one at scouts, one at church, one who lives on the same block. Regardless of how many "best" friends your child has, each one is very close.

Empathic children need to learn how to sort friendships into categories. Because it is so easy for them to get close, quickly and deeply, they assume everyone else does, too. As if!

One way to protect your child from hurt is to teach the art of testing relationships. Don't instantly go from being strangers to close friends. Linger at the level of being acquaintances. Sure, the new kid on the block seems friendly. But is he also honest, loyal, worthy of your trust? While it's fine, even charming, to say to a new neighbor, "Want to be friends?," the first day is too early to offer, as some kids say impetuously, "I'll be your best friend."

Even as adults, some of us haven't learned to test our friendships. How many sad stories have you heard where a woman assumed that sex with a stranger made them best friends? Adults, like children, benefit when we take closeness slowly, one step at a time. While empathic children may stumble as they learn to sort out their relationships, a framework for understanding degrees of friendship will help them to gain a cumulative understanding.

A disgusted historian once wrote: "History is one damned thing after another." Help your child to construct a more meaningful history.

Limits on Television

TV won't give your child a more meaningful history. Instead, it will convince them that violence is an acceptable part of life. Over 3,000 studies on the effects of TV violence show negative consequences for children.[*]

*Carl M. Cannon, "Honey, I warped the kids: the argument for eliminating movie and TV violence." Utne Reader, May-June 1994, No. 63, p. 95

Government hasn't been able to curtail our media to a meaningful degree, nor is that necessarily the job of government. Parents, consider yourselves hired.

Parents of empaths, in particular, need to be wary. We wouldn't tolerate a foul-mouthed human baby-sitter, or a violent one, so why let an electronic baby-sitter talk trash? One hour of prime-time viewing subjects your child to 9 acts of violence, on average; 21 violent acts per hour for cartoons.*

How can that *not* make violence seem acceptable... and TV viewers a little crazed? Real-life violence has escalated such a degree that a six-year-old was recently shot to death by one of her classmates. On a lighter note, I remember back to before my own son was six, and the biggest TV fad was Mighty Morphin Power Rangers. Kids his age were addicted to the violent show and, evidently, some parents weren't far behind. At a neighborhood playground, another little boy started kicking Matt for no apparent reason. "Excuse me, what's going on here?" I asked, trying to break up the fight. "Let's not hit. Let's use words."

The boy's father joined us. "Christopher isn't hitting," Dad explained. "He's just being a Power Ranger."

Even worse than watching the violent kid's shows, what happens when children overhear their parents listening to the news? Research demonstrates that kids believe the news more than other TV programs.

In *Eight Weeks to Optimum Health*, Dr. Andrew Weil recommends going on a "news fast" where one does not read, watch, or listen to any news whatsoever. Just for the sake of strengthening our own immune systems that's vital, he says, because of the anxiety and anger triggered by the news.**

---

* Frances Moore Lappé, *What to Do After You Turn off the TV* (New York:Ballantine Books, 1985), pp. 9-10
** Andrew Weil, M.D., *Eight Weeks to Optimum Health* (New York: Alfred A: Knopf, 1997) p. 78

Consider going on a news fast for the sake of your children, if not for yourself.Empathic children are especially sensitive to the suffering they see. Aside from the horrifying selection of items chosen as "news," what are kids to make of the performances by news anchors? I wonder most about that. How will kids sort through the attractively disguised lack of genuine human emotion? To me, news broadcasters are some of the scariest people on TV.

Sometimes relatives or friends try the sheep-like argument that your child will suffer socially if deprived of trash TV. I know how uncomfortable it can be to fight this kind of pressure. In the thick of the Power Rangers craze, some parents and kids gave me so much grief over my decision to boycott the cute little kickers that I began to doubt myself. "What can I do? How can I keep Matt from becoming a social outcast?" I asked his preschool teacher. Wisely she suggested buying a little paperback book about them to read him. Crazes come and go. A conscientious parent can always find a way to educate children enough to keep them from feeling left out.

Fortunately, empaths will never be left out for long. By their very nature, our consciousness joins with others. When I need an extra ounce of strength to tilt the scales away from "what everyone's doing" and towards my own beliefs, I remember a favorite bumper sticker: "Be counterculture. Raise your own children."

Spiritual Basics

Recently a mother brought her daughter to me for a third eye opening. Keisha had learned a great deal from her mother about religion, she just didn't know about spirituality. When I talked with Keisha, I asked her:

"Which part of you do you think *has* spiritual experiences, anyway?"

She answered, "Your unconscious."

No wonder the poor kid didn't have much spiritual experience. She expected God would come to her in sleep or hit her over the head like a hammer, striking from some mystery place underneath her skull. Sure, grace is amazing. It can appear in any form to thrill your soul. But the Aha! to your soul or mind or heart is transmitted through your consciousness. Being awake in your consciousness, you can count your spiritual blessings, even speed the pace of their coming. Keisha was thrilled to realize that she could bring herself, her everyday consciousness, to meet God halfway.

As a parent, you may wish that this meeting would take place in a particular house of worship. Whatever religious training you provide, it's important to help your empathic child understand that she has a spiritual nature. Unfortunately most kids in America today are taught about having sin, not consciousness.

In her research on Highly Sensitive Persons, Dr. Elaine Aron discovered that virtually every HSP she has encountered is spiritually awake. Similarly, the empaths in my classes have, without exception, been spiritually vibrant.

Whatever your family religion, be it organized or disorganized, you can help your child by developing an appreciation for the spiritual side of life. Even pre-schoolers can be shown that people and things have an inside as well as an outside. When your child has a scrape, for instance, remind him that seeing blood is a shock because you expect it to be inside, not outside. Blood keeps your body healthy, even if you don't usually see it.

Older children can learn in a more sophisticated way that inner life has great importance, though it doesn't show on the outside. To boot a game on your home computer, the programming disk must first be installed. In truth, the part of life that *doesn't* show is the most essential.

With increased mainstreaming of differently-abled children in classrooms, children are reminded that physical problems need not keep a person from being inwardly whole. When kids ask their inevitable questions about people who look different, it can be a great teachable moment. Outer blessings, like physical health, bring only a superficial contentment until they are supported by spiritual joy. Spiritual life, unsupported by material life, is likewise incomplete.

Well, hello! as your teenager might say. What goes up must come down, which is why in the next chapter we'll explore, in detail, the art of balancing spiritual growth with material grounding. In simple ways, children can start paying attention to both.

Why insist on telling children they're spiritual? Isn't that as superfluous as selling ice to Eskimos? No, because kids don't necessarily appreciate how awake they are. Self-knowledge is especially valuable for children who are empaths because they are destined to have inner experiences that are intense, complex, fascinating, profound, and sometimes confusing. Your child needs to appreciate how quiet experiences of *inner* learning are the basis for what shows outwardly.

Self-Authority

As I write these words, the calendar on my desk flags my attention. It's Workman's *The Little Zen Calendar*. Today's saying, by Dogen, reads:

"Do not think that buddhas are other than you."

One of my hardest life lessons has been to claim spiritual self-authority. For decades I made my guru the all-powerful authority over my spiritual life; my highest aspiration was to live enlightenment in his terms. Certainly I didn't consider myself Buddha material. Since then I've learned more about honoring my spiritual truth. And my sweetest victories as a teacher have involved opening students up to their own self-authority. Recently, a student wrote me a thank you note:

"I've studied with many teachers but I was unprepared for the impact your class would have on me. You woke up the knowledge that I could accept my truth in my own terms. After all these years, I'm finally having many deep experiences. I've stopped trying to fit into anyone else's framework."

That's the spirit! Anyone, at any age, can learn to empower herself this way, but especially fortunate is the empathic child who learns about self-authority as a natural part of growing up.

Spiritual self-authority means confidence in recognizing the truth for yourself. You decide what rings a bell rather than waiting until someone else informs you that yes, you're in the presence of certified tinkle. Courage is needed to declare this form of spiritual independence. It's harder than it looks. Worshipping idols (including alleged spiritual authorities) has tempted the multitudes since Biblical times.

Today, within this lifetime, the same Moses-leading-the-tribe-through-the-desert lesson must be learned repeatedly. When spiritual truth speaks to you as a still, small voice within, will you ignore it or listen?

As a parent, you can teach this vital lesson by making a clear distinction between authority and self-authority. Often children are scolded out of their self-authority when their parents confuse teaching them to respect *authority* with teaching them to disrespect *self-authority*. "I'm the grown-up," goes this school of parenting. "I know what's best. Shut up and do what I say."

Kids mix the most profound knowing with perfect inexperience. We need to honor one, guide the other. During one summertime walk with my son, I asked him what he wanted to talk about. Matt answered with full-force five-year-old enthusiasm:

"Mom, I want you to tell me about all the religions in the world. Then I'll tell you how to make them better."

Self-authority showed in his confident curiosity. I nurtured that during the conversation. Of course, I also made it clear that he was not to go up to people and lecture them about religion or anything else. (Particularly his "improvements," I thought.)

Reality squashes our children's excess confidence thoroughly enough. We don't have to smash it for them. Of course there are times for full-force discipline, backed up by authority. When your daughter refuses to clean up her room, sometimes the best tactic is to say: "Yes you will, because I say so."

Afterwards, though, she also may need a tender talk about her feelings. No matter how ridiculous the point of view she needs to express, a wise parent listens with respect. Since your child is an empath, she'll be able to tell when you are really honoring her self-authority. She'll feel it if you are Holding a Space during these discussions, versus just going through the motions of letting her talk.

All children watch what their parents are doing. Empaths, in particular, tune in to the truth of what their parents are *being*. Empaths will learn all that you can teach them about both kinds of authority: the kind that pushes outward, the kind that flows inward.

Skillful parenting doesn't require that you model both kinds of authority equally well. Some of us are more comfortable as one who imposes *authority*, while others are at our best when nurturing *self-authority*. Regardless, each of us is asked go back and forth, doing first one, then the other. Like it or not, you are your kid's both-ways-authority figure.

Late one August afternoon, I saw an exhausted-looking mother unload a mini-van full of kids at the neighborhood pool. The youngest boy, clearly, had been bickering with her. She grabbed him by both shoulders and stood facing him as he whined, "Do you mean that I have to go to my swimming lesson even when I don't want to, just because you're my Mom?"

"You got that right." she snapped back. Did all three of us notice that this was a glorious moment?

What Not to Tell Your Child

Parents have also been overheard trying to comfort their sobbing child by saying, "You're okay." Ugh!

Sure, the parents have a point. The child is not, technically, dead. Scraped knees or hurt feelings can heal. Besides, no matter how great any problem appears, as my sixth grade teacher used to proclaim with obnoxious cheerfulness, "All will be the same a thousand years hence."

However, I'm confident that even in the year 3,000, it still won't be wise for parents to force their kids to feel okay instead of upset. Three cheers to the child who would answer back, under these circumstances: "I'm not okay and if you think so, you're not okay either."

The one thing the statement "You're okay" does well is to cause COGNITIVE DISSONANCE, which means simultaneously believing two things that clash. Even a robot can't operate under two sets of instructions, each of which contradicts the other.

You know better. I know better. So we're wise to ask our children, "What's going on?" or "How can I help?" instead of making the killer pronouncement about okayness. When raising an empath, straightforward communication carries a greater weight of importance. We are charged with the task of teaching our children honesty. Without the habit of searching for truth, however inconvenient, our rising empaths will find it hard to claim the use of their gifts.

The more they know, the deeper they see, the more they will need to sort through experience to find the truth. Hurt, sadness, anger, fear— each needs to be recognized for what it is. When parents repeatedly mis-name or deny emotions, children become confused about their own feelings. Later, when they use gifts like Emotional Touch or Emotional One-ness, their confusion will multiply.

In *Raising a Son*, authors Don and Jeanne Elium warn parents to al-low all feelings, though it's still important to make a distinction between *feeling* the emotion and *acting* on it. When an emotion like anger is not allowed, a child may call it "sadness" for the rest of his life, and suffer accordingly.* Instead you can give your child permission to have all emo-tions, learn their rightful names, and consciously choose whether to act on them.

That's emotional intelligence. All children need this. However, empaths may benefit in ways never envisioned by Daniel Goleman when he wrote his bestseller on *Emotional Intelligence*. Empaths start flying from birth.

---

* Don and Jeanne Elium, *Raising a Son* (Hillsboro, OR: Beyond Words Publishing, 1992) pp. 93-108

Learning the rightful names for feelings protects them from being confused as they travel, helps them when Coming Home to sort out what they've learned.

- Children who specialize in emotional forms of empathy need to personally own the full range of emotional truth. Otherwise the habit of dishonesty (either in the form of lying to others or as self-deception) will confuse them out of knowing what they really do know.
- Physical empaths may need to talk about their bodies a lot. Therefore, you may often have to remind them which aspects of physical functioning are appropriate for conversation, which are not—different from saying, "Shush, that's dirty."
- In addition, your rising physical empath may dwell on aches and pains to a degree that you, personally, find sickening. Nevertheless, it's vital to refrain from labeling physical suffering as hypochondria or self-pity. From an empathic viewpoint, the child is developing physical awareness that, over time, will serve her well.
- Intellectual empaths often complain, "I'm bored." Avoid writing this off with, "You shouldn't be." Sooner or later, your son must learn how to assign himself new projects to examine. Maybe you can guide him to link intellectual travel with another modality, like analytically learning the fine points of a sport (which develops physical awareness) or applying a bit of music theory to a favorite CD (which strengthens the language of Clairaudience).
- Spiritual empaths may shock or embarrass you with intense reactions to people, contradicting your own expectations like crazy. Mr. Day, that kindly old crossing guard, is scary? Mrs. Knight, your neighbor across the street with the immaculate home and the nicest manners, is aurically angry all the time? Don't scold your son for what he notices. It's probably true, if

bothersome. Good, polite manners must still be taught in greet-
ing these people, but not because "That's ridiculous. There's
nothing wrong with Mr. Day." or "You're wrong about Mrs.
Knight. She has a heart of gold."

▫ Keep in mind that young empaths sometimes tell you most
about their perceptions of evil. That's because they expect the
world to be good. Don't over-react, which would teach them
either fear or undue fascination with wickedness. Instead, listen to your daughter's insights and move on. Later encourage
conversation about the beautiful things she sees spiritually, because any child who can see a blacked-out third eye can also
see one that shimmers with gold.

Honesty

Who will be your child's most influential model of honesty? You, of course.
No matter how wealthy you may be, you can't hire servants to do this job
for you... any more than you can pay them to take on your labor pains.

Honesty is a complicated business. Perfectionist empaths (now that's a
really scary combination of attributes!) are well aware that total truthfulness is hard to achieve. In the jury box, witnesses swear to tell the truth,
the whole truth, and nothing but the truth. Courtroom situations aside,
who has time to ramble like that? It's sound-biting off more than most
people can chew.

Fortunately it requires neither unlimited time, heroic talent, nor a tow-
ering intellect to model honesty for your child. Although you could drive
yourself crazy by demanding an absolute, idealized consistency, there's an
easier way. Take it one situation at a time. In your heart of hearts, you
know when you're doing wrong. So when that Jiminy Cricket voice within
starts to chirp, listen and take action.

As parents, we need to let our kids know about some of the conversations we have with ourselves. "Hold on," you may hear yourself say on

occasion. "What I just said was convenient, but it wasn't completely true. What I really meant to say was...."

As for making mistakes around your child, who can avoid that forever? At least you can show your commitment to making things right afterwards. "Never go to bed angry," my mother advised me on my wedding day, a good policy for handling any mistake. What matters most is that, however long it takes, you do your level best to make things right.

One of the toughest ways to model honesty, perhaps, is to let your empathic child know of your efforts to correct a long-standing mistake. One dinnertime, I told my family how, at age 16, I had stolen a stylish, pastel blue sweater from a Bloomingdale's department store. This day, decades later, I finally decided to get it off my chest. So I had gone to the nearest Bloomingdale's to turn myself in.

Making restitution, Matt heard, was more awkward than I'd expected. The staff was unprepared for my offer to pay for the sweater plus interest, and I had to repeat my confession to several salespeople before resolving matters with the security guard. Even though we spoke to each other over the telephone, I felt the soles of my feet tingle with fear as though I was standing on a high bridge that shook in the wind. Part of me wondered if, after all those years, I might be taken to jail. Instead, it turned out, all I had to do was write out a check for restitution.

Leaving the store, I still shook with the gravity of having shoplifted and, after all these years, being caught. Although I had expected to feel noble, mostly I felt lousy. Yet relief was there, too—in my feelings and in my gut.

Back at the dinner table, both my son and husband listened with their typical powerful empathy circuits connected. Matt, in particular, listened solemnly to every part of the story, asked questions, and felt every nuance.

Even though the story reflected badly on me, I'm glad I'd told him. When you take action around an empathic child, he'll grow from the truth. You'd want to protect him from too harsh or histrionic a journey. But showing him an occasional rocky stretch of road will clear the way for his empowering honesty.

Teaching the ABC's of Empathy

When you're ready to help your child make the transition from natural empath to skilled empath, you can start teaching techniques from this book. Here is the sequence I recommend:

I. Teach Coming Home

For the sake of security, you teach your child her street address and phone number, don't you? Young empaths gain security from becoming consciously aware that who they are energetically represents another kind of home.

Before the teenage years, children learn best in a physical way, so their version of Coming Home may involve activities like self-massage, yoga scaled down to kid size, or simply admiring themselves in a mirror.

You can also invite them to look at their auras in the mirror or teach them the Aura Bounce and Rub. Children enjoy giving their own auras a love pat.

After the age of ten, kids are ready to close their eyes and start to inwardly notice what's going on with them. It's easy to teach them the technique for Coming Home. Sit next to your child, not touching. Talk your child through the steps. After you child has the hang of this, Coming Home together can be a way to keep you close. Sit together. Come Home at the same time. Afterwards take turns discussing what you noticed.

2. Hold a Space—or Not

You know the secret by now: Empaths don't need to learn how to do this so much as learn how to *not* do it.

Teach your child that Holding a Space is optional. Bullies, for instance, don't deserve your child's attention. Ignoring them isn't just smart behavior; it's good advice for the sake of your child's empathic gifts. Entanglement with a bully is confusing and draining. As James Redfield noted in *The Celestine Prophecy*, some confused souls get their jollies by arousing anger in others, then feeding off it. Alert your child to this dynamic.

Depending on the religious upbringing you have chosen for your child, you also may wish to explain how to Hold a Space for a spiritual teacher, like Jesus or the Buddha. Invite your child to pull up an extra chair in the same room with you. Together, imagine the Buddha is sitting right there. You can have a pretend conversation, silently or out loud.

Helene, who is an adult, did a technique like this as a spiritual exercise in the religion of Eckankar. Every morning for a month, she called on the Eck master Wah Z, pulled up a chair for him and invited him to join her in contemplation.

But one day, Helene was especially rushed. All she could spare was ten minutes, and she clean forgot about setting out the extra chair for Wah Z. Suddenly she heard his voice, clear as a bell:

"What about my chair?"

In the Jewish tradition, Passover is one of the most sacred and beautiful ceremonies. It includes setting a place at the table for the prophet Elijah. At a point in the ritual, a door is opened so that he may enter.

Any religious tradition that honors angels or masters will be strengthened when you teach your child to Hold a Space for someone sacred. There's a wonderful term for this, practicing the presence of God. Empathic children instinctively know how.

3. Join in Spirit

Your empathic child has a knack for this, too. So why not teach the fundamentals at an early age? Explain that sometimes he will have a thought about someone who could use his help. An image could come to mind or a feeling, a smell, or simply a name. Any of this amounts to what is called "a vision."

A VISION is an experience of a spiritual nature that is different from what has been going on previously. By analogy, when you watch TV sometimes a little news bulletin flashes across the screen. "We interrupt this regular broadcast for... whatever." Inner visions arise just as suddenly.

Unfortunately, most of these visions are ignored—and for a ridiculously simple reason. As you know from our previous discussion of personal inner language, most people are not primarily seers. They're touchers, feelers, listeners, and so forth. As you develop a sense of your child's strongest inner languages, guide your child to value her experiences of deeper touch, inside feelings, and sound within sound. These insights really do count as spiritual experience.

And because I believe in opening up spiritual language to everyone, rather than the current bias that favors clairvoyants, I recommend that you teach your child not to call these experiences "visions" at all. SPIRITUAL MESSAGES is a more useful term.

Teach your child that some spiritual messages come as an answer to prayer. Others come seemingly out of the blue, floating into our lives as a kind of grace. Yet others come in the form of a spiritual invitation because, right at that instant, a certain person needs us.

When this happens, your child may choose to take a few minutes to feel connected in a loving way with the person who has popped into his mind. In order to be invited to Join in Spirit with someone, he need not know that person well. It could be just an acquaintance. Your child needs to know that it is perfectly okay to decline any of these invitations, regardless of how well he knows the person. If he says no, that person's spirit will go on to find help elsewhere. When sharing your love feels right, however, you'll end up with the glow that comes from performing spiritual service.

Here's a story from one of my students to illustrate Joining in Spirit. Your child may like the story because it includes... pizza.

Vanessa is a grown-up who hated pizza. It didn't usually agree with her—the same with her brother, Mark and his wife, Donna. Nevertheless, one dinner time Vanessa suddenly got a terrible craving for pizza. Mark did, too. So the three of them decided to go to the nearest pizza parlor. The cashier by the cash register stared at Vanessa as though she knew her.

Despite being a complete stranger, the cashier walked over to Vanessa midway through the meal, and without saying so much as a "Hello" beforehand, blurted out:

"Tomorrow I'm going to the hospital for an operation. I'm very scared."

As they talked, it turned out that Vanessa had recently recovered from the very same kind of operation.

"The operation isn't dangerous," advised Vanessa. "And you'll feel much better after you've recovered. Just give yourself a good long time, six weeks or so, to recuperate."

The woman from the pizza chain left their table, relief written all over her face. She went back to her counter to work.

Back at Vanessa's table, Mark and Donna discussed this remarkable coincidence. "I'm worried about her," said Donna. "Do you suppose she has anyone to look after her?"

"Don't worry," Vanessa said. "I'm sure she does." She stopped thinking about the incident.

Next morning, Vanessa was getting ready to do her usual prayers. The face of the pizza woman flashed into her heart. Vanessa realized it was an invitation to Join in Spirit. The invitation was repeated, and accepted, for several days in a row. It gave Vanessa a good feeling. She knew she was being of service.

4. Honor Personal Boundaries

Just as your child may need reminding to tie his shoe laces, from time to time, he may need an occasional prodding to set personal boundaries. Teach him to affirm boundaries for himself, as needed: "I have strong, healthy personal boundaries." And when you listen to his stories about things that upset him, make sure he learns objectivity about other people's boundaries.

For instance, when he's caught in an argument with a friend, he needs to use ordinary social skills. On one hand, he might need to ask the other kid, "What's wrong?" On the other hand, he might need to ask himself,

"Who owns this problem?" These are basic skills about Emotional Intelligence that non-empaths need to learn, too.

Although it can be tempting to over-use empathy in an attempt to figure out what someone else is really thinking, it's more straightforward to simply ask. This is a matter of honoring everyone's personal boundaries.

5. Reject Psychic Coercion

Psychic coercion is a more esoteric concept than personal boundaries. It may be too confusing to explain before your child is 10 or older. When you feel your child can handle it, explain the basics. It's okay for people to wish we were a certain way, either in looks or behavior or beliefs. But on The Learning Planet, each of us must choose for ourself. Nobody has the right to expect your child to be anything he doesn't want to be.

Rules are different. Parents, teachers, and other authority figures have rules about behavior. Parents' rules must be honored while the child lives under your roof. But that's not the same as allowing someone to push on you by repeatedly sending out messages about what you should like or dislike.

For instance, Joe was given accordion lessons as a boy. His parents were proud of his playing. He gave command performances at all family events. When Joe became a teenager, however, he decided enough was enough and refused to play any more.

Joe's father was furious. He commanded Joe to keep playing. When that didn't work, Joe's father stopped talking to him unless he would agree to play the accordion. The man expected his son to play on demand. He didn't understand that Joe had the right to be different. The battle of wills went on for three years until, finally, Joe left home after his high school graduation.

Yes, as psychic coercion goes, this example is pretty extreme. In a less dramatic case, Joe's father might have acted coercive by nagging or secretly praying that Joe would change his mind. Either way, this unfair "shoulding" would have amounted to psychic coercion.

Insisting that Joe finish high school, by contrast, would *not* have been psychic coercion. Parents have the obligation to set standards. Certain behaviors can reasonably be required while others are merely desirable. Playing the accordion does not fall into the category of required filial duty.

Likewise it is coercive for friends or relatives to demand that your child pursue a particular sport, weigh a particular weight, have a particular sexual orientation, or believe in a particular religion.

Ironically, psychic coercion in the name of religion, or virtue, is one of the most common evils of life on earth. On this Learning Planet, nobody has the right to interfere with an individual's free will, aside from parental responsibility or the risk of significant harm (e.g., lawbreaking).

How can you teach your child to escape the spiritual confusion caused by psychic coercion? Rather than resisting it, your child can learn to consider it irrelevant. When she feels herself being pressured, she can remind herself that she knows her own mind. Provided that she doesn't break reasonable rules of behavior, provided that she expects to face the consequences of all her actions, whatever your daughter does is her business. Insistence on her right to personal boundaries and free will sends psychic coercion right back where it belongs, to the sender.

Empathy, of course, is the precise opposite of psychic coercion. When someone identifies with you, projects onto you, pushes ideas or feelings on you, that is coercion. By contrast, empathy means letting someone be, then coming along for the ride.

Connect to Protect

As a parent, you may be interested in research findings about preventing emotional distress in children reported in the Journal of the American

Medical Association.* What is the greatest deterrent to high-risk behavior by teenagers (i.e., drugs, alcohol, early sex, and cigarettes)? The answer, according to a $25 million federal study, is "feeling loved, understood, and paid attention to by parents."

According to this research, feeling *connected* to parents was five times as important as spending time with them. It was six times as important as sharing activities with them.

Although this study did not make a distinction between empaths and non-empaths, which type of child do you think is more likely to notice the absence of genuine connection? Love, understanding, and attention can be given on a superficial level. Or we parents can connect to the fullest — neither every minute of every day nor with the perfection of a saint— but coming as close as we can.

Am I the only parent to wish I didn't have my share of human failings? The worst part is, I didn't notice most of these imperfections until I felt my innocent little child observing them. Honestly, the one consolation in having a shadow self is that you can turn your back on it!

There I'd be at the lunch table with my comfortable non-company manners, shifting the fork nonstop from mouth to plate, in flagrant disregard of all I'd read about how a civilized person was supposed to put the fork down between bites, and I felt Matt watching. Serve me right if he'd start to eat just like me!

Once he saw me start a petty fight with a friend. It wasn't that Matt was judging me, he simply noticed everything. So it couldn't escape him that this particular argument was clearly my fault. Considering that my son had started life so emotionally whole, I hated for him to see me stressed out and crabby. He might catch it like measles.

Since learning about the AMA study, I still reserve the right to *not* cozy up to my kid at the times when even *I* can't stand myself. Nonetheless I hear an encouraging message in the research: *Your child will prosper if you'll just have the humility to come as you are.*

* Michael D. Resnick et al., "Protecting Adolescents from Harm," Journal of the American Medical Association, September 10, 1997, pp. 823-832

What a hopeful thought that your kid would even want you! Of course, when she sprays you with spit-up or scowls at you like a sulky four-year-old terrorist, you still love her. Every once in a while, amazingly, you re-realize that your kid still loves you and needs you, no matter what. Connecting the best you can could be good for you both.

Like your willingness to connect with your child, all the ideas in this chapter can't be instantly set into motion once and for all. The need for patience reminds me of a conversation Matt had at Six with his grandmother. "So you're learning to spell," she said. "Tell me, can you spell the word "of."

Matt thought for a long time. "F-o-o" he answered.

"That's interesting" Grandma said. "But it's not the usual spelling. People usually spell it "o-f."

"Grandma," Matt said, "It's so weird. I can read and write. I just can't spell."

Parenting an empath isn't an open-and-shut case, any more than spelling. You keep at it and the rewards keep coming. Would you have it any other way?

Personal Notes

My biggest Aha!s about parenting from this chapter:

Parents whom I would like to tell things I have learned about raising an empathic child:

Other lifestyle Aha!s that are lively for me now, as I grow into my adult identity of being an Empath:

A milestone in my personal appreciation of spiritual self-authority:

So many empathic children grow up without an adult to mentor them. If I were to volunteer to mentor a child, who would it be?

Spiritual exercise: If I were to move back in time, remembering myself at a vulnerable age, what advice would my Inner Wise Adult give me about becoming an Empath?

13. Grounding

To understand grounding, consider what happened to Alice's size in *Alice in Wonderland*. Thanks to an assortment of magical substances (Remember "Eat me" and "Drink me"?) she grew bigger or smaller, quite beyond her control, until she mastered the art of changing sizes intentionally. Outside Wonderland, we empaths need to master something comparable. We, too, grow bigger and smaller... with alarming frequency. Only, for us, these size changes aren't necessarily physical.

In this chapter, you'll gain a practical understanding of the metaphysical ways that empaths change sizes. Spiritual expansion and grounding are the technical terms for it. And very inclusive terms they are. That fight with your best friend, that nasty firing from your job, those 20 new pounds on the scale—experiences that previously may have seemed to be just "bad things happening to good people"— often are manifestations of grounding. It's vital to recognize these experiences for what they are, cycles of spiritual expansion.

All people, but empaths especially, need to understand how this works. We empaths tend to be so good at reaching for the skies but, alas, so helpless when we fall back down. We're thrilled to Fly in Spirit but resentful that, later, we must deal with gravity. As if earth's grounding principle were as flimsy as a dandelion gone to seed, so we could just make a wish and blow it away!

Luckily we can do the next best thing. We can apply our free will to the process that will, inevitably, take place. Either we can actively choose our favorites or we can settle for what most people do in life: passively wait for the other shoe to drop. To be empowered by empathy, your training won't be complete until you understand the cycle of spiritual expansion, grounding, and spiritual integration. Probably you prefer expansion, so let's start our investigation there.

Spiritual Expansion

One side of life's spiritual equation involves getting bigger. Empaths are really good at getting bigger in consciousness. In fact, any technique for empathic travel, even the simplest act of Holding a Space, brings SPIRITUAL EXPANSION. That means having your consciousness grow and your vibrations move faster. Think back to peak experiences where you went, "Wow, this is bliss!" If you could, you'd have stayed in that transcendent space for years. You were more awake then, more aware of beauty, of wonder, of love, of meaning, of angels, or of God. If you're like most empaths, moments like these are what keep you going in life.

What causes spiritual expansion, anyway? Empathic travel, prayer, meditation, contemplation, fasting, and mindful service can all start it. Wearing white clothes, only white, every day, will create a certain degree of spiritual expansion. Even doing nothing at all can bring expansion sometimes... when spiritual growth comes as a kind of amazing grace.

Ever had a time when you felt so out of sorts, all you could do was crawl into bed and go through "it"—whatever "it" was? Neither asleep, awake, or dreaming, you'd just lie there and buzz. For all you knew, you had insomnia or a two-hour flu. Well, guess what? You were being treated to an extreme form of spiritual expansion. No kidding? Sure, and despite the inconvenience, if you'd only known at the time what was happening, you'd have been jubilant, for all the while God was drawing you one step closer.

Spiritual expansion comes in other varieties, too. For instance:

▫ Sometimes you'll receive a big blast of spiritual energy, what Rev. Ann Makever Myer, author of *Being a Christ*, calls a LOVE FEEDING from spirit, which permanently opens you up to a more refined *quality* of awareness, leading to more Celestial Perception.

▫ Or it could be a POWER FEEDING from spirit, where your subtle energy circuits are being rewired so you can bring through a larger *quantity* of energy and spiritual awareness.

▫ Sometimes you may have a rush of KUNDALINI energy. That's life force energy, related to mystical experiences, sex, and whooshes of electricity that go up your spine. Whether or not you've consciously asked for more kundalini to flow through you, having more of it enables your spirit to come more fully into your body, according to Mary Ellen Flora, author of *Kundalini Energy*. In her teaching she emphasizes that too much kundalini, too fast, can create discomfort; you always have the right to just say no, commanding this powerful force within either to move more gently or to switch off entirely.

▫ HOT FLASHES come under the category of kundalini experience. They're not just a nuisance—menopausal women have the option of growing into a higher spiritual awareness. Hot flashes may be the most widespread, and under-rated, forms of spiritual expansion.

When you're very fortunate, you'll receive another form of spiritual expansion, a PEAK EXPERIENCE, moments of golden awareness where your consciousness expands to its fullest. Abraham Maslow, the founder of humanistic psychology, has found that all self-actualized people have had peak experiences.* One of these will alter your reality forever. And even if it clocks in at two minutes, you'll count that time among life's ultimate treasures, akin to the seven wonders of the physical world.

Yet all forms of spiritual expansion, even the small and undramatic variety, change us forever. We empaths live for the thrill of heightened consciousness. And if we can't order on demand the big, whack-my-head-open-and-pour-ecstasy-into-every-fiber-of-my-being ones, we'll go for what we can get, such as the subtler thrills of Flying in Spirit.

In our enthusiasm, we're apt to forget the price. *Every expansion brings the need for the opposite kind of experience.* It's grounding, the second side of life's equation.

Grounding Required

GROUNDING shrinks us back down to size. The spiritual equivalent of gravity, it reminds us that our contract as humans is to grow spiritually while here on earth.

Physically, our bodies are closer to mud than to light. Subtler (auric) forms of our bodies notwithstanding, earth's physical laws of nature apply to us as long as we live in human bodies. Since grounding's inevitable, the best we can do is to actively choose forms of grounding that are voluntary and relatively enjoyable; otherwise we'll be clobbered by the more negative varieties.

Most people never exercise their choice about grounding, any more than they travel to Wonderland and receive a free bottle of DRINK ME. It's important to know that your opportunity to exercise free will about grounding is huge. A skilled empath's lifestyle includes making informed choices. When you consider your options, you'll be grateful you have free will. Some of the items far down the list are awful.

---

* In fact, having a peak experience became one of Maslow's criteria for self-actualization, as described in *Toward a Psychology of Being,* John Wiley & Sons, 1968, 1999. See the chapter on "Peak-Experiences as Acute Identity Experiences." pp. 115-125

Bad things still will happen sometimes—due to karma and maya, among other factors (see Glossary)—but even then, have perspective! Heavy life experiences have value in the long run because of another inescapable spiritual principle. Yo-yo experiences aren't restricted to diets. Every human being, without exception, yo-yo's between expansion and grounding, up and down, again and again. And the result is SPIRITUAL INTEGRATION.

When you think about it, you've been reclaiming closeness to God ever since you squeezed your way into a place that was too small for you (a.k.a. birth). First you become inwardly big. Then you shrink back down, resting before the next Hegelian cycle of expansion-grounding-integration. For instance, let's say that:

- You fall in love.
- The love affair ends with a rip roaring argument.

From the perspective of spiritual integration, your heartbreaking relationship wasn't a waste. It was, in fact, a blessing. First you expanded through your emotions, then you had a chance to collect yourself in solitude. Eventually, bridging these two extremes will help you to love more deeply—small comfort though that may be during the interim, when you're alone and miserable.

Grounding is necessary. It's unavoidable, too. Regular spiritual practice will speed up our spiritual cycles, not eliminate them. Sooner or later, we're going to receive the slings and arrows of outrageous fortune. And we'll hate them. But they will integrate us.

Everyone loves the journey out: chocolates and romances; movies that enrapture you while tears of healing drip down your face; concerts that make your whole body tingle; math classes where you break through to new realms of understanding; the exquisite, never-recaptured meditation that sets a new standard for your spiritual life. Any one of these goodies will require subsequent grounding. Will you choose to yo-yo with gusto? Or will you blissfully forget there is a price to pay... until you come to the end of your twine?

A Personal Tale of Grounding

Until the age of 40, I fought being on this planet as though it were a prison. Sure, I'd go through the motions of everyday life. But all I valued was the expansion part. I wanted wings but no roots.

As a college student, my quest for spirituality led me to take one LSD trip. I yearned for the cosmic kind of experience I had read about in Aldous Huxley's *The Doors of Perception*. But during my trip, God didn't show up in full splendor according to my specifications. Instead, I found myself at the dinner table with a friend, eating a frustratingly ordinary green pepper. By my standards, very little was happening. Silently I implored God to make himself known.

A cat walked into the room as if on cue.

"All I get is this stupid cat? How repulsive." I thought, feeling horribly cheated. Deep within, however, another thought sounded. "Why do you keep waiting for God to step out of creation to show himself to you? All creation is full of God, even that cat."

Thank Cat, I got the message. I turned to meditation and a drug-free lifestyle. Some peak experiences came my way, and still, for decades, that was all I valued.

Like many spiritually minded people, Quaker, Jewish, Hindu, Presbyterian, Episcopalian, or New Age (and I explored each to some degree), my aura was in pretty good shape... but only from the waist up. The first three chakras were as closed off as they could be, considering that I was still, technically, alive. Denial of being grounded showed in my walk, my voice, everything about me—obvious to anyone with the sense to notice.

Caught up in spiritual expansion with no taste for grounding, I was living only half a life. And having scant respect for material life, life showered me appropriately with *scarcings* (the kind of blessing appropriate to a recluse). Contemptuous of worldly success, I earned just enough money to get by and had few friends, zero sex life, and no sense of connection with society at large. At one point, all my earthly possessions fit into five cardboard boxes. At least that came in handy for moving from one apartment to the next, which I did often.

By the time I turned 40, I was ready to start grounding. Miraculously someone I hardly knew brought me a birthday present, a tee-shirt with a picture of Planet Earth and the words, "I'm not just a tourist, I live here." Something clicked. As a result, my life improved at least 200 percent.

Empathy works better—correction, all of life works better—when we are completely willing to be who we are. I discovered that living in my physical form with great gusto wouldn't make my soul shrink... just the opposite.

By now, I have learned to pay my dues for spiritual expansion. I choose the healthiest forms of grounding possible. Some grounding experiences still come beyond my control, but afterwards I pick myself up again, remembering _life is either bliss or lessons._

When I come to a place of peace between growth cycles, I give thanks for having more clarity and love, plus clearer empathy. Incidentally, I'm pleased to report, the lower half of my body is now aurically among the living.

Many spiritual seekers, like me before I turned 40, assume that all we need do is cram ourselves full of spiritual light, which is tantamount to assuming that a balanced diet can be derived from eating nothing but candy. We figure all the other stuff will work out naturally if we stay spiritually pure, and then life will be perfect....

And life _is_ perfect, just not in that way. A telling symbol of the human need for grounding is the chakra known as the third eye. Commonly it's understood to be only about spiritual expansion, yet it also reveals one's willingness to see life on earth as it is. Refusal to put one's feet on the ground compromises third eye functioning, delaying spiritual progress. Thus, even for the purpose of having the most fabulous spiritual life imaginable, each of us needs to integrate spiritual expansion. Especially empaths—who are so predisposed to spiritual expansion that we do it as automatically as breathing. Spiritually committed to rapid inner growth, we may as well learn to love grounding, too.

The Grounding Cord

Everyday habits of grounding are a good place to start. Some fortunate empaths have (or develop) a spontaneous knack for connecting up with life at the level of their bodies and the environment. That helps them integrate spiritual awareness relatively easily.

Most of us, however, need an extra push in the direction of objective reality. This technique helps. I've adapted it from a technique in *Kundalini Energy* by Mary Ellen Flora.

1. *Sit in a chair* so that your feet touch the floor and your back is straight.
2. *Feel the energy in your body.* Also feel energy around your body but, for now, let yourself be more interested in the physical part.
3. *Notice the boundary around your physical body.* There's a name for it: skin. You may feel that your energy extends outside of your skin as well as inside it. For now, though, pay attention only to the energy within your skin. This is what matters for grounding. (Exception: If you notice light coming out of your third eye, don't try to switch that off. It's your spiritual sight, after all. When your third eye is open, you can be awake in that light along with any other activity.)
4. Bring attention to the base of your spine. *Draw out an imaginary cord to the center of the earth.* Make it thick and dark. Feel how this GROUNDING CORD attaches you to Mother Earth.
5. *Intensify your experience of the Grounding Cord:* Imagine a funnel of white light pouring in through the top of your head (or don't imagine it but tune in on the fact that this is already happening). Breathe *in* and draw that light through your body. Breathe *out* and send your leftover energy down through the Grounding Cord. Continue until you feel very comfortable with the presence of the Cord.
6. *Open your eyes and walk around for a few minutes, feeling the Cord.* Then sit down again.

7. Now focus just on the area at the base of your spine plus the Grounding Cord. *Take seven Grounding Breaths into the Cord.* Each breath pumps rapid bursts of energy down your Cord into the earth.

8. When you feel ready, open your eyes. Notice that, any time you think of it, you can become aware of the Cord *while your eyes are open.* It's like Coming Home, which you can also do with your eyes open. From now on, several times a day, do the technique for Coming Home while your eyes are open. Include your Grounding Cord as part of your picture of who you are.

The Grounding Cord—Q&A

Q: PEOPLE HAVE ALWAYS CALLED ME SPACED OUT. COULD I BE IMMUNE TO GROUNDING?

A: Nobody can afford to be immune, not if you want a balanced life. When you feel spaced out or oversubjective, take a break for grounding. By integrating your spirituality in this way, you'll feel more comfortable inside your skin. Others will feel more comfortable with you, too.

Q: JUST HOW MUCH GROUNDING WOULD YOU SAY IS ENOUGH?

A: Balance is the goal. All of us need different things at different times, and you're the best one to know what you need.

Being an empath, you have a built-in gift for expanding. Most of the empaths I've met do not have the opposite gift. (Non-empaths do, usually.) Probably you'd do well to spend far more of your disposable time on grounding than on expansion. I do. Currently I balance 30 minutes of spiritual exercise with a whole day's activities. In addition, I stay aware of my Grounding Cord off and on all day. Plus I spend several hours on activities that are grounding—the healthiest ones I can choose.

Q: HOLD ON. I'VE ALWAYS HEARD OF GROUNDING REFERRED TO AS A GOOD THING. COULD THERE BE UNHEALTHY WAYS OF GROUNDING?

A: You bet. Unpleasant ways, too. Here comes the complete list.

22 Ways to Ground

Some the following grounding methods are healthy, others not. Some may be acceptable to you but unavailable. At least the list is long enough so that even if you limit yourself to what seems appealing, you'll still have plenty of choices. As you'll notice, the list starts with fun stuff, then works its way down. Take your pick.

I. Sex

Of all the ways to put yourself in your body, this has to be the most fun. As with the advertised merits of various cars, however, your actual mileage may vary. Sex turns up the amount of energy running through you. Imbalances, therefore, become more extreme. It's vital to find a partner with whom you can share respect and tenderness. Sex that you *don't* wholeheartedly enjoy won't ground you well.

2. Aerobic Exercise

Although you can't cuddle up to a Stairmaster it, too, can be good for sweat and heavy breathing. Vigorous exercise takes us out of the ozone and into our bodies. And for those who approach exercise more as a duty than a desire, an added attraction is that it feels so good when it's over.

3. Sleep

Sleep disorder experts will tell you that most Americans don't sleep nearly enough. How about you? Do you consider sleep a waste of time? When we don't rest enough, we'll spend more of our waking hours half asleep. How cheering, then, that sleep can be considered an act of grounding—not that sleep integrates every aspect of spiritual growth but, rather, that some types of integration require nothing less than the full-body, rumpled, uncontrolled surrender of sleep. If you go through a period where you need more sleep than usual, sure you might want to check with a doctor. But sometimes no medical reason turns up. In that case, count your blessing and name it "grounding."

4. Hiking

Walking outdoors has a wonderful grounding effect. After 20 minutes, you'll feel more alive in your body, more connected to nature. Walk in the woods, at the beach or the mountains. Each has its own special excellence for grounding.

5. Massage

Receiving is more fun than giving but, either way, massage will put you in your body. During times when your budget won't permit a weekly session, see if you can set up trades with a friend and be blessed by both ends of the process. Another possibility is to contact the nearest massage school to learn if volunteer subjects are needed by students. They must practice on many warm bodies to become licensed; *someone* needs to be on the receiving end of all those free massages.

Should all else fail, massage yourself. Foot Reflexology is especially good, since it enables you to access nerve endings to your back and other hard-to-reach places. Other possibilities include buying a massage machine (not necessarily expensive) or try stuffing a couple of tennis balls into a sock, throwing this contraption on the floor, then strategically placing your body over it until the balls push against tender parts of your back. Rocking back and forth feels great.

6. Stretching

Cats, the most spiritually expanded of household pets, also are the biggest stretchers. Hmm, why might that be?

Try stretching first thing in the morning, even before you even get out of bed. Stretch mid-day and night. Stretch after meals. Stretch before meals—could it be a deterrent to eating junk food? Stretch at home; stretch (your shoulders at least) while driving in traffic; stretch at work. Stretch secretly if you must. Wiggle your toes or practice Kegel exercises.

Go ahead, send a rush of electricity through your body. Stretching is one of life simplest pleasures, and it also happens to be a quick and easy way to ground.

Incidentally, stretching also keeps your muscles flexible which, in turn, helps keep your bones in alignment. According to chiropractor, Marilyn Holbeck, "Stretching is so important, I'd estimate that 80% of the people who come to see me wouldn't have to if they would only stretch every day." And all you need do, she says, is work major muscle groups in different directions, holding each stretch for a few seconds.

7. Socially Unmentionable Acts of Grounding

Backstage at Conan O'Brien's TV show, the writers have a ritual known as "The Farting Wolf." According to *Entertainment Tonight,* "Whenever one of the writers has to pass gas, he... dons a flimsy paper wolf mask, climbs onto a coffee table, arches his back, locks eyes with one of the other staffers, then lets one rip."

Maybe you don't want to go that far in the cause of grounding but, to put it in the more delicate language of Ayurvedic physicians, *don't suppress physical urges.* What happens, they say, when you habitually postpone the urge to pass wind, cough, and so forth, is that you create a subtle imbalance throughout your mind-body system.

Think about it. When you deny the urge, you're detaching from your physical needs—not the best thing to do if you want to become more in touch with your body. So one way to promote grounding is to visit the restroom when needed, and otherwise find discreet ways to sneeze, scratch where it itches, etc. (Admittedly, giving yourself permission to belch may not be the very first thing you associate with the lofty task of becoming a skilled empath.)

8. Sitting or Standing

Are these the most thrilling activities you can imagine? Hope not. Still, you're likely to enjoy them more than most of the next items on this list. Of course, the sitting or standing referred to here should be done smack dab on the earth.

Cement pavement won't do as much good, nor will a lawn chair, even in the most beautiful of gardens. Something powerful happens when you make direct contact with the earth. Bare feet work best. And whereas any soil or lawn will ground you beautifully, mud—glorious mud—reigns supreme.

9. Pregnancy

Overpopulation notwithstanding, pregnancy is a fine (if extreme and temporary) solution to the problem of insufficient grounding. Morning sickness and childbirth may make you aware of your body in ways too disgusting to dwell on. But rejoice. The sum total is grounding galore. Taking care of an infant is, similarly, about as down-to-earth as this life gets.... It's also rewarding, of course, and will cause of some of the greatest expansion experiences of your life, which are sure to be balanced with plenty of grounding.

10. Pets

Petting an animal grounds you. So does supplying its food, disposing of its wastes, and all the other responsibilities of pet ownership. Giving baths to a reluctant critter, like a dog, earns you especially high marks, grounding-wise. If you and your dog should have a close encounter of the skunk kind, I hope you'll console yourself with grounding thoughts as you pour on yet one more bottle of tomato juice.

II. Cleaning

When it comes to grounding there's no place like home—at least if your job is cleaning it. Vacuuming, laundry, and the rest are perfect opportunities to ground, assuming that you can stay awake. Cleaning forces you to pay close attention to your immediate environment.

Beth is an author and speaker of international renown. Whenever she does an interview on national TV, she makes a point of scrubbing the kitchen floor as soon as she gets home. As she told me, "I've learned from experience that I need to do something like this. Otherwise life finds another way to knock me down a peg or two. These interviews make you feel so big, it can't last."

She's right on both counts. Media interviews can make your aura grow huge, especially if your intent is to help people. Even a taped interview causes you to Hold a Space for the audience. When that audience numbers in the millions, your energy field whooshes outwards in full auric bloom.

And yes, housecleaning does put us in place, along with the rest of the furniture.

12. Getting Yourself into Hot Water

Emergency grounding alert! You feel yourself expanding way beyond your comfort zone. It's the middle of the night and none of the higher items on this grounding list appeal to you. Then try this first aid tip for quick grounding. Immerse your feet into a bathtub or bucket with the hottest water you can stand. After three minutes, dunk your feet into ice cold water. After another three minutes, go back to hot.

Alternate hot and cold dunks until you calm down. To finish, towel dry your feet and drink some water. Welcome back!

13. Weather Reports

Once a day, try a bold experiment for a person in this day and age. Go directly outside and do your own weather report. Yes, you can be your own best meteorologist.

Did you know that the weather experts on TV literally show you an illusion? The map of swirling weather patterns they point to is actually a blank prop with no patterns on it at all. The visuals are added separately, one of the minor miracles of TV technology—not to mention a tribute to the coordination of the performer.

To me, this illusion symbolizes the phoniness of weather as explained by an official pundit, however charming. Why not dunk yourself in the weather all by yourself? Smell the incoming snow. Listen for thunder or stillness. Gauge the day's humidity, splat!, on your skin. Each time you do research and, especially, when you manage to drench yourself in rain, know that you are getting gorgeously grounded.

14. Gardening

A wise gardener has observed that gardening brings perspective about everything in life—except gardening.

Obsessive or not, gardening is great for grounding. The reason is practical. All grounding techniques work best if they're done with conscious awareness of being physical. With gardening, you can't get away with absent-mindedness. An over-watered plant screams at you from its newly created bog. Or think of what happened to Howard, an old friend of mine. He became so distracted, daydreaming while he rode his mower across a vast lawn, that the machine ran away with him until he mowed clear through a thick hedge.

Another friend of mine, a professional psychic, has literally planted herself on occasion. Or, as she described it to me, "I've dug myself a shallow grave. It's in a scenic place a short walk from my house. I'll go lie there for hours at a time."

Sound appealing? Well, maybe you'd prefer to pull up dandelions and crabgrass. Either way, you're grounding.

15. Hard Work

What does work mean to you? Promotions? Frustrations? Piles of money? How about... grounding? Admittedly not the first thing that comes to mind about employment, the truth remains. Work is a grounding Godsend.

Why? To succeed at a paying job in the real world you must produce results that are meaningful, or at least concrete. Regardless of your job description, you'll do this better when you pay close attention to what you are doing, which brings grounding. Reality checks can bolster your paycheck. Indeed, work is one of the few ways to ground where success at connecting with earth energy literally pays off.

How you pace yourself at work can also promote grounding. When the work flow is slow, will you decide to goof off or will you choose to pitch in extra hard? Each time you choose the latter, you'll gain extra grounding points. On the other hand, you don't want to work so hard that you ground yourself clear into the grave. Let your pacing, like your alertness on the job, reflect a commitment to *balanced* integration of your spiritual consciousness.

16. Helping Others to Physically Heal

As an empath, you're used to giving service. But sometimes you can ground yourself better by switching empathy off and doing a more physical kind of service, like helping someone who needs nursing care or companionship. Looking after an invalid for a couple of hours is a kind thing to do. It also can remind you how lucky you are to be able to ground awareness in *your* body-mind-spirit.

To make your service to others most effective (and to enhance the grounding benefits for you) studying energy work with a professional healer whose work you admire. Healing Touch and Reiki are easy to learn, relatively inexpensive, and they'll increase your physical awareness many fold. Another benefit is that you can use them to heal yourself as well as others.

Being an empath, you may discover that your use of healing procedures develops an extra dimension. For instance, one of my favorite techniques from Healing Touch is called "Pain Drain." It's a method where you use your hands and awareness to help a client release physical pain. Believe me, it comes in handy with kids.

While doing Pain Drain on my toddler, empathy struck. I discovered that I could describe what the pain felt like while I worked to release it. Did it feel stinging? Splintery? Dull? Soon Matt's friends were calling for Pain Drain, too, and they seemed to enjoy the verbal validation about their pain even more than the healing.

Is pain description taught as part of Janet Mentgen's Pain Drain technique? No, it's just a bonus for empaths. You'll find similar extras whatever healing methods you study.

Incidentally, you may also find (like me) that physical healing is completely counterproductive for grounding. In a healing situation, before I know what hit me, I've expanded enormously. Holding a Space for the patient, I feel streams of energy flow through me and become wonderfully inspired but not the least grounded. Even if I'm visiting at a hospital bedside where I am supposedly *not* doing anything but paying a social call, this energy flow begins. In fact, it's harder for me to switch empathy off with people who are physically ill than with any other life situation.

You, however, may be different. Depending on your personal assortment of gifts, you may be fabulous at turning empathy off when you're around patients, and physical healing on that basis could be extremely grounding. Many empaths find this. See for yourself.

17. Eating Meat

When your body-mind-spirit is hungry for grounding, meat will do the trick faster than any other food, especially red meat.

Okay, I know the above advice will make some readers squirm. Vegetarianism has great appeal to spiritual people, and its health benefits are a matter of scientific fact. Personally, I've been a vegetarian off and on from the time I had my first apartment in 1967. Nonetheless, meat is a powerful option for grounding. Don't rule it out.

There may be times in your life when meat can help you ground better than anything else. At such times, your body will nudge you with daytime cravings or nighttime dreams. And then, responding to your body's desire for meat can be the most spiritual choice you could make. Listening to your body is a sacred responsibility. Maybe that's why the Dalai Lama has said that, although he values the ideal of vegetarianism, for health reasons he, personally, eats meat.

Still not persuaded? Remember that grounding integrates every step of our spiritual progress. Thus, it prepares us for the next step of expanded consciousness. Spiritual seekers of the highest order can slow themselves down because of rigid beliefs about food. Avoid that miss-steak.

18. Junk Food and Drunk Food

One man's meat is another man's bag of potato chips. Vegetarian options for grounding with food are abundant. Your body's wisdom can direct you to the options that work best for you.

Beer is the grounder's drink of choice, unless mother's milk is available. (Works for babies!) Just one bottle of beer does the job. Leave the rest of the 99 bottles of beer on the wall for another day—also hard liquor, appropriately called "spirits." Liquor expands, rather than grounds.

Oily foods, like nuts or chips, may not be recommended by the diet police but they can work wonders for grounding. Diet experts have despaired over the tendency of Americans to get fat, even when we stick to low-fat diets. The reason need not be gluttony. It could be over-feeding in the attempt to get grounded. Oily food happens to be very grounding. Even if you avoid it completely, your need for grounding may cause you to choose the next item from this list anyhow....

19. Putting on Weight

Eating a lot of any food can help you hold onto a higher state of consciousness. Statues of the Buddha show him chubby for good reason.

It's not that a pudge-producing lifestyle will automatically make a person more spiritually evolved. Rather, a person's evolution sometimes leads to the need for more padding. Take menopause, for instance.

According to Susun S. Weed, author of *Menopausal Years, The Wise Woman Way*, hot flashes are virtually synonymous with menopause. "From an energy viewpoint, a hot flash is a release of kundalini (cosmic) electricity, which 'rewires' the nervous system, making it capable of transferring and moving powerful healing energies for the entire community."[*]

And what else is—or should be—synonymous with menopause? Gaining 10 pounds. Weed recommends this. The herbalist explains, "Fat cells make estrogen. Weighty women have a later menopause, less severe hot flashes, a more gradual Change, and denser bones (less osteoporosis)."[**]

As an aura reader, I'd add the spiritually obvious. Heavier people often carry bigger auras, which is good because it means that they can hold and move more spiritual energy.

Even if you're not menopausal, even if you're not female, it's important to understand the relationship between weight, grounding, and spiritual expansion. As noted by psychic Marcy Calhoun in *Are You Really Too Sensitive*, food causes sensitives to "come back into their bodies and be grounded." Of course Calhoun also reports in later pages that improving her diet helped her to drop unwanted pounds. Iris Saltzman, Sue Greer,

[*] Susun S. Weed, *Menopausal Years: The Wise Woman Way* (Woodstock, NY: Ash Tree Publishing) p. 57
[**] Ibid., p. 28

Vivian Bochenek, and Rosalyn Bruyere all have confirmed that the endocrine system becomes extra vulnerable with the growth of intuitive work.* Obesity may be the result until the system is brought back into balance. Kathlyn Rhea specifically lists foods that help balance the adrenals in her book *Mind Sense*.

Despite conscientious attempts at healing and balance, some empaths remain overweight. If that's your predicament, I dare you to take a counterculture perspective. Assuming that you have worked through stuck emotional pain and tried other ways to ground yourself (higher-up items from this list) and they haven't worked, consider the possibility that maybe, just maybe, those pounds are meant to be there. Jesus told his disciples that even something as seemingly trivial as the fall of a sparrow has a place in God's plan.** If "even the hairs of your head have all been counted," why shouldn't your weight be in that same category?** Allegedly excess pounds may be just what you need to carry your full share of spiritual heft.***

Yes, I'm inviting you to consider a very radical idea, since we Americans tend to equate extra pounds with sin. But it's true: *Usually people with heftier bodies carry a bigger energy field.* Once I read about scientific research that showed a correlation for male business executives between physical girth and power—the bigger they are, the better their job titles.

And there's a related research study you can do for yourself. Next time you see an advertisement with before-and-after photos for someone who graduated from a weight-loss program, read the auras in both pictures.

□   Most commonly, the Before Photo shows a big aura. Granted, the photo is purposely designed to make the dieter look lousy.

---

* Belleruth Naparstek, *Your Sixth Sense* (New York: HarperCollins, 1997), pp. 164
** *Good News Bible*, Mt. 10:29-31
*** For brilliant advice on overcoming "appearance obsession," see Linda McBryde, M.D.'s *The Mass Market Woman: Defining Yourself as a Person in a World That Defines You By Your Appearance* (Eagle River, AK: Crowded Hour Press, 1999) See www.massmarketwoman.com.

Her expression, the lighting, her hairstyle and clothes, are all supposed to convince you that her former obesity was a nothing short of a disease. Socially, that's true enough. Prejudice against the overweight runs rampant. But check out the aura in that before picture. It's big, too, which means the person can hold and move lots of energy.

□ By contrast, the After Photo, all glammed-up, cheerful, and expensively dressed, is a model of social success. But the aura to go with the client is small and, often, way out of balance.

The moral of this story, I believe, is that each person has a most comfortable size for spiritual health. Some people beam out their full auric wattage with bodies that are naturally slender; most need a heavier body to hold their full energy. And why would anyone care about having a full-sized aura? You feel more alive. Your presence impresses people more. Your learning accelerates. If you're an empath, you'll have more to give.

20. Smoking

Nobody's a bigger anti-smoking fanatic than an ex-smoker. Put me in that category. Nevertheless, no list of grounding methods should omit smoking. It's one of the most powerful ways to ground because each puff temporarily closes a person off to spiritual vibrations. That's right. Cigs shrink auras.

One exception: If you're involved in a Native American ceremony to connect via Mother Earth's energy with the Great Spirit, your ancestors, or totem animals, that's a holy rite, and tobacco could help you integrate spiritual awareness, in keeping with the power of your intention for that ceremony. However, the typical teen smoker isn't planning to connect with God when she lights up. If you're hooked on a tobacco product, smoking has become a way to slow down your spiritual growth.

Here's the good news. When you quit smoking for good, your aura is going to puff right out again.

Then the bad news—yes, it's common knowledge that ex-smokers gain five pounds or more. But why? Most people assume that cigarettes keep your mouth too busy to snack. When you take away those nicotine pacifiers, oh boy! in go the cookies. Please! Let's construct a more sophisticated explanation by putting together what we've already learned:

- Spiritual expansion makes a person's aura bigger.
- Carrying more energy in your aura is more comfortable if the physical body can anchor it down with some extra pounds.
- Smoking shrinks a person's aura.
- When a person stops smoking, his aura expands and his body packs on enough pounds to ground it.

Coolfont Spa in West Virginia offers Breathe Free®, a smoking cessation program developed by Martha Ashelman. Recently I read auras for graduates of the week-long program, comparing their current auras with what showed in photos taken the day of their arrival. Without exception, by the end of the week their auras brightened significantly. Individually, results of aura readings were even more fascinating. Each non-smoker's aura in the group showed distinctive vulnerabilities that had contributed to a smoking addiction. For instance:

- Murray suffered from long-standing clog in his throat chakra. "Why bother?" It said. "Nobody's interested in what I have to say." Smoking masked his feeling of hopelessness.
- Dolores showed a pattern of interpreting conflicts in ways that made her an emotional victim. Instead of getting mad, she'd feel hurt. Smoking kept her numb to the pain she was holding.
- Carl had a remarkably bright aura, even when hooked on tobacco. His energy field showed a first-rate talent for Physical Oneness (which he acknowledged once I described it to him). With his newly cleaned-up aura he'll be able to travel big time.

All the Breathe Free graduates appreciated my insights about what had kept them hooked. Any anti-smoking approach would be enriched by self-awareness about personal energy dynamics.

- ▫ Which problems, reflected in my aura, contribute to a smoking addiction and still need to be addressed?
- ▫ Which other forms of grounding could be substituted for cigarettes?
- ▫ Which gifts of my soul show up in my aura, strengths I can use to stop smoking?

Every responsible smoking cessation program would benefit from empathic readings to answer questions like these.

21. Taking a Vacation from Spirituality

To everything there is a season. No matter how much you love exploring your gifts as an empath, some days your interest will be less than zero. The same goes for prayer, meditation, listening to your Higher Self, and anything else you call "spiritual."

When this happens (and it will) don't force yourself to go through the motions of spiritual exercise. Do a different technique that day, that week, that month. Or do nothing at all for a while. Relax, your spiritual self won't perish.

While the need for grounding is particularly intense, you could even go through a full-blown loss of faith. Ironically, this seemingly un-spiritual crisis could be orchestrated by your very own soul. When you return to faith, you will be whole in a way that includes more of who you really are.

Many empaths beat themselves up over loss of faith or what they interpret as spiritual laziness. Lighten up! Empathy techniques bring expansion. To integrate them, we need grounding. Ultimately our own souls set the pace. We can help by enjoying this rather than guiltifying it.

22. Chronic Physical Pain

Pain has got to be the worst case version of grounding. Loving pain would be weird. Nevertheless, from the perspective of grounding, let's give pain its due. Pain happens to be a very effective way of pushing awareness right back into your body.

Life being unfathomable, there's no one simple explanation for physical pain or long-term disability. One inevitable consequence, however, is that *pain grounds consciousness.* Even if you learn to transcend it, pain continually serves as a downer, bringing you back from a spiritually expanded state to sensations that are tight, contracted, and unpleasant—in other words, as grounded as physical experience can be.

A healthy lifestyle can minimize the odds of your living in pain. For preventing illness, for faster recovery, go back to the top of this list about methods of grounding. Make sure you're taking enough of the "Eat me" to balance out your "Drink me." With wisdom and luck, your empathic lifestyle will lead to grounding in its more enjoyable forms.

22 Ways to Ground—Q&A

Q: Would you comment on a problem I've been having for years? It think it might have something to do with spiritual expansion. There's a kind of insomnia I get sometimes where I lie in bed and my consciousness changes. I haven't done anything to make this happen and I know it isn't sleep. I get very big. Sometimes I go shooting out to the stars.

A: That's expansion, all right. Your spirit believes you're ready, even if your personality has its doubts.

Don't call it insomnia, though. How about this? You're having your vibrations raised.

Q. This happens to other people, too?

A. Spiritually, it's the quintessential turn-of-the-millennium experience. So don't worry about it. Just follow up within 24 hours by doing something to ground your consciousness, which will help you to integrate the experience smoothly.

Q: WHAT DO YOU THINK ABOUT TAKING DRUGS FOR EXPANSION? OR JUST PLAIN FUN.

A: It's a bad idea. So many natural ways can get you high more safely—and legally. Drugs really distort auras too, and the yuck takes a long time to wear off.

If your motive is recreation, legal forms of fun lead to better consequences for the body and environment. If your motive is escapism or the need to belong, drugs create more problems than they solve. If your motivation is spiritual experience, you're better off using empathy techniques or any other path that gives you a balanced spiritual expansion.

Q: DO YOU COUNT YOGA FOR GROUNDING?

A: Some forms of yoga emphasize grounding, whereas others emphasize expansion. Usually yoga combines expansion and grounding—the same with Tai Chi, Qui Gong, and related disciplines. These schools of wisdom from the East primarily strengthen your energy field, with wonderful side effects for your body. If you tend *not* to be very grounded, these disciplines won't help ground you at all. For this purpose you'd do better with something more purely physical.

Q: EVERY DAY I TEST FOR FLOWER ESSENCES AND TAKE THE ONES I NEED. THEY SEEM TO WORK WONDERS AT BALANCING ME OUT. WOULD THAT BE GROUNDING?

A: Flower and gemstone essences work like crystal healing or homeopathy. Primarily they act on your subtle bodies. When you reach a point in your spiritual evolution where you identify yourself first as energy (and your physical body comes second), these technologies will be among your best grounders.

Q: BEFORE THEN?

A: So long as your body feels like "the real me," essences and crystals will expand your consciousness, not ground it.

*P*ersonal *N*otes

People I know who fall into being over-objective:

People I know who fall into being over-subjective:

Good role models for me, people who have fabulous objective-subjective balance:

How I would summarize my own Personal Tale of Grounding:

My favorite ways to ground:

My *least* favorite ways to ground:

What I have done today to ground my energy:

Friends who might benefit if I could tell them about the relationship of smoking and/or overweight to grounding:

14. The Power of Empathy

Being an unskilled empath is not an empowered state. Frankly, it reminds me of the time I got locked in a confessional.

Here's how that one happened. While attending a retreat held in a former convent, I wandered around after lunch and found, to my delight, a confessional. Although I had never been in one before, I had always been fascinated by them. No members of a congregation were around to be offended at what I wanted to do, and I was sure God wouldn't take offense. So, Catholic or not, I opened the door and slipped inside.

Out poured my prayerful version of what I thought it would mean to confess. The recitation of my imperfections took all of five minutes. I felt greatly relieved. But when I tried the door, it wouldn't budge.

Evidently God wasn't convinced I had finished. So I prayed more, now with an extra sense of urgency. Again, I finished. Again, the door stayed locked shut.

Now I listened harder—not for a response from the Almighty but for signs of human life. Eventually I heard the approach of other retreat participants. Yelling and pounding on the door, I got their attention. Mercifully, they let me out. Only then did I learn that I had been locked in the priest's side of the booth.

Could I have been any more ignorant about what I was doing? Once more, I'd been a fool for love. In typical unskilled empath fashion, I'd traveled with no idea where I was going, and even more clueless about how to return.

Clueless empathy isn't empowering. But self-knowledge and the techniques in this book have been helped you and me to gain a new kind of power. It's the power to use our gifts on purpose, in a balanced way.

Even if you don't breathe a word to your friends and co-workers about what you've been doing, the change in your breath will show. Yes, your higher consciousness will show in your breath, your speech, and your silence.

Skilled empathy brings about nothing less than a higher state of consciousness. Think about it.

You have learned (in a deeper way than ever before) who you are as an ENERGY PRESENCE—and to trust your language for this, which is highly personal. For example, the truest thing I can say about myself is not that I'm a woman, a mother, a wife, a Caucasian of German and Russian descent, an American, a writer, or anything like that. I am dancing light, a chime in the silence. I am an image that emerges in silence from life's stereogram, The Magic I. However you describe yourself as a presence of pure energy, that YOU has learned to Fly in Spirit.

You have learned to FLY AT WILL into another person's aura, freeing yourself from the limits of habitual ways of being. Empathy, you know now, means more than a psychological turn of mind. It means opening your mind, body, spirit, and heart to experience of a different order. What a sublime opportunity! Flying in Spirit, you have gone far beyond the realm of mere psychology. Inner space has become the final frontier.

You have experienced ONENESS, a transcendent connection with people who are not (apparently) yourself.

You have discovered YOUR EMPATHIC GIFTS—and through conscious appreciation, you have transformed them into genuine gifts, rather than afflictions. Empowerment comes when you grow wiser every day in the use of your gifts. Stability comes from integrating your experiences of spiritual expansion, grounding yourself deliberately. No more waiting for the other shoe to drop!

Even if you don't breathe a word to anyone about your newfound skill as an empath, you'll help others by your example. But I hope you'll do more. Spread the word that empathy means more than your friends have thought. Lend them your book—even better, buy them a copy of their own. Teach them about Coming Home, how to Hold a Space. Travel with them.

It will be to your advantage for as many people as possible to become skilled empaths. Think of the Hundredth Monkey Effect: On the level of our consciousness, all human beings are interconnected. When enough people master any type of knowledge, everyone else learns that same knowledge more easily. For example, when bicycles were first invented, learning to ride took a long time. Cycling was strictly for grownups. Today enough people have learned for riding to be an easier skill to acquire— and they learn it far younger age. In my neighborhood, for instance, there's a kid who can ride a two wheeler with no problem at all, and he's just three years old. How old were you when you learned? The human race has evolved greatly since then.[*]

Because of the Hundredth Monkey Effect, it will help you personally whenever a person makes the leap from unskilled empath to skilled empath.And empaths have never been more ready to learn. Human consciousness, for everyone on the planet, has been evolving at an ever-accelerated pace. Having worked since 1971 as a spiritual teacher, this is obvious to me (likewise to my fellow teachers of all forms of personal development). Our jobs have been made far easier. What once took students weeks or months to discover, now can be crammed into a couple of hours.

Some of my current students stumble into class, not even sure why they've come. Friends drag them in while they giggle, embarrassed. When I ask what they know about subjects like empathy and auras, they confess total ignorance.

[*] See Rupert Sheldrake's fascinating *A New Science of Life: The Hypothesis of Morphic Resonance*, Inner Traditions: Rochester, VT. 1995

Many of these newcomers practice their childhood religion, but feel it hasn't grown with them. Others practice no formal religion at all. Regardless, when I read their third eyes, I usually discover huge consciousness.

At the opposite extreme, I have students who have actively followed one spiritual path or another for decades. They, too, have huge consciousness (and, to be fair, usually considerably more of it than the spiritual newbies).

But what 99 percent of all my students today have in common, when they begin to study with me, is the combination of very *big* consciousness and very *small* spiritual empowerment.

Based on my experience with students like these, bolstered by having read countless auras on the street, and from photos in magazines and newspapers, I've discovered two fascinating things.

- People alive today can't avoid having access to higher states of consciousness.
- Unless they know they have consciousness, people can't make it move. This is the spiritual equivalent of having a million-dollar bank account without knowing how to withdraw your own money.

As if the lack of spiritual empowerment wasn't bad enough, the psychological consequences are worse. Empathy denied, or not used with skill, causes self-doubt and other chronic problems. Yet, with such a small shift of emphasis, Flying in Spirit could lift every empath to a well-deserved and healthy self-confidence.

Write a Mission Statement

One of my students, Lewis, is a relative latecomer to spiritual seeking. When he first came to study with me, he was highly talented as an empath but utterly unskilled. Even after making considerable progress, he was still confused about his SPIRITUAL MISSION on earth. How could his spiritual abilities express themselves in his life work?

When we talked, he said, "I should be a healer. Several psychics have told me so. But I've studied a couple of healing techniques and they don't seem to stick."

Together we explored the real nature of his gifts. We found two major strengths, Emotional Oneness and Intellectual Shape Shifting—the latter being a much rarer gift. To supplement this, his most active inner language turned out to be Analytical Awareness.

By trade, Lewis is a master electrician. Power-related problems are easy for him to fix—on mechanical levels, anyway. Intellectual Shape Shifting gets him on the right wavelength. Lewis takes his empathic strengths all the way to the government's halls of power, where he's in charge of ensuring that, literally, the lights stay on.

Ironically, Lewis has been giving away too much of his own personal power. Otherwise why would he believe that his personal mission must involve physical healing? When you search the radar screen of his gifts, physical forms of empathy don't register a single blip. Aurically he's grounded enough to be healthy ... and sexy enough to enjoy that earthiness. But that doesn't mean his soul has packaged him up as a physical healer. Healing does NOT thrill his soul.

Many people, not just Lewis, need to learn *you don't have to be a healer just because you have a gift for moving energy.*

A common misunderstanding today is that only two "career paths" are open to people who become interested in subtle perception. Either you become a healer (like Rosalyn Bruyere or Barbara Brennan) or you do psychic readings (like James Van Praagh or Laura Day). Such a limiting perspective! It's like saying that women who work outside the home must be either nurses or teachers.

Instead, it's time to acknowledge that spiritual gifts like Lewis'—and yours—are part of a unique spiritual mission. You may be paid for this spiritual work... or not. It may have a quick easy label... or not. Regardless, rest assured that every time you consciously Fly in Spirit, you're giving spiritual service. It counts as much as if you could proudly point to your diploma on the wall and say, "I'm a graduate of the Acme School of Healing." Here on The Learning Planet, as you may know, credentials bear only the most superficial relationship to a person's real abilities.

Another student of mine, Donna, works as a statistician, having the full set of outer-world qualifications. Yet her real love is helping people grow emotionally and spiritually. In recognition of her extraordinary talent, Donna has been given office space rent-free, plus a full load of client referrals from local physicians and therapists. Who needs the degree on the wall? Not her clients, who call her a Holistic Health Consultant.

Finding a life mission is a challenge for most of us. But it's easy compared with what you've been through already in becoming a skilled empath. Of course you, like Donna or Lewis, will be happiest when you can match your true inner gifts with your outer work in the world. Connecting inner and outer life isn't a frill—more like underwear. Aurically speaking, it wakes up the High Heart chakra. Most people haven't done that yet, but you can. The means is finding, then doing, the work that thrills your soul. I've published a video about this (see the back of this book for details).

Meanwhile, an alternative way to access knowledge about your real work, and awaken your High Heart, is to give yourself some quiet time for reflection. Use clairsentience, or clairvoyance in front of a mirror. Plug into your own energy field and question about your special excellence.

Ask to be shown your life work. Maybe you'll find patterns of success and joy. Maybe you'll be shown persistent patterns of pain or rejection. Keep looking, gently, until you find a pattern of spiritual service. It's there. Map out what you do energetically. Then write a spiritual mission statement.

□ Draw it. Or write it out as a poem.
□ Feel free to use words or pictures, charts or outlines.
□ Include your empathic gifts and your most lively languages.

When you're satisfied that it resonates with your truth for now, put what you have created in a place of honor. I put mine on the wall of my office like a college diploma. Why not? We need to give ourselves license to be powerful empaths.

Getting Out of the Way

Don't stop searching until you find your mission, including the piece of it that involves empathy. Then do it. Or, to be more precise, become conscious that you do it—including the fact that you have been engaged in your mission, on a spiritual level, since birth.

Often appreciating your mission will include noticing what it means to GET OUT OF THE WAY. Your cute but limited individual personality, the one you meet when Coming Home, needs to step aside at certain times so you can *simply be*. For many highly spiritual people, your mission on earth is primarily just that: to be. Choosing out-in-the-world activities that thrill your soul is a plus, but not a requirement for you to fulfill a mission related to your way of, spiritually, being.

In this context, I remember interviewing Janet Mentgen, the founder of Healing Touch, for a magazine profile. Healing is her passion, she told me. In one of my textbooks for studying Healing Touch, I'd seen a photo of her demonstrating a healing technique. When I looked at her aura, I was awed by her ability to get out of the way. Transparently she let huge amounts of spiritual light move through her. I'd never seen anything like it.

"Do you have any tips for getting out of the way?" I asked her during the interview, feeling slightly idiotic to be asking. After all, it's not as though she was Heloise, a professional giver of household hints. Graciously, this extremely soft-spoken woman listened to my request for the Cliff Notes version of becoming a world-class energy mover. I'll never forget her answer, it was so perfect.

"Have tips?" she said slowly. "Sure don't."

Collections and Recollections

Memories of great teachers, like Janet Mentgen, are what I collect the way some people collect postage stamps. Whatever else you may like to collect, when you can Fly in Spirit, you'll never lack for valuables. More and deeper than ever, you'll collect ways that spiritual beings can be human, in all their glory.

Some of the memories in this collection may be sad ones. For example, I think of my father, Ernie Rosenbaum, whom I now can appreciate as one of the most gifted empaths I've ever known. Ignorant about his gifts, he was *un-empowered* by empathy.

In his happier moments, Dad loved music, especially playing music for guests. In his glory, he was a kind of empathic disc jockey, sorting through his huge music collection to find the perfect cut from the perfect record. Then Ernie would watch his friend listen, and glow enough for them both.

At mid-life my father nearly died from a sudden attack of a digestive disorder. In the hospital, what brought him back to health was the musical need of his roommate, a Greek sailor who spoke no English. Ernie vibed out which music the sailor would like, asked my mother to bring it from home along with a record player. Once Dad found the right music, both men healed "in record time." The sailor was soothed by the sounds of home; my father sailed into the man's relief and delight.

But life for an unskilled emotional empath means life on a nonstop journey: now sailing, now swimming, now lurching forward on the roller coaster. Lack of skill as an empath takes its toll on health, both psychologically and physically. By the age of 42, my father began to have heart attacks. Sure, doctors explained this in strictly medical terms. I felt they missed the point, which was my father's emotional pain. Whatever the cause, increasingly my father came to live in the sterile world of hospitals, with their Latin diagnoses, unnatural odors, and rooms that were mostly walls and sickbeds.

By 55, Ernie's arteries had hardened prematurely, doctors said, causing senility. Medically he was a long list of diseases. Personally, the part I found hardest to take was the loss of his intelligence. Truth to tell, he could barely think.

When I came to see him for the last time, the look of death clung to him. Ernie had always carried a huge aura, 250 pounds of him beaming out a love of life that struck you like an almost physical force. Now he lay in a hospital bed, physically and aurically shrunken. Pitifully small in his faded blue gown, he acknowledged his visitor with a vacant look in his eyes.

In years past I had paid respect to dying relatives, made small like this, tucked like dolls into their hospital beds. This time was different. I was saying goodbye to my father. Memories could have flooded me with love and wonder, gratitude and rage. Instead I felt empty. All my spiritual beliefs couldn't take away the grim reality of loss. Now was the time to tell Ernie goodbye.

My mother, who visited every day with what was left of him, tiptoed out of the room to leave us alone. What could I say to a man whose mind was gone? For once I had no words. Finally inspiration came.

"Dad," I heard myself say. "If we held hands and I meditated, do you suppose you could feel it?"

He gave a childlike smile. Feeling other people's feelings was still his favorite thing. I held Ernie's hand, closed my eyes, and Flew in Spirit to the highest heaven I could reach. He joined me there. I could feel his presence in the twinkling silence. Minutes later I peeked at him and saw him sitting, eyes closed, aurically beaming. It was our last conversation. I left him that way.

So many people, like Ernie, slip in and out of deep knowing. But it's never quite conscious, which means that they can never claim its full power. Your life is going to be very different. Go on, show the world how to be an empath with loving purpose and great power.

*A*ffirmations

1. When I show up to life in a grounded way, life shows up to me in a powerful way.
2. My Inner Child is the empath within. I release the belief that I carry within me a wounded Inner Child. My Inner Child is so healthy, it's dazzling.
3. I give thanks for finding my perfect mission in life. For me to envy others is silly, silly, silly.
4. I release the struggles I've gone through to find my gifts as an empath. I have found gold in that mud, so I am ready to accept my own greatness.
5. I believe in my wisdom. Especially when others push me away, I trust that my truth has value.
6. Today I replace old habits of viewing myself as weak. God, you're hired: Teach me how to live in perfect balance.
7. I choose to love my body as it is right now. I release the habit of putting my body last. My body is a perfect instrument for service as an empath.
8. I trust my emotions, even when I don't enjoy them. Every precious drop of wisdom within me has been earned. As a skilled empath, I am a fountain of joyful wisdom.
9. Lucky me, I'm such a talented empath, I can fulfill my life's purpose using empathy just *part time*.
10. It is not required that I suffer because I'm an empath. I remember that I'm always free to Travel in Spirit—or not. I have a talent for happiness.

Annotated Bibliography

READING PEOPLE LIKE A BOOK—that's an expression I hear a lot, but not from the kind of people who are attracted to my work. The expression implies glibness, as though there were a particular slice of information one could neatly dispose of, like eating a roast beef sandwich.

Usually this delicatessen-style "reading" is an attempt to master someone's PERSONALITY—the social level of behavior that extreme non-empaths equate with the totality of an individual. By contrast, empathy enables you to explore PERSONHOOD—mysterious depths that involve many layers of who an individual actually is.

Just as your reading of people becomes inexhaustible when informed by your gifts for empathy, so the following books offer you far more than one quick read. Each invites you to enter a world that can enrich you immeasurably. I've categorized these books by the empathic talents I've noticed most strongly in their authors. With publications from small presses I've included websites or email addresses to help you find them.

Physical Oneness
The wisdom of the ancient Druids has shape-shifted into a powerful book of daily meditations.

> *The Celtic Spirit: Daily Meditations for the Turning Year*
> Caitlín Matthews
> New York: HarperSanFrancisco

Physical Intuition
Powerful training includes a thorough knowledge base about grounding.

> "Healing from the Core" audiotapes
> Suzanne Scurlock-Durana
> www.healingfromthecore.com

Emotional Oneness
Purity of heart: just how would that show up in an empath, anyway? Listen and marvel.
"Listening to the Heart in Spirit" audiocassette
Marya Michael
75734.1375@compuserve.com

Emotional Intuition
Not all HSP's are empaths but, so far, I have yet to find an empath who isn't a sensitive.
The Highly Sensitive Person: How to Thrive When the World Overwhelms You
Elaine N. Aron
New Jersey: Birch Lane Press. 1996

Intellectual Shape Shifting
Scholarly, thorough, pioneering—sure, and the work of a superb Intellectual Shape Shifter. Enjoy her!
The Acquarian Conspiracy
Marilyn Ferguson
New York: J.P. Tarcher. 1980

Spiritual Oneness
All empaths will function best if we make care of the soul a lifelong priority. As we honor our own souls, we enhance our service.
Care of the Soul: A Guide for Cultivating Depth and Sacredness in Everyday Life
Thomas Moore
New York: Harper Perennial. 1994

Glossary

Analytical Awareness To explore the level of Celestial Perception by means of intellectual agility. A complex language for deeper awareness. To be used effectively, Analytical Awareness requires patience and suspension of disbelief.

Animal Empaths Ability to move in consciousness to the wavelength of one or more non-human animal species.

Astral Projection An out-of-body experience into another plane of reality where one experiences oneself in a light body that seems as real as the physical body.

Auric Modeling The process (usually unconscious) where people's auras intermingle and spiritual learning takes place. Occurs whenever two or more people are together.

Auras Subtle bodies, made of electro-magnetic energy, that interpenetrate the physical body. Storehouses of information about different aspects of the individual.

Boundaries Drawing the line between oneself and others. Clear personal boundaries are a prerequisite for being a skilled empath.

Celestial Perception Awareness of levels of reality that are deeper and more glorious, such as angels, auras, and deep human secrets.

Chakras Energy centers within the human aura. Databanks of information about areas such as communication, sex, and power.

Clairaudience To hear truth about life at the level of Celestial Perception. A language for deeper awareness.

Clairsentience To touch the truth about life at the level of Celestial Perception. One of the most universal languages for deeper awareness.

Clairvoyance To look into life at the level of Celestial Perception. Best known (but not the most common) language for deeper awareness.

Co-dependence Obsessive concern with controlling another person's life; depending on others to make oneself happy.

Coming Home Choosing to make oneself the primary focus of attention. A core technique for becoming a skilled empath.

Compassion Sharing the suffering of another, not to be mistaken for empathy. Compassion draws on one's personal past experiences of suffering. Empathy opens one up to otherness, including nuances of emotion not personally experienced before.

Consciousness The aspect of human beings that is most transparently made in God's image. How people radiate life force energy. How we receive information about other beings who also have consciousness, such as people and pets. The basis of spiritual experience and, also, physical matter.

Crystal Empaths The ability to join in consciousness with crystals and gemstones, resulting in knowledge or healing by means of telepathic communication with members of the mineral kingdom.

Darshan The contagious glow from someone with high consciousness or charisma. Traditionally, the evolutionary boost from being in the presence of a saint. Currently, a major reason for watching movie stars.

Elemental Empaths The ability to join in consciousness with nature spirits and angels that protect the earth, in order to facilitate joy, agricultural abundance, and healing at many levels of the environment.

Emotional Intuition A gift for empathy on the emotional level. The ability to experience, from a distance, what is going on with another person's feelings.

Emotional Oneness A gift for empathy on the emotional level. The ability to experience, within one's own feelings, what is going on with another person's emotions. This gift can be confusing until one becomes a skilled empath. Not to be confused with projection. *See* Projection.

Energy Holders People who move through past experience more slowly than others, so it takes them a long time to release memories and attachments. Their uncommon thoroughness in processing inner experience makes them a rich resource for healing others.

Energy Movers People whose auras pulsate so actively that they awaken consciousness in others without even trying. Their transformative abilities may not be appreciated by those who have contact with them, setting off a backlash reaction.

Enlightenment Spiritually awake to the fullest. Identifying with the self as pure energy, silence, and bliss. Psychologically and physiologically, functioning with a minimum of internal stress.

Environmental Empaths Having a gift similar to that of Elemental Empaths, these empaths also heal the planet and awaken joy. By contrast, environmental empaths work by connecting to the consciousness of Mother Earth, humanity, and animals, rather than elementals or angels.

Emotional Intelligence Skill at being aware, at the psychological level, about oneself and others. This form of intelligence is unrelated to the forms of empathy described in this book. A useful supplement to empathy.

Emotional Oneness An empathic gift for being aware of emotions belonging to other people in terms of one's own self.

Emotional Intuition An empathic gift for being aware of emotions belonging to other people as separate from one's own self.

Empathic Sharing Connecting at a subtle body level to any living being. Taking on experiences that are physical, mental, spiritual, or emotional.

Empathy, Non- The mind-body-spirit set-up of the majority of human beings, who have different spiritual specialties, e.g., dispassionate insight, quick and complete grounding of spiritual experience. Non-empaths use the same languages for Celestial Perception as do empaths. However, except for special situations (such as falling in love or the birth of a child) non-empaths do not have empathic gifts such as Physical Oneness or Emotional Intuition.

Empathy, Skilled The experience of true otherness, gained by Flying in Spirit into another person's aura. Sharing energetically, activating soul-level gifts, gaining wisdom and giving service.

Empathy, Unskilled Taking on experience of others energetically without conscious awareness, control, or enjoyment of the process.

Face Reading Interpreting physical face data, with a loving intention, to reveal character. One step inward in perception from reading expression and body language.

Flying in Spirit A non-corporeal shift, by means of consciousness, into another's way of experiencing life, whether physically, mentally, emotionally, or spiritually. Not astral projection. (*See* Astral Projection.)

Gardening Empathy The ability to join in consciousness with things that grow, resulting in diagnosing, healing, and/or telepathic communication with members of the plant kingdom.

Getting Big The process of connecting one's personal consciousness with an individualized source of consciousness with the highest transpersonal wisdom, such as an Ascended Master or Archangel. A prerequisite for skilled empathic travel.

Grounding Coming down to earth. Integrating spiritual experience. The opposite of spiritual expansion.

Grounding Breath Quick shallow breaths, out and in, through the mouth only. Combined with the intention to ground one's energy, this breathing pattern helps to integrate spiritual eperience into the physical body.

Gustatory Giftedness Language at the level of Celestial Perception that involves smell and taste.

Higher Self The expanded, wiser version of one's everyday spiritual self. An energy-based identity with enormous love, intelligence, and joy.

Higher States of Consciousness Spontaneous experiences of reality where Higher Self awareness is consciously accessible and Celestial Perception is available at will.

Highly Sensitive Persons   Individuals who are neurophysiologically wired to be extra-responsive to life, from infancy on. This important term was developed by psychologist Elaine Aron.

Holistic Knowing   Language for Celestial Perception. Ability to hold awareness of several people at once. Connecting with the wholeness of a situation.

Holding a Space   Paying attention to people in a deeply receptive way. Unfocused sharing of consciousness with others. The basis for activating intense experiences of empathy.

Hot Flashes   A kind of kundalini experience where a woman is rewired to grow into a higher spiritual awareness. Commonly under-rated.

Hypochondria   Fabricating an illness by blowing ordinary physical sensations out of proportion. Apparent hypochondria can be the sign of an unskilled empath.

Imagination   Creative exploration by means of thought. A spiritual faculty.

Inner Dictionary   A set of information written in consciousness deep within the individual. Consulting this Dictionary (usually through the Questioning technique) enables a person to interpret Celestial Perception in a way that is productive as well as meaningful. Each person's dictionary is unique, flowing out of subjective perception and connected to spiritual work which only that individual can do.

Intellectual Shape Shifting   A gift for empathy on the intellectual level. Ability to intuitively experience another person's thought process—not to be confused with mind reading.

Intention A conscious inner statement that sets a desired dynamic into motion. The basis for some of the most powerful techniques that involve consciousness, will, or intelligence.

Joining in Spirit Responding to another person's need for support or healing. Paying attention on the level of consciousness. Service best undertaken consciously and as a choice, rather than as an unskilled empath's reflexive reaction to another person's need.

Karma Reactions to a person's actions, short- and long-term consequences. Part of the unfathomable complexity of life on earth.

Kundalini Life force energy that accelerates both spiritual expansion and grounding. Related to mystical experiences, sex, and whooshes of energy that travel up the spine.

Language A means to intensify and remember what happens during empathic travel. Highly personal, individual sensitivities, such as Gustatory Giftedness and Clairaudience.

Love Feeding from Spirit A sudden blast of spiritual energy which permanently opens a person up to a more refined *quality* of awareness, leading to more Celestial Perception. Can be accompanied by physical discomfort, emotional anxiety, the need to sleep, or insomnia.

Maya Illusions about the nature of reality, including the habit of identifying the self with the physical body, material possessions, or other limited, changing aspects of life.

Medical Empaths Empaths with a spiritual gift for walking around inside another person's body with their consciousness, plus diagnostic ability.

Medical Intuitives Psychics who specialize in receiving health-related diagnoses in a detached manner.

Molecular Empathy A rare gift for Holding a Space with others at a molecular level, moving them forward in their spiritual evolution.

Naming An ability used by (but not limited to) poets for using the sacred ability of true speech, awakening consciousness.

Non-interference A spiritual law which decrees that nobody has the right to push another person off a spiritual path. Suggestions and information may be offered once or twice but efforts beyond that will set in motion karmic difficulties for everyone concerned.

Otherness Direct experience of another person's body, mind, heart, or spirit.

Out-of-body Experiences Experience of the self where awareness is not localized in the physical body, e.g., looking down on one's body, along with that of others in a room. Can be a component of peak experiences.

Peak Experiences Flashes of higher states of consciousness that can include clear experiences of God. Acute-identity experiences common to self-actualized people. A term coined by pioneering psychologist Abraham Maslow.

Physical Intuition A gift for empathy on the physical level. The ability to experience, from a distance, what is going on with another person's body.

Physical Oneness A gift for empathy on the physical level. The ability to experience, on a personal level, what is going on with another person's body. This gift can be confusing until one becomes a skilled empath.

Power Feeding from Spirit Rewiring of a person's energy circuits which permanently opens up a person to receiving more spiritual awareness, leading to more Celestial Perception. Related to the flow of kundalini.

Primary Sensor Hand Each hand has a specialty when it comes to Celestial Perception. The Primary Sensor Hand is the more valuable tool for *receiving* information about auras. The other hand is the Power Hand, more valuable for *sending* out energy for healing.

Projection Unfinished psychological business from one person being attributed to somebody else. Not to be confused with the otherness of genuine empathy.

Psychic Ability Distinct from empathic abilities, a detached knowing that pops into awareness, revealing specific information that can be evaluated in terms of accuracy.

Psychic Knowing An intuitive language similar to Truth Knowledge, except that it supplies information across time or space or both.

Psychic Coercion A destructive pattern that makes it hard to know one's own mind, caused by another person's repeated thinking, wishing, praying, or willing how someone should act, think, believe, look, etc. Psychic coercion is avoidable on both the giving and receiving ends.

Psychic Ties Connections from one person to another, on the level of the emotional body, where energy flows back and forth. Although these ties usually operate unconsciously, a skilled empath can check for their presence and release them.

Questioning A technique for gaining spiritual clarity. Connecting with the wisdom of one's Higher Self.

Religion A set of traditional beliefs and practices. A lifestyle. Although religions are ultimately based upon spirituality, participation in religion does not guarantee spiritual experience. Nor does spiritual experience require any religious affiliation.

Self-authority Making oneself the ultimate human decision maker about what constitutes personal spiritual truth. A requirement for skilled empathy and long-term experience of higher states of consciousness.

Sex Energetic sharing with another person that includes an erotic, physical component. Can be a means to experience otherness.

Soul Expression of the spirit in its complete human form—an earthy, here-and-now part of the individual. Includes aspects that are more animal-like than usual conscious identity but also aspects that are more spiritual. Soul is best able to recognize choices that accelerate a person's spiritual evolution.

Spirit The unique spark of God that constitutes a distinct individuality.

Spiritual Expansion Experiences that raise spiritual vibrations. Includes peak experiences.Will inevitably be followed by Grounding.

Spiritual Invitation An opportunity to grow spiritually, evidenced by increased interest, charm, enthusiasm, or curiosity... plus a sense of delightful familiarity.

Spiritual Mission Statements Insights about how to use one's spiritual abilities in life. Purpose. Not necessarily related to employment in the material world.

Spiritual Oneness To explore another person's spiritual experience at the level of Celestial Perception. The only universal gift for empathy.

Spirituality Direct experience of God, either being expressed in life or in God's formless presence. Spirituality is experienced by means of being awake (i.e., one's personal consciousness).

Sympathy However well intended, sympathy is a socially sanctioned substitute for emotional forms of empathy. Sympathizers feel virtuous, whereas empaths actually feel.

Synesthesia Experiencing one sense in terms of another, e.g., wine-tasting in terms of color and texture. A universal ability activated at the level of Celestial Perception.

Truth Knowledge A simple, no-frills form of intuitive language. Awareness slips to a deeper level without effort.

Vibe-raising Breath Breathing in through the nose, out through the mouth, when attention is directed inward. This pattern opens the crown chakra, peels off surface stress, and makes spiritual awareness clearer.

Visions Experiences of a spiritual nature that are different from a person's previous context of experience. Not always easy to recognize at first, and not necessarily involving clairvoyance. More appropriately named "spiritual messages."

Index

A

B

$\mathscr{S}$tudy with Rose

This book is packed with tested techniques
to help you become a skilled empath,
able to turn your gift(s) OFF at will
then turn your empathy ON, full force, whenever you wish
for maxium service to others and
the greatest benefit for your own growth.

Sometimes students wish to supplement this book
by studying personally with Rose.
She regularly teaches on three continents, including
Empath's Empowerment Intensives.
For information about all these courses,
visit her website, www.rose-rosetree.com.
If she isn't offering a course near you, perhaps you
or an organization you know would like to sponsor a workshop.
Email her to discuss: Rosetree@Starpower.net.

You also might enjoy a personal session with Rose,
either a teaching session or one dedicated to aura transformation,
where she helps you to become clearer as an empath
by facilitating removal of limiting patterns from your aura.
These phone sessions are just as effective
as if you and Rose were in a room together.
Details about these personal sessions are at:
www.rose-rosetree.com.

More Books for an Empath's Library
by Rose Rosetree
Available through Women's Intuition Worldwide, LLC

Become the Most Important Person in the Room: Your 30-Day Plan for Empath Empowerment
This easy Empath Empowerment® program has you read one short chapter daily, then do just 10 minutes of follow-up. Watch your life change! Humorous and practical, it's must reading for any born empath.

Read People Deeper: Body Language + Face Reading + Auras
Gain energetic literacy skills and apply them to 50 different categories that matter most for everyday life, both business and pleasure. This how-to contains a powerful technique for reading auras from regular photos. You'll also enjoy leading-edge discoveries about body language and the 5,000-year-old art of physiognomy, reading faces for character.

Cut Cords of Attachment: Heal Yourself and Others with Energy Spirituality
Use this book as a how-to and/or a consumer guide for healing imbalances in your emotional and spiritual life. Presenting leading-edge techniques, Rose can help you to read those 50 databanks in any chakra. This book was the first in English on the topic of cutting cords with quality control, summarizing the best of what Rosetree learned in 20 years as a healing practitioner: 12 Steps to Cut Cords of Attachment®.

Aura Reading Through All Your Senses
Here Rose pioneers her easy-to-learn method of Aura Reading Through All Your Senses®. Improve relationships, health, even your choices as a consumer. Over 100 practical techniques make deeper perception both fun and practical. An international bestseller!

The Power of Face Reading
Rosetree has been called "The mother of American physiognomy." Her system of Face Reading Secrets® presents soulful interpretations of physical face data, with nuanced and highly accurate readings about personal style — an easy, useful reference book with over 100 illustrations. It's like a birdwatcher's guide for people.

Let Today Be a Holiday: 365 Ways to Co-Create with God
Don't just serve humanity. Get a human life! Rose helps you balance both aspects of your full potential. Browse the 450 techniques, plus thought-provoking ideas. Or use *Holiday* is a daybook. Either way, you'll strengthen the connection to your most important relationship of all, the one with your spiritual Source.

The Roar of the Huntids (A Novel for Empaths)
This spiritual thriller is a coming-of-age story about Energy Spirituality. Set in the year 2020, the story is spiced with social and political satire, plus a fast-moving plot, romance, and quirky characters (some of whom are empaths and some who are definitely not).

Wrinkles Are God's Makeup: How You Can Find Meaning in Your Evolving Face
In the 5,000-year history of reading faces for character, this is the first to explore how faces change over time. Using comparison photos, you learn to become a spiritual talent scout.

Order books at the author's website, www.rose-rosetree.com.
Many of Rose Rosetree's titles are available in foreign editions.
For inquiries about distribution in (or outside) the U.S. or foreign rights acquisitions, contact Deanna Leah, President of HBG Productions, deanna@hbgproductions.com, available by telephone at 530-893-4699.

By 2010, Rose had over 270,000 copies of her books in print.

Rose Rosetree

Her how-to books (including a national bestseller in Germany) and blog, "Deeper Perception Made Practical," are available online at www.rose-rosetree.com. Rose has trademarked the pioneering systems of Empath Empowerment®, 12 Steps to Cut Cords of Attachment®, Aura Reading Through ALL Your Senses®, and Face Reading Secrets®.

Over the past 40 years, this Brandeis University graduate has given more than 900 media interviews, her work praised in publications as different as *The Washington Post, The Washington Times, The Los Angeles Times,* and *The Catholic Standard.*

Clients include Long & Foster, Canyon Ranch, Posh Supper Club, The Food Marketing Institute, George Washington University, USA Today, The Inner Potential Centre in London, and VOICE in Japan.